Language, Gender and Videogames

Frazer Heritage

Language, Gender and Videogames

Using Corpora to Analyse the Representation of Gender in Fantasy Videogames

palgrave
macmillan

Frazer Heritage
Department of Psychology
Birmingham City University
Birmingham, UK

ISBN 978-3-030-74397-0 ISBN 978-3-030-74398-7 (eBook)
https://doi.org/10.1007/978-3-030-74398-7

Cover credit: Contributor: Giuseppe Ramos/Alamy

This Palgrave Macmillan imprint is published by the registered company Springer Nature Switzerland AG
The registered company address is: Gewerbestrasse 11, 6330 Cham, Switzerland

For my family and friends

Acknowledgements

There is a saying that it takes a village to raise a child—and this book is my child. It is only right to thank the people who helped bring it to fruition.

First and foremost, I would like to thank Professor Paul Baker. I was fortunate enough to have Paul as my supervisor for my Ph.D. Without his tutorage, help, and guidance, this work would not be what it is today.

I would also like to thank all members of the Department of Linguistics and English Language at Lancaster University, where I studied for my Ph.D. and worked as an Associate Lecturer during this period. The members of the department were not only very encouraging at every step of the way, but also provided thoughtful and interesting discussions, along with regularly providing feedback on ideas and concepts.

I would also like to thank my colleagues at Birmingham City University, where I currently work as an Assistant Lecturer in the Department of Psychology. The department has been incredibly welcoming and offered so much support throughout the publication process.

While writing this monograph, I also served as the secretary for the British Association of Applied Linguistics' (BAAL's) Language, Gender, and Sexuality (LGaS) Special Interest Group (SIG). The members of this SIG have been lovely and incredibly encouraging—I would like to thank all of them.

I would like to thank the three anonymous reviewers who read my initial proposal for the monograph, and the anonymous reviewer who checked the final manuscript. All of your comments were appreciated.

On a personal note, I would like to thank several of my friends and family members for constantly supporting me and believing in me. There are too many to name here, but all are loved.

Finally, I would like to thank Cathy Scott and at Palgrave Macmillan and Redhu Ruthroyoni at Springer Nature for sorting out the administrative side behind the monograph. Both Cathy and Redhu have been stars throughout this process and have made writing my first monograph a truly enjoyable experience.

Contents

List of Figures

List of Tables

1
Introduction

Listen to My Story, This May Be Our Last Chance

It is late one cold winter's night in the early 2000s, and I have been crying for the past three hours. Three words have shattered my composure and have made me feel as though my guts have been ripped out: 'I love you'. However, these words were not said by a lover, a close family member, or even a dear friend. They were whispered by Yuna, a character from the 2001 videogame *Final Fantasy X* (Square Enix, 2001; released on the Playstation 2 in the UK in 2002). I had spent more than a hundred hours playing this game: facing new challenges, forming bonds with the characters, and fully immersing myself in the narrative. Without spoiling the ending, Yuna had just confessed her love for the main (male) character and the game came to a close. Needless to say, the combination of the story ending and the confession of this love created an emotional conclusion to a fantastic videogame (in fact, I could think of no more appropriate opening heading for this book than the first line from *Final Fantasy X*).

F. Heritage, *Language, Gender and Videogames*,
https://doi.org/10.1007/978-3-030-74398-7_1

But how did we get here? How did it come to be that I, like many others, sat bawling my eyes out over nothing more than pixels? For centuries, games have been interwoven into the fabric of cultures. For example, *The Royal Game of Ur* is believed to have been played in cultures dating as far back as 3,000 BC (see Finkel, 2007). In the 1970s, however, two different games emerged that would change the face of gaming forever and would ultimately lead to the birth of games like *Final Fantasy X*. First, in 1971, Gary Gygax and Jeff Perren created the game *Chainmail* (Gygax & Perren, 1971; see also Birnbaum, 2004). The aim of this game was for a player to take control of a few figures and they would have to try and destroy another figure within two hits. *Chainmail* ultimately led to the creation of *Dungeons and Dragons* (Gygax & Arneson, 1974), which has been hailed as a pioneer of role-playing games (see Egenfeldt-Nielsen et al., 2015).

While these role-playing games changed the face of table-top gaming, a different game was released a decade before. This game would ultimately transform elements of *Dungeons and Dragons* and introduce an entirely new genre. As such, it is worthwhile looking to what was arguably the first videogame created—*Tennis for Two* (Higinbotham & Dvorak, 1958). *Tennis for Two* had the players control different lines, which were meant to represent tennis players. The players had to knock a pixel over a solid line on the screen. Therefore, the videogame looked like a game of tennis from the side. *Tennis for Two* signified that it was possible to combine technology with gaming. This combination paved the way for more videogames. One such videogame, which arguably massively changed the face of gaming, was *Pong* (Atari, 1972). *Pong* was a virtual simulation of the table-top sport game *ping pong* (sometimes called *table tennis*). In this videogame, players would control a small bar and would attempt to knock a ball (a pixel) across the screen and try to get the pixel behind their opponent's small bar. What made *Pong* so different from *Tennis for Two* was that it was made massively available to the American public, and it was successful in terms of sales.

While these two games (*Dungeons and Dragons* and *Pong*) have been massively popular, the genre has developed since they were created. In today's age, it would be seen as strange to be crying at a replication of *ping pong*. So, how did we move from chunky pixels that could just about move across a screen, to almost movie-quality like cutscenes seen in modern videogames? You also might now be wondering, what does *Dungeons and Dragons* have to do with anything? Finally, you may be thinking, what do either of these have to do with language and/or gender? These are the questions which will be answered in this chapter. This chapter provides a broad history of gaming and the schools of thought which underpin the research. Throughout, I attempt to interpret any questions that you, the reader, might have about any of the different sub-disciplines in which the entire monograph is based.

Moving from *Pong* to More Recent Games

There is a wealth of literature that has looked at developments in videogames since *Tennis for Two* was released (see, e.g., Egenfeldt-Nielsen et al., 2015; Kent, 2010). To discuss all of the videogames which have occurred since *Tennis for Two* would be an entire book within itself. However, it is worth noting some of the significant developments and why these are important to the current monograph.

Arguably, the first major development came with *Colossal Cave Adventure* (Crowther & Woods, 1977). Prior to *Colossal Cave Adventure*, most games were relatively short: players could spend maybe an hour or so playing a game, but ultimately would either finish the game or leave it. If the player left the game, they would lose any progress they had made. However, in the run-up to *Colossal Cave Adventure*'s release, games were beginning to get progressively longer—players were struggling to play through an entire game in a single sitting. *Colossal Cave Adventure* allowed players to save their progress, and this became revolutionary: this feature paved the way for much longer videogames. Imagine, for example, if those hundred or more hours which I had racked up on *Final Fantasy X* had been in one go: I would have had to have played it without sleep or any other commitments for at least a week. However, *Colossal Cave Adventure* did not have any visual elements to the game—it was all based purely on text. Thus, players could build their own 'text world', whereby they were able to use the written information to construct mental conceptualisations of the society the game is set in (see Gavins, 2007). The structure of these games also bore some resemblance to the later created 'Choose Your Own Adventure' books (see, e.g., Pickard, 1979). These kinds of books were popular in the late 1970s and early 1980s, and they allowed the reader to select how they wanted their story to pan out.

This kind of text-based fantasy would go on to influence the next development within videogames: the 'point and click' sub-genre of videogames (see Marchiori et al., 2011). In these games, the player would be presented with a visual object that they would click on, which in turn would reveal a text box that had more information about that object. The language used within this text box could add to the broader immersive narrative, give clues to the player, and ultimately shape the players' experience. One of the best examples of this is *Monkey Island* (LucasArts, 1990). Players were able to click on items for more information, and this, in tandem with the visual elements, allowed them to conceptualise the broader society and understand the different narratives within the game.

More recently, the language within games has changed again, and titles, such as *The Witcher 3: Wild Hunt* (CD Projekt Red, 2015), *Final Fantasy XV* (Square Enix, 2016) and *Kingdom Hearts 3* (Square Enix, 2019) now have professional voice actors speak the dialogue. This speech is overlaid on to the game, so players can both listen to what the characters have to say and can read subtitles of these audio files. Indeed, research has already been conducted into the use of accents and how they map on to different identities within videogames (see, e.g., Goorimoorthee et al., 2019). These developments show that language has been central to videogames since the late 1970s, although as time has progressed, so has what can be included within a videogame. What is needed now are dedicated analyses of how language is used within videogames. In particular, given the greater complexities of language available in more recent videogames, this book is concerned with looking at the complex narratives and linguistic features used within videogames to represent complex social phenomena and how the language in this medium can normalise attitudes towards identity.

Dungeons and Dragons and the Influence on Videogames

Earlier in the chapter, I noted how *Dungeons and Dragons* would go on to change the face of the videogame industry. Games such as *Dungeons and Dragons*, and the ensuing videogames which it inspired (such as *Pool of Radiance* (Strategic Simulations, 1988)) drew on a lexicon associated with the fantasy genre, established long before those games. For example, there were different races (such as *elves*, *humans*, and *dwarves*) and different classes (such as *paladins*, *rogues*, and *warriors*). These kinds of words drew on associations with previous literature—such as the work of J. R. R. Tolkien and his famous *Lord of the Rings* series (Tolkien, 1954a, 1954b, 1955). By placing high fantasy narratives (and the language associated with them) into an interactive form, games like *Dungeons and Dragons*, and indeed later games like *Pool of Radiance*, were (and still are) able to bolster people's expectation of the occurrence of words associated with the particular fantasy genre. More recently, games, such as *World of Warcraft* (*WoW*) (Blizzard Entertainment, 2004–onwards), regularly update their massively multiplayer online game. Each iteration and expansion of the game also contains language associated with the fantasy genre—and indeed, draw upon the different races and classes mentioned above.

At this point, it is worth making a distinction in different types of fantasy videogames, specifically within the ones which involve the player taking up a perceived 'role'. One type is c-RPGs (see Fizek, 2012), while the other is MMORPGs (see Harding-Rolls, 2006). c-RPGs are offline role-playing games, such as *Final Fantasy X* mentioned earlier. These kinds of videogames do not require an internet connection to play, and unless there is a function that allows for close-range connections, typically allow a player to play the game completely by themselves. This kind of videogame requires publishers to spend extra time ensuring that all functions and language are perfect (or as close to perfect as possible) before it is published. Typically, the only way any errors within these games can be fixed is with downloadable content or by releasing a second version of the game (which is very expensive to do). MMORPGs, on the other hand, stand for Massively Multiplayer Online Role-Playing

Games. These games require internet access to play and allow for thousands, if not millions, of players to congregate and play the videogame together. One of the best examples of this is *WoW*, which had a peak subscription of 12 million players in 2010 (Lee et al., 2011). In these games, developers regularly allot for times where they are able to update features, including linguistic changes to the content they have previously published. Another element comes into play here, though. MMORPG developers typically create 'chat' windows, which allow the players to talk with each other (see Baker, 2008a). The language produced in these chat windows, although not wholly 'spontaneous' (because the players have a chance to edit what they write), is different to the language which may be used by an NPC (non-playing character). NPCs are programmed to give specific language, which is the product of a scriptwriting team, and thus not likely to reflect some of the ludolects used by players. Ludolect here refers to a specific subset of language which is associated with people involved with videogames: be that the players, the developers, or people that report on the game (see Ensslin, 2012).

Gender and Videogames

By this point, you may be looking at the title of this book and thinking to yourself 'I picked up this book because it says that it looks at gender in videogames—where is the gender?' That is what this section now turns to.

As technology has developed, so too has the capability to represent gender—be that gendered social actors, such as characters or the concept of gender more broadly. For example, contrast the simple bars of *Pong* to more recent videogame characters—such as Laura Croft from the *Tomb Raider* franchise (see Eidos interactive 1996–2009; Square Enix, 2009–onwards). Although not much can be said about *Pong* from the perspective of how it represents gender (other than possibly about the male-dominated design team), there have been a number of academic debates about how characters like Laura Croft are represented within videogames (see MacCallum-Stewart, 2014). Scholars have noted that the representation of Laura Croft has changed across time and that she is less sexualised in the more recent games in comparison with earlier games. MacCallum-Stewart (2014) draws attention to this change and suggests that when more women were part of the design team, the representation of Laura became less sexualised. Although we cannot say for certain that there is a causal relation between women being included on the design team and a less sexualised representation, we can certainly say that there has been a diachronic change in how gender is represented in the series (this is discussed in more detail in Chapter 2).

There have also been a number of studies which have examined the representation of gender across games and the cognitive impact it might have on players (e.g. Dietz, 1998; Yao et al., 2009). Typically, the studies argue that there is a general cultivation effect on players of videogames (see Gerbner et al., 2002; Martins et al., 2011; Morgan et al., 2017 for discussion of cultivation effects). In essence, the notion of cultivation is one which suggests that repeated patterns of representations will encourage consumers of media to accept those representations and reproduce them. Indeed, with regard to the representation of gender within videogames, folk-feminist and media critic Anita Sarkeesian has discussed this kind of cultivation. She notes:

> One of the really insidious things about systemic and institutional sexism is that most often regressive attitudes and harmful gender stereotypes are maintained and perpetuated unintentionally. Likewise, engaging with these games is not going to transform players into raging sexists. [...] However, media narratives do have a powerful cultivation effect, helping to shape cultural attitudes and opinions. So, when developers exploit sensationalised images of brutalised, mutilated, and victimised women over, over, and over again [it] tends to reinforce the dominant gender paradigm which casts men as aggressive and commanding and frames women as subordinate and dependent. (Sarkeesian, 2014)

One really important aspect that Sarkeesian draws attention to is that 'engaging with these games is not going to transform players into raging sexists'. Indeed, there is a growing body of work which argues that perceptions of gender-based violence remain localised to in-game contexts (see, e.g., Williams, 2006). Therefore, what this book focuses on is probably best described as normalisation effects—that is to say, how ideals of gender in broader society are represented through the medium of videogames, what writers of videogames think is acceptable for gendered characters to do and say, and how videogames normalise particular genre-based conventions for the representation of gender (i.e. what is acceptable in a videogame but not in society in a broader context). In other words, repeating patterns of representation can lead to an 'incremental effect' (Baker, 2006, p. 13) that slowly builds up a picture of what we expect gendered characters to look like, how they behave, and how language is used both by and about them (this idea is conceptualised in more detail in Kelly et al., 2020). Such representations and ideologies might end up influencing how a player ends up behaving in the real world—but nevertheless, the relationship between the text and player's actions is more complex than 'monkey see, monkey do'.

However, returning to Sarkeesian's discussion of gender in videogames, it is worth noting the controversy surrounding her claims. In 2014, an online (anti)feminist-movement called '#Gamergate' received worldwide attention, of which Sarkeesian was a central figure. The movement was called # (hashtag) Gamergate because the it started on Twitter (users on Twitter can search for topics using the #) and because it was meant to draw parallels to Richard Nixon's 'watergate' scandal. #Gamergate started as a call for ethical standards in videogame journalism, but quickly (d)evolved into arguments around the representation of women in the gaming industry—as creators, critics, and characters of videogames (see Massanari, 2017 for a full overview). Although there were a number of problematic claims—on both sides of the debate—it is worth bringing to the fore that there are criticisms about the representation of gender in videogames (I return to some of these criticisms in Chapter 2) and that these should be investigated. However, whether or not these criticisms about how gender is represented within videogames (or indeed how it is researched) are upheld and validated through rigorous research, is a different story. As such, it is worth critically and systematically examining how gender is constructed within this medium.

To date, as will be discussed in more detail in Chapter 2, there have been a number of studies which have examined the visual representation of gender within videogames. These research pieces typically tend to examine normalised ideals for body types and research has shown that these body types may make players feel dissatisfied with the way they look (see, e.g., Martins et al., 2011). Outside of videogames as a text, there have been a number of visual content analyses of gendered bodies in magazine articles about videogames (see, e.g., Miller & Summers, 2007). These research articles draw on the notion that representations normalise gender norms—both in terms of what players might feel they need to look like and what gendered social actors should look like. There has also been work which has examined how players engage with characters who are of the same gender as themselves within games (see, e.g., Gray, 2014; Richard & Gray, 2018). While all of these fields and data types are useful for understanding videogames in a broader context, there still appears to be a lack of research which examines the language within videogames, and how this can have a normalisation effect in terms of attitudes towards gender.

Language and Gender

A different point you might now be thinking to yourself is: 'OK, you've now spoken about fantasy videogames and gender in videogames—but I picked up this book because it said that it was about language. Why is language important to the study of videogames? And what does the study of language have to do with gender?'. But first, it is possibly worth answering the question: 'why is language and gender research important? And how is this kind of research relevant to society?'.

It is no secret that words are important. Words carry meaning—and this is something which underpins most research into the social use of language. Take, for example, the words *bachelor*, *bachelorette*, and *spinster*. If you were to think of three adjectives to pre-modify each term, the likelihood is that *bachelor*, *bachelorette*, and *spinster* would all be pre-modified by different adjectives. Indeed, as Baker (2008b) notes, the word *bachelor* is more likely to occur with terms like *eligible*, *handsome*, or *wealthy*. By contrast, *spinster* is more likely to occur with terms like *frustrated*, *old*, and *lonely*. In addition, the word *bachelorette* (a gendered term derived from adding the gendered suffix '*-ette*' to *bachelor*—a coinage born from a strive towards equality) still is likely to be modified by different adjectives to both *bachelor* and *spinster*. A search in the Corpus of Contemporary American English (COCA) (Davies, 2009) reveals that this term is likely to be modified by adjectives such as *lucky*, *blonde*, and *fake* (COCA and other corpora are discussed in more detail later in this chapter). Interestingly, this term is also used as part of noun phrases such as *bachelorette party* and *bachelorette weekend*, implying a level of care-free fun (and possibly shenanigans) associated with this group of people. While some terms denote the same concepts (in the above examples, unmarried people who are male or female), they may have different associations. These associations help people build mental pictures of what to expect of gendered social actors and these expectations can form potentially harmful stereotypes. For instance, if I called a restaurant and said 'I'd like to book a table for 10 bachelorettes', they might be inclined to think the party will be noisy, rowdy, and potentially might want to refuse the booking. If I called a restaurant and said 'I'd like to book a table for 10 spinsters', the restaurant might be expecting a group of old women to turn up—and the restaurant may make certain food/drink pre-orders or rota on specific members of staff according to these stereotypes. But language also becomes problematic with gender in a different way here—what do we say if we want to refer to unmarried people whose gender identity falls outside of a gender binary? (other than 'they are an unmarried person who is non-binary'). We could potentially use the term *single*, but these terms can still apply to men and women—there are no terms which are unique for non-binary people. Therefore, we can quickly see that just a small amount of words that denote relationships are all tied up with connections to gender identities, and these can be difficult to accurately portray.

Having now demonstrated just one facet of language and gender—that there are subtle biases related to gender in language—it is now important to note, however, that language and gender research is a rich and ever-growing field of scholarly inquiry. There are a number of subfields within the study of language and gender, but they can broadly be divided into two camps: studies which look at the representation of gender (e.g. Baker, 2014; Heritage, 2020; Hunt, 2015; Wilkinson, 2019) (a definition for representation is given later in this chapter), and language use (e.g., Baker, 2014; Coates, 1996; Hall, 1995; Jones, 2012).

This is not to say that these two are mutually exclusive—and indeed, in the case of videogames where the language is scripted but then spoken by gendered voice actors pretending to be gendered characters, these camps very easily blur into each other.

All of the research within these sub-fields is of great social importance: ranging from looking at how ideologies towards sexuality are discussed in parliamentary language—which could influence the kinds of social policies implemented (Love & Baker, 2015) to how different groups of people use language to sustain ideologies about people based on their gender (see Heritage & Koller, 2020) which plays into creating 'us vs them' divides. These 'us vs them' divides based around gender and sexuality can become so extreme that they ultimately encourage people to murder others based on their gender and how they present their gendered bodies (as discussed in Heritage & Koller, 2020). Important in all of these social implications is that the language used about gender (and intersecting identities—such as sexuality) is (re)produced and reinforced. With regard to videogames, as texts which can repeat and (re)produce ideologies to several players, they are the perfect vehicles for the normalisation of certain ideologies.

Similar to how the developments of technology have allowed for more affordances in the representation of gender, so too have they allowed for more affordances in what kinds of language can be included. As will be discussed in more detail in Chapter 2, there are a number of studies which have looked at the (visual) representation of gender within videogames—that is to say, a number of studies have examined the way in which bodies of gendered characters are portrayed on screen (see, e.g., Martins et al., 2011). Less common, however, is research which has looked at language within videogames, and less so language that is related to gender. At this point, it is worth discussing how this book uses the term language. Broadly speaking, throughout this book, I am concerned with language as it relates to words and grammar. While some scholars are interested in the representation of gender in any form of communicative mode (e.g. Machin & van Leeuwen, 2016 examine the communicative mode of sound), I specifically analyse lexico-grammatical language. In addition, this book is only concerned with written/spoken modes of language. This is not to invalidate other's research into other modes of language—indeed, a good amount of work has been done on sign language, which is an equally valid but different form of language (see Johnston & Schembri, 2007). However, analysing additional modes beyond written/spoken modes would be beyond the scope of this book. Although visual analyses can be useful in the study of gender—as visual communication still conveys ideologies—ultimately, this book focuses on how lexis and grammar are able to communicate gendered ideologies due to the already existing wealth of research which focuses on visual communicative modes in videogames.

Although videogames alone are not likely to cause a particular political policy to be implemented—nor are they likely to encourage someone to go out and murder people who have different gender performances to their own (despite moral panic sometimes instilled by the media)—it is important to note the influence that games can have. Ultimately, the language used in videogames is a way of normalising what is seen as acceptable for talking about gendered characters (or indeed, what is seen as normal for how gendered characters talk). When this kind of language is problematic but repeated, it solidifies this problematic representation into common thought—that, even if it is a small number, some people will begin to think that those problematic ways are acceptable (see Stubbs, 1994, 1996). While previous research has analysed this idea as it relates to visual elements (see, e.g., Machin & van Leeuwen, 2016; Sarkeesian, 2014), little attention has been paid to how the lexico-grammatical structures in videogames allow for these representations.

Discourse, ideology, and representations

Throughout the previous section, one word which regularly came up was representation, and representations are closely linked to ideology. It is worth discussing these two concepts, and in particular, in relation to the related concept discourse. As will be discussed in more detail in the next chapter, I take a critical approach to discourse, and as such analyse discourses in terms of how they are used to represent and convey ideologies about gender. It is worth, however, turning to a working definition of each of these terms.

Broadly speaking, the view I take to discourse sees discourse as language in use as a social practice. However, discourse draws on shared social and cultural knowledge and ways of seeing the world, typically with respect to social groups. This knowledge, the view of what is accepted as the norm, and these ideas can be challenged, subverted, or indeed sustained through language use as a social practice (see Koller, 2012). This could be, for example, discourses on gender and sexuality—in which language is used as a way to lexicalise what the expected norms for people of a certain gender are (see, e.g., Baker, 2014). This view to discourse is summarised and justified in greater detail in Chapter 2 (but see also Fairclough & Wodak, 1997, p. 258)

Ideology is tied to discourse, in so far as discourses do ideological 'work'. That is to say, when language is used as a social practice, ideas and discourses relating to specific groups of people or concepts can be lexicalised in a way that shows how we view those people or concepts. For example, if someone were to say, 'I hate women', this would draw on a discourse that is misogynistic (i.e. uses language to collectivise women and negatively evaluate that social group), but would also show that person's ideology towards women (they have an ideology which draws on assumed cultural and social knowledge which positions women as lesser to men). Obviously, this is an overt example, and ideologies can often be much more subtle. It should also be noted, however, that the relationship between ideology and discourse is not one way, and that while ideologies can be conveyed through discourse practices, they can also shape discourses and discourses can have an impact on people's ideologies (see Koller, 2014).

Finally, the last term which creates a central tenant of the arguments in this book is the relationship between discourses and representations. I view representations as depictions of a social phenomenon or groups as manifested through a process of semiosis via drawing on discourse. The process of semiosis is the process of making a 'sign' (in this case, language such as words and grammatical structures) have meaning and how those signs are both interpreted and reproduced. Importantly, the process of semiosis is dependent on social and cultural factors. Take, for example, the name *Chad*. The word *Chad* by itself does not mean anything in particular—the most one might think is that it is a man's name (it has previously undergone a process of semiosis by which it has come to be used as a name for a man). However, certain communities online have put this noun through another process of semiosis and to them a *Chad* is a man who exhibits not only good looks, but desirable features of masculinity (see Heritage & Koller, 2020). With regard to other gendered terms, this could be, for example, using language to prescribe certain characteristics to women within a particular context. Such repeated representations can become problematic if a social group is only ever represented in one particular way.

With regard to the present monograph, representations, especially those of gender, are localised to a particular text type—videogames. In videogames, gender can be represented in a number of ways. One way is visual (see, e.g., Machin & van Leeuwen, 2016). The other way, though under-researched, is to examine the language used within videogames. In other words, people who create videogames are able to draw on certain discourses about gender when they write the language to be used in the game. These discourses allow for certain ideologies of gender to be represented (i.e. ideologies about gender can be lexicalised and conveyed in the text), and gender in itself can be represented in certain ways. Linking this back to the work on language and gender discussed earlier, these kinds of discourses, ideologies, and representations, can be conveyed through language about or by characters.

Corpus Linguistics

But how can we investigate discourses and ideologies, especially those which relate to gender? One such way in which we can investigate language is to closely analyse a small section of language. Such close readings can be highly fine-grained and can reveal how different elements of the language can build up to broader pictures in how we represent gender. However, I take the opposite approach: this book uses 'big data' to examine what discourses are being drawn on and then uses those findings to direct the analysis to closer readings.

The kind of 'big data' approach I take is to use a collection of methodologies called corpus linguistics. The word corpus (plural corpora) originates from the Latin word for 'body', and thus the field is concerned with analysing 'bodies' of texts. These bodies can be small, but representative, data sets of a few tens of thousands of words (see, e.g., Bednarek, 2015; Heritage & Koller, 2020). For example, Cutting (2000) used a corpus of only about 25,000 words, but this was highly specialised (see also Koester, 2010 for a discussion of small corpora). We could also create bodies of texts which total a few million—if not billion—words. For example, we might take a representative sample of American English (such as COCA, see Davies, 2009) or British English (Love, 2020). Typically, computer programs are used to examine patterns of language which would not normally be possible if the text were read through manually (see McEnery & Hardie, 2011). This could be, for example, running statistical tests on the data to see what words are over/under-used within a particular collection of texts in comparison to language used in a more general sense (see Brezina, 2018). It could also be examining what words occur most frequently in a given data set. While this is typically grammatical words (such as *the*, *and*, or *a*), this approach can also reveal what is salient through content words.

There have previously been several useful synergies between corpus linguistics and discourse analysis (see, e.g., Baker et al., 2008; Taylor, 2013, 2014, 2020). There have also been a number of these synergies which have focused on gender and sexuality (see, e.g., Baker, 2014; Heritage & Koller, 2020; Taylor, 2013; Wilkinson, 2019; Zottola, 2021). In this latter camp, studies typically examine explicitly gendered or sexuality-based terms—such as *man*, *woman*, *boy*, *girl*, *bisexual* and *transgender*. These explicitly gendered and sexuality-based terms are used as they clearly bring gender and sexuality identities to the fore. Related, and important to remember, is a question from language and gender studies—'yes, but is it gender?' (Swann, 2002, p. 43). Swann argues that, as interesting as some uses of language may be, these uses do not always indicate that there is some sort of gender bias and that some uses may not be due to the gender of language producer. To that end, corpus approaches which examine explicitly gendered terms offer a useful method. That is to say, by looking at these explicitly gendered terms, an analyst can be more confident that what they are examining is directly related to the representation of gender (and/or sexuality), as opposed to some other identity. Similarly, Swann's criticism also draws attention to the idea that one speaker's use of language (or indeed a small number of speaker's language features) might not be due to the gender of that/those speaker(s) but could be a product of that/those speaker's idiolect(s). Therefore, using a corpus approach allows us to examine a massive and representative sample. We are able to examine both explicitly gendered terms and multiple people's speech to see if any difference can be examined across speakers and with statistical data to guide the analysis.

Corpora thus offer a way of looking at videogames from a 'big data' perspective—this methodological approach allows a researcher to examine the representation of gender across several games and characters. Such analysis might allow a researcher to examine how gender is represented within a genre, or look at what gendered terms might appear in a specific game that is different to others within a genre. Although I have not gone into detail about the specific methods used in corpus linguistics in this chapter, these are discussed in more detail in Chapter 3.

Summary of the Chapter

This chapter has looked at the very core principles and outlined the key tenants of three different fields: ludolinguistics, language and gender, and corpus linguistics. In particular, I have discussed the kind of genre that this book is concerned with (fantasy videogames), how videogames have been influenced by other texts, and how they have developed. As videogames have developed, the technological affordances for different representations of gender (and the language that can be included in a videogame) have changed. It is therefore worth considering looking at the language used within videogames, as a way of normalising the kind of roles gendered characters have, the kind of language gendered characters use, and how gendered characters are discussed. I argued that one way to examine these representations of gender is via corpus linguistic methods—using computers to analyse big sets of data and to examine specifically gendered lexemes within videogames.

Although this chapter has introduced some of these fields, I have only given a very basic and simplified overview of the disciplines. In later chapters, I discuss some of the nuances of the fields, and how they shape the analyses presented later in this book.

So Why Write This Book?

So, why have I decided to write a book titled 'Language, Gender, and Videogames: Using Corpora to Analyse the Representation of Gender in Fantasy Videogames'? Broadly speaking, there are two reasons for this: the first is that there is a dearth of literature which has previously applied corpus methods to such a text type (though, see Heritage, 2020, 2021). This dearth of literature is explored in more detail in Chapter 2. This monograph thus contributes to previous scholarly literature, as it attempts to demonstrate that it is possible to apply such methods to this text type. The second reason why I have written this book is to account for a few methodological criticisms lobbied at previous studies into the representation of gender in videogames (again, this is discussed in more detail in Chapter 2). Therefore, this book attempts to provide directions for more systematicity in the study of gender representation in videogames.

Outside of these academic reasons, i.e. to bridge gaps in the literature and to suggest new directions for research, I wanted to write this book in a way which is accessible for a range of readers. Simply put, in this book, I assume that a reader has no background knowledge of any of the major fields which I draw on—language and gender studies, corpus linguistics, and ludolinguistics. I have tried to make this book as accessible as possible for all readers. It is my hope that readers from a variety of fields and backgrounds can learn about the potential synergies and uses of applying corpus methods to videogames as a way of exploring the construction of (gender) identity.

As noted in the above discussions, this book is particularly concerned with examining the representation of gender (and, to a lesser extent, sexuality), in videogames. I am particularly interested in looking at the representation of gender through the examination of the language (i.e. lexis and grammar) within videogames. In this book, I use a corpus approach to the data—though, this will be coupled with a close reading of the data as generated via corpus methods. This is not to invalidate the work of scholars who have looked at videogames from a qualitative perspective and/or have taken broad overviews of a single videogame, but this book is concerned with the application of pre-established methods which move beyond this kind of analysis.

Although there has been significant work on multimodal approaches to the representation of gender in videogames (see, e.g., Machin & van Leeuwen, 2016), this book does not seek to address the multimodal nature of videogames. The reasoning for this is manifold: first, visual analyses of gender representation in videogames have been done before, while close examination of lexical and grammatical structures has not. Second, multimodal analyses of these games could be an entire series of monographs in themselves—and multiple pages could be written on just a small handful of images. Third, the interpretation of visual images can be highly subjective—more so than interpreting data from a corpus. Finally, on a more practical level, multimodal analyses would require a lot of copyright permissions from the different videogame developers—which would probably limit the number of images which could be reasonably analysed.

Another aspect to not expect from this book is an analysis of videogame paratext. As will be discussed in more detail in Chapter 2, analyses of 'the language of gaming' (see, e.g., Ensslin, 2012) tend to focus on the language around videogames—such as in magazines about videogames, in online fora, or among players. This book is not concerned with player-generated language—instead, I am interested in the language used within videogames, as generated by large companies who likely spend a lot of time and money in the production of language which they deem 'acceptable' to players. This is an important distinction and one which sets the current book apart from a lot of previous studies.

Throughout the analysis chapters of this book, I often will draw on other discursive models of analysis, which move beyond just corpus methods. These models have been selected because they have been married with corpus methods in previous research. Given the array of models, I will discuss the frameworks where appropriate, to save readers of this book having to flick between the analysis chapter(s) and a different chapter where the framework is outlined.

This book is structured as follows: first, in the next chapter (Chapter 2), I give more detail about language, gender, and videogame research. I have discussed some of the core concepts about these fields in this chapter, but Chapter 2 seeks to provide a more insightful and in-depth discussion of these fields. Chapter 3 seeks to discuss corpus linguistics in more depth, with a focus on corpus approaches to the language in videogames. The reason why this chapter is separated from Chapter 2 is that it is arguably more methodologically oriented (as corpus linguistics is a scholarly field based around collection of methodological approaches to language).

Chapter 4 stays in a methodological vein and discusses some of the issues associated with building a corpus of videogames. In particular, one of the few studies which has looked at the language used in videogames only used the language from 'a typical playthrough' (Goorimoorthee et al., 2019, p. 274). However, this quickly becomes problematic when considering that players have different choices and that these choices will influence what language a player engages with. I discuss four potential methods for collecting data for videogame corpora, which underpin the data collection methods in the subsequent chapters.

In Chapter 5, I turn to analyse the representation of gender in a reference corpus of fantasy videogames. I take a representative sample of language from 10 videogames, totalling approximately 330,000 words. In this chapter, I focus on using corpus-assisted methods (discussed in more detail in Chapter 3) and explore how the gendered pronouns *he* and *she* as well as the gendered nouns *man* and *woman* are used. In this chapter, I pay particular attention to the kind of verbs that gendered terms occur with and how these different verbs can sustain problematic ideas about gender.

In Chapter 6, I analyse a single videogame series—*The Witcher*. In this chapter, I take a much more corpus-driven approach to the data (again, discussed in more detail in Chapter 3). I explore the different keywords for each game, semantically group these words, and demonstrate the importance of moving beyond lexical semantics of non-gendered words. I ultimately argue that corpus techniques can reveal that some words which are not ostensibly gendered might reveal a gendered bias—as evidenced through collocates and collocational networks of the word *trophy*.

In Chapter 7, I look at the re-release of *Classic World of Warcraft* (*Classic WoW*) (originally released in 2004, but re-released in 2019, see Blizzard Entertainment, 2004–onwards), as it draws attention to several of avenues for research into the language of videogames. *Classic WoW* was very popular back in 2004—achieving a score of 94/100 on Metacritic (see Metacritic, 2004). When Blizzard re-released *Classic WoW*, they were already halfway through their seventh expansion, *Battle for Azeroth* (*BFA WoW*). Even while writing this book, Blizzard has not stopped maintaining its servers and is still developing new expansions. However, *Classic WoW* was re-released 15 years after the original version, meaning that the language (and the language about gender) might have changed and indeed might be different in *BFA WoW*. It is this change which is the focus of Chapter 7.

Finally, in Chapter 8, I synthesise the findings and discuss the implications for future research. It should also be noted that throughout, I provide the references for each chapter at the end of that chapter (i.e. each chapter has its own independent bibliography). It is my hope that this will make future research easier for readers.

Ludography

Atari. (1972). *Pong*. Sunnyvale, California: Atari.
Blizzard Entertainment. (2004–onwards). *World of Warcraft*. Irvine, California: Blizzard Entertainment.

CD Projekt Red. (2015). *The Witcher 3: Wild Hunt*. Warsaw, Poland: CD Projekt Red.
Crowther, W., & Woods, D. (1977). *Colossal cave adventure.* No publisher.
Eidos Interactive. (1996–2009). *Tomb Raider*. London, UK: Eidos Interactive.
Gygax, G., & Arneson, D. (1974). *Dungeons and dragons.* Lake Geneva, Wisconsin: TSR inc.
Gygax, G., & Perren, J. (1971). *Chainmail*. Evansville, Indiana: Guidon Games.
Higinbotham, W., & Dvorak, R. (1958). *Tennis for two.* No publisher. Exhibited at Brookhaven National Laboratory.
LucasArts. (1990). *Monkey island*. San Francisco, California: Lucasfilm Games.
Square Enix. (2001). *Final Fantasy X*. Tokyo, Japan: Square Enix.
Square Enix. (2009–onwards). *Tomb Raider*. London, United Kingdom: Square Enix.
Square Enix. (2016). *Final fantasy XV*. Tokyo, Japan: Enix.
Square Enix. (2019). *Kingdom hearts 3.* Tokyo, Japan: Square Enix.
Strategic Simulations. (1988). *Pool of radiance.* Mountain View, California: Strategic Simulations, Inc.

Bibliography

Baker, P. (2006). *Using corpora in discourse analysis.* Bloomsbury.
Baker, P. (2008a). *Sexed texts: language, gender and sexuality*. Equinox.
Baker, P. (2008b). 'Eligible' bachelors and 'frustrated' spinsters: Corpus linguistics, gender and language. In K. Harrington, L. Litosseliti, H. Sauntson, & J. Sunderland (Eds.), *Gender and language research methodologies* (pp. 73–84). Palgrave Macmillan.
Baker, P. (2014). *Using corpora to analyse gender*. Bloomsbury.
Baker, P., Gabrielatos, C., KhosraviNik, M., Krzyżanowski, M. ł., McEnery, T., & Wodak, R. (2008). A useful methodological synergy? Combining critical discourse analysis and corpus linguistics to examine discourses of refugees and asylum seekers in the UK press. *Discourse & Society, 19*(3), 273–306.
Bednarek, M. (2015). "Wicked" women in contemporary pop culture: "bad" language and gender in Weeds, Nurse Jackie, and Saving Grace. *Text & Talk, 35*(4), 431–451.
Birnbaum, J. (2004). *Gary Gygax / Dungeons & Dragons interview.* Game Banshee. https://www.gamebanshee.com/interviews/28268-gary-gygax-dungeons-dragons-interview/all-pages.html. Accessed February 2021.

Brezina, V. (2018). *Statistics in corpus linguistics: A practical guide*. Cambridge University Press

Coates, J. (1996). *Women talk*. Blackwell Publishers.

Cutting, J. (2000). *Analysing the language of discourse communities*. Brill.

Davies, M. (2009). The 385 + million word corpus of contemporary American English (1990–2008+): Design, architecture, and linguistic insights. *International Journal of Corpus Linguistics, 14*(2), 159–190.

Dietz, T. (1998). An examination of violence and gender role portrayals in video games: Implications for gender socialization and aggressive behavior. *Sex Roles, 38*(5–6), 425–442.

Egenfeldt-Nielsen, S., Smith, J., & Tosca, S. P. (2015). *Understanding video games: The essential introduction* (3rd ed.). Routledge.

Ensslin, A. (2012). *The language of gaming*. Palgrave.

Fairclough, N., & Wodak, R. (1997). Critical discourse analysis. In T. A. van Dijk (Ed.), *Discourse studies: Multidisciplinary introduction* (pp. 258–84). Sage.

Finkel, I. L. (2007). On the rules for the royal game of Ur. In I. L. Finkel (Ed.), *Ancient board games in perspective* (pp. 16–32). British Museum Press.

Fizek, S. (2012). *Pivoting the player: A methodological toolkit for player character research in offline Role-Playing games* (Doctoral dissertation, Bangor University).

Gavins, J. (2007). *Text world theory: An introduction.* Edinburgh University Press.

Gerbner, G., Gross, L., Morgan, M., Signorielli, N., & Shanahan, J. (2002). Growing up with television: Cultivation processes. *Media Effects: Advances in Theory and Research, 2*(1), 43–67.

Goorimoorthee, T., Csipo, A., Carleton, S., & Ensslin, A. (2019). Language ideologies in videogame discourse: Forms of sociophonetic othering in accented character speech. In A. Ennslin & I. Balteiro (Eds.), *Approaches to videogame discourse: Lexis, interaction, textuality* (pp. 269–287). Bloomsbury.

Gray, K. (2014). *Race, gender, and deviance in Xbox live: Theoretical perspectives from the virtual margins.* Routledge.

Hall, K. (1995). Lip service on the fantasy lines. In K. Hall & M. Bucholtz (Eds.), *Gender articulated: Language and the socially constructed self* (pp. 183–216). Routledge.

Harding-Rolls, P. (2006). *Western world MMOG market: 2006 review and forecasts to 2011.* Screen Digest.

Heritage, F. (2020). Applying corpus linguistics to videogame data: Exploring the representation of gender in videogames at a lexical level. *Game Studies, 20*(3).

Heritage, F. (2021). *Maidens and monsters: A corpus assisted critical discourse analysis of the representation of gender in The Witcher videogame series* (Doctoral dissertation, Lancaster University).

Heritage, F., & Koller, V. (2020). Incels, in-groups, and ideologies: The representation of gendered social actors in a sexuality-based online community. *Journal of Language and Sexuality, 9*(2), 152–178.

Hunt S. (2015). Representations of gender and agency in the Harry Potter series. In P. Baker & T. McEnery (Eds.), *Corpora and discourse studies: Integrating discourse and corpora* (pp. 266–284). Palgrave Macmillan.

Johnston, T. & Schembri, A. (2007). *Australian Sign Language (Auslan): An introduction to sign language linguistics*. Cambridge University Press.

Jones, L. (2012). *Dyke/girl: Language and identities in a lesbian group*. Palgrave Macmillan.

Kelly, C., Lynes, A., & Hoffin, K. (2020). *Introduction: Reorienting the debate*. In C. Kelly, A. Lynes, & K. Hoffin (Eds.), *Video games, crime & next-gen deviance: Reorienting the debate*. Emerald Group Publishing.

Kent, S. (2010). *The ultimate history of video games: Volume two: from Pong to Pokemon and beyond—The story behind the craze that touched our lives and changed the world*. Three Rivers Press.

Koester, A. (2010). Building small specialised corpora. In A. O'keeffe & M. McCarthy (Eds.), *The Routledge handbook of corpus linguistics* (pp. 66–79). Routledge.

Koller, V. (2012). How to analyse collective identity in discourse—Textual and contextual parameters. *Critical Approaches to Discourse Analysis Across Disciplines, 5*(2), 19–38.

Koller, V. (2014). Applying social cognition research to critical discourse studies: The case of collective identities. In C. Hart & P. Cap (Eds.), *Contemporary critical discourse studies* (pp. 147–165). Bloomsbury.

Lee, Y., Chen, K., Cheng, Y., & Lei, C. (2011). World of Warcraft avatar history dataset. In *Proceedings of the second annual ACM conference on Multimedia systems* (pp. 123–128). ACM.

Love, R. (2020). *Overcoming challenges in corpus construction: The spoken British National Corpus 2014*. Routledge.

Love, R., & Baker, P. (2015). The hate that dare not speak its name? *Journal of Language Aggression and Conflict, 3*(1), 57–86.

MacCallum-Stewart, E. (2014). “Take that, Bitches!” Refiguring Lara Croft in feminist game narratives. *Game Studies, 14*(2).
Machin, D., & van Leeuwen, T. (2016). Sound, music and gender in mobile games. *Gender and Language, 10*(3), 412–432.
Marchiori, E. J., Del Blanco, Á., Torrente, J., Martinez-Ortiz, I., & Fernández-Manjón, B. (2011). A visual language for the creation of narrative educational games. *Journal of Visual Languages & Computing, 22*(6), 443–452.
Martins, N., Williams, D. C., Ratan, R. A., & Harrison, K. (2011). Virtual muscularity: A content analysis of male video game characters. *Body Image, 8*(1), 43–51.
Massanari, A. (2017). #Gamergate and the fappening: How Reddit's algorithm, governance, and culture support toxic technocultures. *New Media & Society, 19*(3), 329–346.
McEnery, T. & Hardie, A. (2011). *Corpus linguistics: Method, theory and practice*. Cambridge University Press.
Metacritic. (2004). *World of Warcraft*. Metacritic. https://www.metacritic.com/game/pc/world-of-warcraft. Accessed February 2021.
Miller, M., & Summers, A. (2007). Gender differences in video game characters' roles, appearances, and attire as portrayed in video game magazines. *Sex Roles, 57*(9–10), 733–742.
Morgan, M., Shanahan, J., & Signorielli, N. (2017). Cultivation theory: Idea, topical fields, and methodology. In P. Rössler, C. Hoffner, & L. Zoonen (Eds.), *The International encyclopedia of media effects*. Wiley.
Pickard, E. (1979). *The cave of time*. Bantam Books.
Richard, G. T., & Gray, K. L. (2018). Gendered play, racialized reality: Black cyberfeminism, inclusive communities of practice and the intersections of learning in gaming. *Frontiers: A Journal of Women's Studies, 39*(1), 112–148.
Sarkeesian, A. (2014). *Tropes vs. women. Feminist frequency: Conversations with pop culture*. YouTube. https://www.youtube.com/watch?v=X6p5AZp7r_Q. Accessed February 2021.
Stubbs, M. (1994). Grammar, text and ideology. *Applied Linguistics, 15*(2), 201–223.
Stubbs, M. (1996). *Text and corpus analysis*. Blackwell.
Swann, J. (2002). Yes, but is it gender? In L. Litosseliti & J. Sunderland (Eds.), *Gender identity and discourse analysis* (pp. 43–67). John Benjamins.
Taylor, C. (2013). Searching for similarity using corpus-assisted discourse studies. *Corpora, 8*(1), 81–113.

Taylor, C. (2014). Investigating the representation of migrants in the UK and Italian press: A cross-linguistic corpus-assisted discourse analysis. *International Journal of Corpus Linguistics, 19*(3), 368–400.

Taylor, C. (2020). Representing the Windrush generation: Metaphor in discourses then and now. *Critical Discourse Studies, 17*(1), 1–21.

Tolkien, J. R. R. (1954a). *The fellowship of the ring*. Allen & Unwin.

Tolkien, J. R. R. (1954b). *The two towers*. Allen & Unwin.

Tolkien, J. R. R. (1955). *The return of the king*. Allen & Unwin.

Wilkinson, M. (2019). 'Bisexual oysters': A diachronic corpus-based critical discourse analysis of bisexual representation in The Times between 1957 and 2017. *Discourse & Communication, 13*(2), 249–267.

Williams, D. (2006). Virtual cultivation: Online worlds, offline perceptions. *Journal of Communication, 56*(1), 69–87.

Yao, M. Z., Mahood, C., & Linz, D. (2009). Sexual Priming, gender stereotyping, and likelihood to sexually harass: Examining the cognitive effects of playing a sexually-explicit video game. *Sex Roles, 62*(1), 77–88.

Zottola, A. (2021). *Transgender Identities in the press: A corpus-based discourse Analysis*. Bloomsbury.

2

Language, Gender, and Videogames

A Century of Progress?

The representation of gender within literature has long been a sticking point of feminist critique and a cornerstone of feminist research. In 1929, Virginia Woolf critiqued the representation of gender within literature and stated:

> All these relationships between women, I thought, rapidly recalling the splendid gallery of fictitious women, are too simple. […] And I tried to remember any case in the course of my reading where two women are represented as friends. […] They are now and then mothers and daughters. But almost without exception they are shown in their relation to men. It was strange to think that all the great women of fiction were, until Jane Austen's day, not only seen by the other sex, but seen only in relation to the other sex. And how small a part of a woman's life is that. (Woolf, 1929, p. 107)

More recently, as noted in Chapter 1, there have been several feminist critiques about the representation of gender within videogames as a new literary genre (see Sarkeesian, 2014).

F. Heritage, *Language, Gender and Videogames*,
https://doi.org/10.1007/978-3-030-74398-7_2

Since Woolf's socially aware literary commentary, there have been many socio-political changes that have influenced women worldwide. Women across the world have fought for and won many socio-legal rights. In Western society, this includes (but is not limited to) rights such as the right to vote, the right to equality in the workplace, and the right to marry other women if they wish (for an overview, see Tickner & Sjoberg, 2013). It is reasonable to suggest that the representation of women will also have changed as they gain socio-political rights. In other words, the representation of gender within videogames might be vastly different compared to how women were represented in the books Virginia Woolf was reading. However, research has suggested that while there have been socio-political and legal changes to protect those who face prejudice due to their gender and sexuality, the biases may still be present but coded in more tacit ways (see Love & Baker, 2015). Therefore, even though the society in which videogames are produced is different to the society in which Woolf lived in, it is nevertheless worth examining whether or not the language used within these texts uphold similar values to those which were subject to Woolf's criticisms.

Similarly, the nature of Sarkeesian's feminist criticisms raises questions about how videogames represent gender and if they reflect contemporary socio-political views on gender. In particular, if there are tacit gender biases at play, how are these linguistically formulated? Moreover, there are several criticisms of Sarkeesian's work from a methodological standpoint. Although I do not have the space to provide a nuanced account of all of these criticisms, it is worth noting that the examples Sarkeesian uses as the foundation of her analysis are specifically picked to highlight the points she wants to make. In other words, Sarkeesian starts with a hypothesis and shoehorns in data from popular videogames to fit that hypothesis. This approach is problematic because it is not true to the data itself, as the data may have multiple positive representations but may be selected based on a single negative aspect. Methodological criticisms such as this spark a discussion of what methods are most appropriate for exploring the representation of gender in videogames. As I touched upon in Chapter 1, I would argue for the use of corpus linguistics—as it is a method which takes a more representative approach to language. Although I discuss corpus linguistics in more detail in Chapter 3, it is worth noting that some of the studies discussed in this chapter use corpus linguistic methods. Therefore, it is worth reiterating that a very basic definition of corpus linguistics is that it is a collection of methodologies which involve the use of computer programs to examine patterns of language which would not normally be possible if the text were read through manually (see McEnery & Hardie, 2011).

Therefore, this chapter seeks to specifically discuss previous research in language and gender studies, as well as previous work in ludolinguistics. Although I start by discussing these fields as separate scholarly disciplines, the latter half of this chapter seeks to discuss instances where these fields have been combined. Throughout, I make the argument that studies which have looked at the representation of gender in videogames have focused on the language around videogames—i.e. in videogame paratext, such as on websites and in internet fora (see, e.g., Ensslin, 2012) (I also discuss this in more detail in Chapter 4). Studies which have looked at the representation of gender within videogames are much rarer, and when they do occur, they typically do not focus on the lexico-grammatical structures, rather they focus on the multimodal components of the games.

Language and Gender Research—Historical Developments

First, it is important to make a distinction between sex (biological traits associated with being male or female, relating to, for example, chromosomes, hormones, and sexual organs) and gender (socially constructed roles and behaviours deemed appropriate for one's sex). Although historically, the two have previously been viewed as inherently linked and synonymous (see Johnson & Repta, 2012), this is not necessarily the case. Societally influenced medical practices, such as assigning newborn children a sex (and therefore an assumed gender) based on their reproductive organs, have positioned these social constructions into a shared binary: that people are regularly seen as either 'male' or 'female' depending on their external genitals (see Davis et al., 2014). The expected norms for these perceived two genders (male and female) shape an individual's identity (Butler, 1990). Some studies discussed in this chapter, especially those written when structuralist philosophy was dominant in mainstream academic thinking, have conflated gender and sex and have viewed the conflated concept as a binary structure (although I do not view it in such a way).

Scholarly pioneers of the third-wave feminist movement[1] in the early 1990s, proposed that sex is biologically determined, and gender is abstract, socially constructed, and perpetually changing (see Bing & Bergvall, 1996; Butler, 1990, 1997; Eckert, 2014; Jackson, 2012). This notion was further developed in tandem with the post-structuralist philosophical movement, to a point where, the contemporary standard academic viewpoint is that both sex and gender are social constructions (Cameron, 2005; Eckert, 2014; Johnson & Repta, 2012). Throughout this book, wherever possible I will be using the term 'gender' as opposed to 'sex', as the discussions presented throughout the book are concerned with the abstract social construction of gender, while also acknowledging that sex can be relevant in the construction of gender too.

The change in how gender and sex are seen is just one of the many changes that have occurred over the last century. Importantly, the changes in how we view gender have also influenced how we view the study of language as it relates to gender. A large amount of work has summarised the change in approaches to language and gender research (e.g. Baker, 2014; Cameron, 2008, 2009; Coffey-Glover, 2019; Litosseliti, 2006). In short, one way to view the developments in the study of language and gender is through the 4 Ds model. The first 'D' stands for the deficit approach, in which scholars such as Otto Jespersen argued that women's style of speech was deficient in comparison to men's style of speech (see Jespersen, 1922). In his work, Jespersen makes claims which by modern standards would be viewed as sexist—such as the claim that:

[1] 'Waves' of feminism is a metaphor for the social goals of feminism in the 'Western' world at a given point (see Cameron, 2005, p. 483). The goal of first-wave feminism was to achieve the right to vote. The goals of second-wave feminism included, but were not limited to, achieving workplace equality, more visibility of women in the media, access to equal education, and access to birth control. And one of the primary goals of third-wave feminism is/was to show that gender is socially constructed and fluid. Others have begun to argue that there is a fourth wave emerging, which has the goal of moving feminist ideologies and activism into online contexts (see Rivers, 2017).

'the vocabulary of a woman as a rule is much less extensive than that of a man' (p. 249). Simply put, Jespersen's work was a product of the society in which it was written—a society which viewed women as inferior to men.

However, despite how problematic Jespersen's work was, it influenced Robin Lakoff to write a pioneering paper and book—both called *language and women's place* (Lakoff, 1973, 1975). In her work, she suggested that men and women do use different linguistic features—but this is not necessarily the product of a mental deficiency (as argued by Jespersen), rather this difference was due to society viewing women as inferior to men. She also argued that this view of women as inferior to men was self-perpetuating, as men and women were likely to use certain language features to sustain the status quo. Drawing on anecdotal evidence, she argued that women have different features associated with the ways they use language—for example, women use more tag questions and empty adjectives in comparison to men. However, Lakoff's work has been heavily criticised. Cameron (2007, p. 3) highlights the popularity of ideologies similar to those proposed by Lakoff:

> The idea that men and women "speak different languages" has itself become a dogma, treated not as a hypothesis to be investigated or as a claim to be adjudicated, but as an unquestioned article of faith. Our faith in it is misplaced.

In a similar vein, Mills (2003) argues that Lakoff's research demonstrates typical traits of second-wave feminism, as Lakoff only focused on the language used by white middle-class women, which were claimed to be representative of all women. Mills also notes how the feminist movement has shifted to a state where the norm is to view women as a heterogeneous group (a group consisting of different kinds of people), rather than as a homogeneous group (a group where all people are seen as the same).

However, this notion that women were being subordinated in society due to language features lead other scholars to examine what has since become termed the Dominance approach—which viewed language as a means of sustaining male dominance. One way in which proponents of this approach claimed that such dominance was achieved was through language which assumed masculine as the norm—such as by assuming the gender of an unknown doctor to be male (see, e.g., Spender, 1980). There was also a strand of research within this approach which examined how men sought to dominate conversations—via the quantification of linguistic features, such as the frequency of overlaps and the length of pauses (see Zimmerman & West, 1975).

Not long after, some scholars began to argue that these perceived differences were not due to men and women having different biological features, and that it was not always due to men seeking dominance, but rather that men and women were effectively raised in two cultures (see Tannen, 1990). This approach became known as the Difference approach. However, Tannen's approach to gender can also be seen as problematic. Giora (2002, p. 330) critiques both the work of Lakoff (1973, 1975) and Tannen (1990), noting:

> Both the "different and deficient" and "different but equally valid" approaches, then, are problematic politically: They result in maintaining inequality. However, they are also inadequate as descriptive theories. There is a growing body of evidence [...] disconfirming the difference view.

The fourth 'D' is the Discursive approach and is usually undertaken by social constructionist feminists. In this approach (which I align myself with), gender is viewed as an identity which is performed via discourse(s) (see Butler, 1990; Cameron, 2007; Meyerhoff, 2014). As Butler (1990, p. 34) states: 'there is no gender identity behind the expression of gender; that identity is performativity constituted by the very "expressions" that are said to be its results'. In other words, Butler argues that anyone may draw upon linguistic traits associated with any gender, regardless of their sex. Hence, Butler's argument suggests that stereotypical masculine and feminine linguistic traits associated with male and female identities are not necessarily bound to an individual's gender identity. Performativity can be an unconscious, learnt phenomena, as a result of individuals identifying with certain 'correct' ways of being gendered within society. Individuals can observe other's performances of gender and emulate them—or, they can choose to subvert them. Therefore, those who use language in ways which Lakoff (1973, 1975) notes do so in a way that conforms to essentialist norms. On the other hand, in some cases, such as drag queens, gender performance can be a conscious act, whereby individuals acknowledge 'correct' gender norms and choose to defy (or sometimes align with) the ones that are associated with their sex (see Barrett, 2017).

Gender Performativity

Coates (1996) builds on the work of Butler through qualitatively and quantitatively analysing authentic data that has come from across a range of different situations (Butler's work is very abstract and discusses gender performativity at a theoretical and philosophical level). Coates draws attention to the fact that, depending on the context, some features may appear more masculine, while others may appear more feminine (see also, Cameron, 2005). Furthermore, Butler's work on gender performativity also acts as a springboard to allow us to understand the performance of sexuality. The performance of sexuality and expectations of sexuality can heavily influence an individual's performances of gender. This influence is highlighted by Cameron (1998), who examined the construction of heterosexuality among a group of male college students. She demonstrates how the construction of a heterosexual identity is heavily gendered, but also how linguistic traits associated with femininity are not bound to linguistic constructions used by women. Hence, gender performances appear to be complex, as do performances of sexuality (see also Cameron, 2005; Cameron & Kulick, 2003). In sum, Coates and Cameron give evidence for Butler's (1990) notion that gender is performed, though Coates and Cameron emphasise that it is also situationally constructed.

At the same time, given the historical prejudice against women in both British and American societies (such as how, in Britain, only a small subset of women were allowed the right to vote in 1918 with this being rolled out to more women in 1923), it is easy to associate the study of gender with the study of women. However, the study of men and masculinity is also an important aspect to the study of language and gender. For example, Connell (2005) argues that masculinity is not only discursively constructed, but it is tied to socio-economic structures. Connell identifies different types of masculinity, which differ depending on the socio-economic class of the performer, and she argues that there are multiple and different forms of masculinity. Connell draws attention to the intersection between different forms of masculinity and socio-economic status. For example, she outlines the concept of physical masculinity, which is associated with the working-class, and technical masculinity, which is a product associated with the upper-middle-class. Within the construction of masculinity, Connell argues that physical, technological, and political power are all associated with masculinity, yet class also plays a significant role in how masculinity is constructed and normalised.

A central aspect of this notion is that hegemonic masculinity is enacting masculinity to make more feminine 'others' subordinate. As Schippers (2007, p. 88) summaries:

> In Connell's theory, subordination is one mechanism for the ascendancy of hegemonic masculinity, but it is not the only one; there are also marginalized masculinities. While hegemony, subordination, and complicity are aspects of the gender order, Connell offers marginalization to characterize the relationships among men that result as class and race intersect.

This appears to strongly link to Crenshaw's (1991) notion of intersectionality, whereby different social identities intersect with one another to create different configurations of (dis)empowerment and different performances of gender. In a similar vein, Beynon (2001, p. 1) argues:

> 'Masculinity is always interpolated by cultural, historical and geographical location and in our time the combined influence of feminism and the gay movement has exploded the conception of a uniform masculinity and even sexuality [and by extension, femininity] is no longer held to be fixed or innate'.

Thus, while Connell proposes that masculinity is based on physical, technological, and political power dependent on socio-economic class, Beynon has argued that the social identities and culture also determine to what degree something is classified as masculine, feminine, or neutral. Thus, the multifaceted nature of identity must be considered in any analysis of gender and the study of gender extends beyond just the study of women.

In a nutshell, there are a variety of aspects to consider with regards to one's identity and categorising broadly by gender identity can be detrimental to research. Research which suggests 'x' feature is used by 'y' gender (sometimes called 'women's language', or 'men's language') is highly problematic. Such a problematic approach to gender might make you wonder how language and gender studies are conducted. As Baker (2014) notes, there are typically two ways to explore the intersection between language and gender: usage and representation. Within the usage camp, Baker's (2014) chapter on how female lecturers construct their identity demonstrates fruitful corpus-based approaches to gender performance (see also Butler, 1990; Cameron, 1998). Note, that even though Baker still looks at the way in which female lecturers speak, the focus is on identity construction, rather than assigning arbitrary features to a perceived gendered speech. In the representation camp, one chapter of Baker's (ibid.) book examined the representation of gay men in the British newspaper *The Daily Mail*. Baker was able to note how the media (re)produced discourses about gay men and drew on stereotypes about them—that gay people are represented as politically militant, have casual and meaningless (sexual) relationships, and are viewed as effeminate. Baker's analysis highlights the importance of examining how gender (and intersecting identities such as sexuality) are represented (and normalised) in the media, all of which are particularly applicable to videogames as a text.

From Speech to Writing

In most of the above studies, performativity has been discussed and explored with particular regard to spoken language. However, there is an ever-growing body of research which looks at how gender is represented at a textual level and the ideologies about gender which are imbued within texts (e.g. Baker, 2014; Hunt, 2015; Gupta, 2016). In order to understand why and how representations, ideology, and gender are linked, it is first discussing the idea of discourse. As noted previously, gender is constructed via discourse(s), but just what is discourse? While I have given a very surface-level definition in Chapter 1, it is worth turning our attention to how discourse is used in this book in greater detail.

There are entire book-length arguments about the definitions of discourse(s) and how it/they can be interpreted (see, e.g., Butler, 1990; Sunderland, 2004). For example, one definition of 'discourse' is the notion that it is 'language above the sentence or above the clause' (see Stubbs, 1983, p. 1; see also, Baker, 2006, p. 3). Baker (2006, p. 3) points out that some could argue that the assumed structure of a recipe can be seen as a 'discourse' depending on definitions like this. This ties in with Bakhtin's (1981) argument that discourse is a set of language features and structures which are associated with a particular genre. Others, such as Foucualt (1966, 1980), argue that discourse is about how we structure ideas as they relate to power and how these ideas manifest as practice. Foucualt's work is particularly concerned with power as it relates to the construction of reality and the (social) practices by which discourses become manifested in reality (see also Weedon, 1987, p. 108).

One of the main issues with the term 'discourse' is that it is used in two different ways: first it can be used as a count noun (e.g. 'the austerity discourse of the UK coalition government') but it can also be used as an uncountable noun (e.g. 'neoliberal centrist discourse') (see Fairclough, 2010; Koller, 2014a). Regardless of whether discourse is used as a countable or uncountable noun, for the purposes of this book, I follow Fairclough and Wodak's (1997, p. 258) definition, which:

> sees discourse – language use in speech and writing – as a form of "social practice". Describing discourse as social practice implies a dialectical relationship between a particular discursive event and the situation(s), institution(s) and social structure(s) which frame it: the discursive event is shaped by them, but it also shapes them. That is, discourse is socially constitutive as well as socially conditioned – it constitutes situations,

> objects of knowledge, and the social identities of and relationships between people and groups of people. It is constitutive both in the sense that it helps to sustain and reproduce the social status quo, and in the sense that it contributes to transforming it.

Thus, throughout this book, discourse is broadly defined as language use as a social practice that is based on (sociocultural) knowledge. Important in this distinction is that discourse does ideological work: discourse is shaped by ideology and continues to shape ideologies.

Baxter (2008, pp. 245–246) draws connections between her work on feminist post-structuralist discourse analysis (FPDA) and Butler's (1990) work on discourse and performativity. In particular, Baxter makes seven links between FPDA and performativity as well as other ways of viewing discourse; the similarities are paraphrased as follows: (1) discourse is a social practice, (2) speaker's/writer's identities are performative (3) speaker's/writer's identities are diverse and multifaceted, (4) meaning is constructed in context-specific settings, (5) there is an interest in the deconstruction of power relations, (6) that discourse(s) are always interwoven with each other, and (7) there is a need for continuous self-reflexivity. These core tenants, which are useful because they account for both speakers and writers, will underpin the later chapters of analyses.

While Baxter provides useful tenants for FPDA, it is worth turning to representations—which in Baxter's framework could also be seen as performative. In this book, I view representations as depictions of a social phenomenon or group as manifested through a process of semiosis via drawing on discourses. That is to say, representations are specifically concerned with the way concepts, events, and groups are portrayed—either through language or some other communicative mode. These representations can be reflections of a writer's performed identity, but in the case of videogames could also be how writers feel a character 'should' perform gender. Thus, ideologies about how gender 'should' be performed are also intertwined with representations and discourse. For the purposes of this book, ideologies are seen as networks of socio-cognitive representations (see Koller, 2012, 2014a; 2014b; Chapter 1). That is to say, ideologies are thoughts, beliefs, and ideals (i.e. mental perceptions) about social phenomena and groups as manifested through discourse.

The above points demonstrate the theoretical underpinnings of moving from language and gender in spoken language to the representation of gender within written forms. Although investigations which look at the representation of gender in written texts are not uncommon, it is now worth turning to a small handful of successful studies to explore trends in the academic literature. Specifically, the following few paragraphs draw upon work which has taken a corpus linguistic approach (see Chapters 1 and 3) to the representation of gender at a textual level.

Two related studies which have used corpora to look at the representation of women within a corpus of newspapers are Caldas-Coulthard and Moon (2010) and Moon (2014). In both studies, the scholar(s) looked at terms that denoted men and women. In Caldas-Coulthard and Moon (2010), the researchers noted how adjectives like *curvy* typically modified female social actors and that the constructions in which it was used typically positioned women as the object of sexual desires. Furthermore, the researchers examined the words *man*, *woman*, *boy*, and *girl* and noted that the representation of gender typically changes depending on the age of the gendered social actor. This study was further supported by Moon's (2014) research, in which she suggests that as women age, they are more likely to be described with adjectives such as *frail* or *bitter* (see also Anderson, 2019; Baker, 2008b). The normalisation of such representations is important because the people being represented often lack power: it is usually those in a position of power—such as the newspaper editors—who can decide who is represented and how they are represented (see Gupta, 2016; Jeffries, 2007).

In other studies, scholars have elected to look at one specific subset of language and examined how people of different identities use language to represent gender (e.g. Baker, 2014; Holoshitz & Cameron, 2014). One of the most notable studies is Baker's (2014, pp. 157–195) analysis which explores how heterosexual men use language in personal adverts. In Baker's study, corpora of Australian, Indian and Singaporean men's adverts were approached using techniques which included a comparison of key semantic categories, collocational networks and concordance line analyses (all of which are discussed in more detail in Chapter 3).

Baker found that men from different areas would desire specific parts of women's bodies and this varied across cultures. However, Baker notes that there were three common and overarching discourses: that women have faced social pressures to act sexually repressed, that women should know their place, and that the men wanted to *spoil* women. All of these contributed towards particular representations of what the heterosexual men desired and normalised certain gendered attributes prescribed to women. Ultimately, a number of these findings and discourses were uncovered through the triangulation of different analytical techniques.

However, sometimes complex methods like this are not needed to explore representation. For example, Holoshitz and Cameron (2014) explored the representation of sexual violence using just one single corpus tool—Antconc (Anthony, 2011). Their study still yielded fruitful findings, despite using corpus tools in less complex ways than Baker's (2014) study. In their study, which examined the representation of sexual violence in the Democratic Republic of Congo and Abu Ghraib in the New York times, Holoshitz and Cameron found that the authors of texts neglected to identify perpetrators of the sexual acts as well as de-emphasised both the sexual nature of the abuse and the experiences of victims. Certain grammatical patterns—such as the nomination of verbs (where verbs are turned into nouns)—were used to imply that the processes or states denoted (i.e. the sexual violence) simply occurred or existed. In other words, by using certain grammatical classes of words, less attention was given to the actions of the perpetrators and the serious nature of crimes.

In a similar vein to exploring how grammatical patterns can place the onus of a sentence on a reported person, Hunt (2015) demonstrated a novel methodology in her gender-based analysis of the Harry Potter series. Hunt examined reference to body parts to determine what characters are shown to do with their bodies and whether or not there is a gender bias within the actions they conduct. She contends that there is evidence for underlying sexism in the series, as the female characters were often described as carrying less important objects than their male counterparts and were helped to their feet more. Furthermore, Hunt analysed these body parts to explore the agency of women in terms of grammatical subject or object position, arguing that women were often placed as the object of transitive verbs.

However, it is also worth drawing attention to the previous work that has examined the representation of men and masculinity with corpus methods. One such study comes from Baker (2015) who examined adjectives which modified *man* in the Corpus of Historical American English (a large data set which has samples of American English written between 1810 and 2009). Baker's analysis draws attention to the multi-faced ways men are discussed—including in terms of their wealth, morality, and physical bodies. Importantly, Baker draws attention to the differences in what is viewed as a 'good' gendered body: for men, it is musculature, but for women, it is based on being beautiful.

Other studies have examined the way heterosexual men construct ideals of other gendered social actors and represent them within their own communities. In Heritage and Koller (2020), we examined a community of men who were known for their extreme levels of misogyny. What we found was that these men would appraise other men in different ways, and the way they appraised the men demonstrated that members of the community conceptualised different types of men and masculinity on a hierarchy. Importantly, the members of this community were neither at the top nor the bottom of this hierarchy, meaning that they viewed some other men as 'better' (i.e. more masculine because they could have sex with women) than themselves and viewed some other 'types' of men as worse than themselves.

Elsewhere, others such as Coffey-Glover (2019) have investigated how men are represented in magazines aimed at women, via feminist critical stylistic analysis. Coffey-Glover took a sample of magazines aimed at women and examined how male social actors were represented in these, in particular through zooming into naming practices for men. Importantly, she argues that there is evidence of anti-beautification discourse within such magazines: that those who are seen to engage in beautification practices (such as grooming) are seen as not-masculine. Such research has serious implications for masculinity and how men negotiate their everyday behaviours. These studies go to demonstrate the need to consider how ideals of gender are constructed, not just by those in the press, but also people of different gender identities.

Something to draw attention to, however, is that regularly the representation of female social actors is contrasted to the representation of male social actors, and only the differences in these representations are examined. However, Taylor (2013) argues for the importance of also looking at similarities in how they are represented—that sometimes, gendered terms such as BOY and GIRL are represented in similar ways. In her study of how these gendered nouns are used in the British press, Taylor points to both differences and similarities—and notes that, for example, both GIRL and BOY collocate with terms denoting relationships. However, Taylor also found some differences—for example, the term GIRL is more likely to be the object of verbs (which bears some resemblance to the findings of Hunt, 2015). Ultimately, the arguments posited by Taylor demonstrate the need to look at both similarities and differences, even though differences may be more pronounced.

The studies noted above are just some of the numerous investigations into the representation of gender in written language. However, these are just some of the many text types that have previously been explored via corpus methods. While an entire monograph could be dedicated to reviewing such a wealth of literature, the next section turns to examine the representation of gender in text types which are more closely related to videogames.

Gender in Videogame Paratext

Before I discuss how language has been used to represent gender in videogames, it is worth discussing ludolinguistics as a broader field. To date, there appear to be four major foci within the ludolinguistic literature: language teaching (see, e.g., Gee, 2003, 2008); lexicography, localisation, and variation (see, e.g., Fernández Costales, 2012; Mangiron & O'Hagan, 2006); player interactions (see, e.g., Potts, 2015; Rudge, 2019), and multimodal approaches to ludolinguistics (see, e.g., Machin & van Leeuwen, 2016; Toh, 2019).

Typically, the data analysed within these can be categorised into three camps: the first is the language used in videogame paratext, such as in online fora and manuals associated with a particular videogame (see, e.g., Balteiro, 2019; Campos-Pardillos, 2019; Ensslin & Finnegan, 2019). The second is player interactions, typically gathered through netno/ethno-graphic methods (see, e.g., Graham & Dutt, 2019; Kiourti, 2019; Rudge, 2019). The third but less frequent is close analysis of videogames as an actual text (though see Goorimoorthee et al., 2019; Heritage, 2020; Machin & van Leeuwen, 2016; Ray, 2019).

Within the ludolinguistic literature surrounding the representation of gender, there appears to be a focus on the representation of gender in videogame paratext. Specifically, there is a growing body of research into gaming 'communities' through the examination of how players and fans of videogames construct gender roles and the representation of gender in videogame-related media, such as in magazines and web-forum posts. This separation of research themes is outlined by Ensslin (2015), who states that 'the discourse of games involves various layers of communicative interaction and multiple types of social actors' (p. 406). She states that there are three social actors within the field of videogame studies: the players, the professionals, and those who engage in debates about games, such as politicians and journalists. She further differentiates these studies from ones that examine games as cultural artefacts which communicate meanings via user interfaces, backstories, instructions, and scripted dialogues.

Gender in Videogame 'Communities'

Before I explore the research which has investigated videogame 'communities', it is worth defining communities. Unlike a physical community (such as a village), the community of videogame players (or gamers) closely resembles an imagined community (Anderson, 1983, 2006; McConnell-Ginet, 2010) which refers to 'groups of people, not immediately tangible and accessible, with whom we connect through the power of the imagination' (Kanno & Norton, 2003, p. 241). These communities often have shared cognitive models of how they perceive other social actors (see Koller, 2012, 2014b).

Within research which examines players as an imagined community, scholars have argued that there is a relationship between time spent on videogames by people within gaming communities and sexist attitudes (Breuer et al., 2015). However, Breuer et al.'s study did not compare the attitudes of the players to the general population. In other words, there is no way to discern whether these attitudes are general attitudes, or specifically created by time spent on videogames. Secondly, even if it were the videogames which caused these sexist attitudes, there may be a difference created by the videogame(s) respondents play. For example, the effect of videogames such as *Candy Crush* (King, 2012–ongoing), a game with the purpose of connecting similar looking pieces of 'candy' (also known as 'sweets'), may be very different from those of *Grand Theft Auto* (Benzies et al., 1997–onwards), which has a reputation for violence—including violence against women. In other words, while videogames may have some cognitive impact on sexist attitudes, the genre and target audience of a game must be considered in analyses (see Martins et al., 2011).

Turning to the language within games, and how players use language to construct (non-)sexist discourses, an element to imagined communities is the idiosyncratic lexical choices of members within a community to create and maintain group identity (McConnell-Ginet, 2010, p. 19). Scholars, such as Ensslin (2012, 2015), have drawn attention to idiosyncratic lexical choices within imagined communities centred around videogames, both on the part of gamers and designers. Such varieties of gamer slang have been referred to as ludolects (Ensslin, 2012; Chapter 1) and are used as informal in-group codes to construct group membership, identity, and status (see also Newon, 2011; Rudge, 2019). One of the more common research areas within the scholarly literature is explorations of how players of videogames use these ludolects, with specific regards to how ludolects can be imbued with ideologies centred around gender (see Braithwaite, 2014).

Indeed, there is a small body of research which has explored the construction of identity in communities of players from single videogames. For example, some have argued that videogame players of

World of Warcraft (*WoW*) (Blizzard Entertainment, 2004–onward) have previously used sexist language in online forums discussing Blizzard's decision to change the language used by a new character (see Braithwaite, 2014). To some degree, the discourses surrounding the specific character became both gendered while also centred on sexuality. Braithwaite's research offers interesting and important findings about the community. However, the description of the methods implemented by Braithwaite is relatively vague, and the analysis could have benefited from some form of quantification in order to obtain a clearer idea of which findings were representative.

Similar work has utilised corpus linguistic methods to explore the representation of gender in *WoW*. Ensslin's (2012) corpus study of the representation of gender has explored how players use metaphors about gender in forum posts, official websites, and in live-chats about the videogame. Although Ensslin's work utilises corpus methods (discussed in more detail in the subsequent chapter), the research focused on how people not affiliated with the game used language. That is to say, the language used by players of the game is likely to be written without the players being paid. These players are likely to only spend a short amount of time (if any) editing the language and thinking about what ideologies they want to convey. This is not necessarily the case for professional companies, many of which spend exorbitant amounts of money on hiring professional writers.

Similarly, Carrillo Masso (2011) has employed corpus techniques to explore the representation of gendered characters in the language used in online forums for the MMORPGs *WoW* and *Diablo* (Blizzard Entertainment, 2005–onwards). Her findings suggest that women are often positioned in different professional roles to men, which raises questions about how these roles are discussed and evaluated within the games. Indeed, Carrillo Masso draws on the work of Macdonald (1995) and argues that the representation of women is a demonstration of binary misogyny: that women are portrayed as either a damsel in distress or a femme fatale (see also Ensslin, 2015, p. 85). She explored the words which were statistically significantly likely to co-occur with the terms *he* and *she*. This then allowed for a quantitative analysis which gave an indication of the prominence of male and female characters and how they were portrayed by people who played the game. From a methodological standpoint, Carrillo Masso's study, like Ensslin's (2012) study, initially presents a promising method for exploring how gender is represented within videogames. However, ultimately, while the scholars refer to their work as looking at the language 'in' videogames, their methods only allow examine representations around videogames.

Probing the line of inquiry about how players in different videogame communities use language to construct group identity, others have suggested that the language in 'let's play' videos[2] and the comments for these videogames on YouTube is homosocial, as opposed to homophobic (Potts, 2015). Although like Ensslin's work, the producers of the language are not affiliated with the official game, Potts' study presents interesting methodological implications. In particular, her multi-method research included elements of corpus linguistic methods which appeared to yield fruitful results. Potts also takes visual aspects into account and suggests that both the players on YouTube and those commenting on the videos present gender identity and sexuality as complex phenomena. Similar to Potts' findings, others have argued that many gamers actively distance themselves from negative stereotypes associated with people who play videogames. These negative stereotypes typically encourage people not in the imagined community to create a mental image of an overweight white heterosexual man who is both sexist and homophobic (see Bergstrom et al., 2016). Potts' findings further suggest that the construction of identity within videogame communities does differ depending on the games and activities around which those communities are centred.

Taken together, the findings from research conducted by Braithwaite (2014), Potts (2015), and Bergstrom et al. (2016) suggests that there are two contradicting conceptualisations of members in videogame communities. One is that they hold outdated views on gender and as such actively reject feminist calls for equality in the language used within videogames; while the other is that they actively position themselves against homophobia and inline with certain feminist ideals. While it is useful to know how players of the videogames react to issues of gender

[2] 'Let's Play' videos consist of one or more people recording their playing experience of a videogame. The videos are often done to establish links between the players and viewers.

and sexuality, it is also important to understand the discourses created and set out by the videogame makers. In particular, I am specifically interested in the language generated by the scriptwriters and publishers of (MMO)RPGs. These creators of the videogames create a product for mass consumption which can position ideological views based on social identity.

Gender in Videogames—As a Text

Before exploring the representation of gender in videogames as a text, it is worth making the case that videogames should be treated as a text in their own right. Although different to texts such as newspaper articles or novels, multiple scholars have proposed that games should be viewed as textual in nature (e.g. Aarseth, 1997, 2004a; Juul, 2005). Even though they must be played through kinetic interaction rather than simply read, watched, or listened to, there are underlying rules which are articulated semiotically—verbally and nonverbally (Ensslin, 2015). But regardless of these rules, videogames have ways of communicating thoughts, ideas, and concepts to the players—even if what they communicate is sometimes very limited.

Some scholars have taken the idea that videogames are a text and applied it to different fields within linguistic scholarship. For example, Gee (2003, 2005, 2007, 2008) has argued that videogames are useful sites for language learners to explore authentic language use. Gee's work argues for the use of videogames as a teaching tool—suggesting that videogames as a text can be implemented into the language learning classroom, so as students might be able to use language in a variety of contexts. Others have argued that videogames should be seen as narrative texts and that they are deeply rich in narrative and ludological structures (Ensslin, 2015; Egenfeldt-Nielsen et al., 2015; Kirkland, 2009, 2015, 2016). Both Aarseth (2004b) and Martins et al. (2011) have pointed out that some games should not be considered a narrative due to the lack of objectives or language. Some, especially older, games such as *Pong* have less obvious and less complex narrative structures in comparison to more modern games (see Fizek, 2012). However, these games are arguably rarer—and indeed, this is an issue with the use of generalisable definitions. With such a wealth of games, and now a rich archive of videogames across the world, it is highly unlikely that a single definition will be able to ever capture all the nuances of gaming, and what elements games can (not) convey. I would argue for the use of a cline, where some games might convey little to no use of narrative elements, while others may be very narrative-driven. However, all games discussed in the later analysis chapters of this book could be considered to be towards the more narrative-driven end of this cline and contain narrative elements. That is to say, games such as *FIFA* (EA sports, 1993–onwards) (a football simulator) or *Call of Duty* (Activision, 2003–onwards) (a first-person shooter game) will not be discussed in later analyses, while certain role-playing games such as *The Witcher 3* (CD Projekt Red, 2015) will be.

Regarding gender in these kinds of games which are more narrative-driven, Carrillo Masso (2011) has argued that gendered messages are semiotically encoded into gameplay, and in turn, this shapes a player's identity. A common finding in the literature which examines how gender is coded into videogames is that female characters are less present in videogames than male characters (Gestos et al., 2018; Ivory, 2006), with some arguing that the ratio of men to women could be as high as four to one (Burgess et al., 2007; Paaßen et al., 2017; Scharrer, 2004). Furthermore, some academic literature suggests that despite their lower frequency of occurrence, women are more likely to be over-sexualised. However, it should be noted that these studies have typically focused on the visual and multimodal elements of representation and have not investigated representation at a lexico-grammatical level (see, e.g., Carrillo Masso, 2019).

Explorations into the representation of gender in videogames typically focus on the visual representation of gender in MMORPGs, such as *WoW* (see Fox & Bailenson, 2009). A considerable amount of work has examined avatar creation and reasons behind why people choose particular avatars. For example, Bergstrom et al. (2012) argue that *WoW* players ascribe healing as a feminine role and tanking as a masculine role. Here, tanking describes when players control characters who are typically adorned with armour. The player tries to use spells and abilities in order to be the only one whom the boss(es) focus their attacks on. By contrast, healers are those who use spells and abilities to restore the hit points of tanks and other members of the party. Typically, healers stay away from the fight so as to mitigate any damage they might take. Bergstrom et al. argue that the players would have a preference for making tanks as male avatars and healers as female characters. The findings seem to be subtly different to Yee et al.'s (2011) notion that when male players enact healing roles in *WoW*, they effectively conform to feminine norms and heal 'in drag', whereby they were more likely to heal because their character was female. Both investigations employ content analysis and explore the player's self-reported roles and avatar gender. The difference in the argument between Bergstrom et al.'s research and Yee et al.'s research is that Bergstrom et al. propose that the men create female healers and male fighting characters because it is the gendered norm for the role they undertake, while Yee et al. argue that healing is more likely to be undertaken because of an avatar's gendered appearance. These arguments raise interesting questions about the representation of gender in other videogames such as: 'what roles do men and women typically have?' and 'how are these roles both realised in language and linguistically referred to?'.

However, *WoW* is an MMORPG, and it is also worth noting that scholars have also looked at how gender is encoded into the narratives of c-RPGs, including, but not limited to the *Silent Hill* series (Konami, 1999–Onwards) (Kirkland, 2009), *Lara Croft: Tomb Raider* (Eidos Interactive, 1996–2008; Crystal Dynamics, 2010–onwards) (MacCallum-Stewart, 2014), and *Dragon Age: Inquisition* (BioWare, 2014) (Pelurson, 2018). Typically, the literature on these games suggests that representations of gender roles, namely masculinity and femininity, are relatively traditional. One of the reasons for this may be because the identities of the writers affect the representation of the characters. For example, when the writing team for the *Lara Croft* series changed from a group of all-male writers to one which included female writers, the visual representation of the protagonist became less sexualised. Although there is no evidence to suggest that this was a causal relationship as opposed to a correlational relationship, the difference in the visual representation of *Laura Croft* was certainly influenced by sociocultural factors, such as the continued fight for gender equality. MacCallum-Stewart (2014) echoes this idea and argues that: 'There is also a considerable difference in gameplay within the new Tomb Raider. New Lara is very much a product of her gaming time, and as such, occupies a substantively different world than her predecessor'. To some degree, MacCallum-Stewart's research suggests that games are a product of their socio-temporal conditions and that there is room for diachronic analyses of the representation in videogames (indeed, I take a diachronic approach to the representation of gender in Chapters 6 and 7).

Other investigations have looked at the audio representation of gender in videogames (e.g. Machin & van Leeuwen, 2016). Machin and van Leeuwen propose that sound is one communicative mode (language is another), and thus explored how this communicative mode could be 'gendered' in two mobile videogames. This research was also coupled with an exploration of how the sound related to the visual aspects of the game (paying particular attention to the bodies of the characters who the player could control). However, while the study yielded interesting results, questions are raised about how gender is represented outside of the genre of mobile games. Indeed, as Martins et al. (2011) note, the processing power of the device which videogames are played on have an impact on how developers can represent gender. The representation of gender in mobile app games is likely to be different from those played on high-performance machines, such as specifically designed gaming computers.

All the research papers outlined above examined the gendered body in some way, as opposed to how the lexico-grammatical features used to represent a gendered group. I would argue that, while some female characters may appear to be hyper-sexualised, the language they use, and indeed language used about them, could be empowering.[3] Conversely, if female characters are not sexualised, but the language used about them is constantly negative or objectifying, there may still be issues relating to how gender is represented. For example, a character may be highly sexualised visually, but may only ever be referred to by other characters as 'strong', 'independent', or 'the best'.

[3] This point is not to invalidate research into the gendered body of characters in videogames. However, I wish to raise attention to the fact that characters are represented in more ways than just visually.

A further criticism of the gender-based content analyses is that, with the exception of a handful of studies (e.g. Heritage, 2020; Martins et al., 2011; Machin & van Leeuwen, 2016), there is a focus on the representation of female characters and femininity. This focus on female representation may be detrimental to the study of the representation of men and masculinity, as well as non-binary gender identities, in videogames. Negative types of masculinity may be prevalent in videogames, and given the effects of normalisation of gender roles, may contribute to sustaining harmful gender-based ideologies.

Indeed, for this reason, I would argue the need for more nuanced analyses of gender in videogames from a post-structuralist perspective at a lexico-grammatical level, as a way of examining discourses. One of the few studies which have examined language use within a videogame is Baker's (2008a) analysis of the interaction between players who identified as homosexual in the game *Second Life* (Rosedale, 2003–onwards). *Second Life* has an in-game 'chat' function, which allows players to type chat in real-time and for nearby players to see what is being said. This study differs from the others as the language Baker analysed was not scripted but spontaneously produced by the players. Although a very short piece of analysis to highlight how performativity can cross communicative modes, Baker found that during a sexual interaction players used language to enact stereotypically hyper-masculine roles, making the avatars appear like nominally heterosexual men, while during a non-sexual interaction the same players made use of camp humour to describe a dungeon area as filthy and needing to be cleaned. To some degree, the player's performances of gender and sexuality provide an insight into what they believe the 'ideal' man should behave and speak like in different contexts. However, while the avatars on *Second Life* use language which is spontaneously produced by the players, the language under investigation in this book is pre-scripted, crafted, and edited by professional scriptwriters.

Elsewhere, in my own research, I have used corpus methods to explore the kind of language which is used to construct the 'ideal' kind of men within *The Witcher* (CD Projekt Red, 2007, 2011, 2015) videogame series (see Heritage, 2021). I utilised corpus methods to explore all the language within the three instalments of *The Witcher* and argued that typically ideals of masculinity were predicated on physicality—so that if a man was unable to enact physical strength, he was deemed to be viewed in negative ways. In that research, I focused on the adjectives that occurred with the term *man* (as well as the ones which occured for *woman*) and examined the contexts in which they were used. I focused specifically on adjectives that denoted both age and the bodies of men—which showed that *man* would be pre-modified by adjectives such as *large* and *big* (typically denoting the size of the man's muscles), but this gendered noun did not occur with adjectives to discuss a lack of strength. When *man* occurred with adjectives for age, old men were seen as in need of being defending and were negatively evaluated because they were infirm and unable to physically look after themselves. These ideals are linked to Connell's notion of hegemonic masculinity (2005), as certain types of men were privileged over other types of men due to their different performances of masculinity. However, with the exception of my own work (see Heritage, 2020, 2021), little has been done to look at the linguistic construction of gender within videogames as texts written by professional writers who must think very carefully about how they represent femininity and masculinity.

Conclusions

There are a number of conclusions which can be drawn from all of this research. First and foremost, one of the most salient points is that gender is something which is both performed and socially constructed. However, it should be kept in mind that gender can still be represented in essentialist or binary ways. That is to say that although gender construction is fluid, and gender is much more complex than just 'men' and 'women', it may be presented in binary ways within data. Thus, while future analysis will also consider how masculinity and femininity are constructed and performed, they may still be performed in ways which appear essentialist, homogenising, and/or problematic.

Overall, there are two major thematic links within the scholarly literature relating to the study of gender in videogames. The first is that a number of studies have claimed to analyse the language in videogames, but in reality, have analysed the language around videogames, such as in player interactions or in blogs and fora. Typically, these studies have looked at videogame communities, and explored how ideals of gender and sexuality are sustained and (re)produced within these communities. However, I have argued that these communities are not reflective of the games themselves—videogame companies spend a lot of money hiring professional scriptwriters to meticulously think of different ways in which characters can be constructed, and this process of meticulous writing and editing is different to the kind of writing associated with posting to a message board.

The second trend is that when videogames are analysed as a text, there is a tendency to analyse the representation of gender in relation to the visual content (though, see Heritage, 2020; Machin & van Leeuwen, 2016). However, as Carroll and Kowtiz (1994, p. 73) write: 'valuable as content analysis may be, it does not give insight into the significant gender differences that exist at the level of the individual linguistic item'. Indeed, Macalister (2011, p. 26) summarises and reiterates the issue with not exploring the linguistic features of a text: 'the point remains that it is important to look beneath the surface features of texts'. In other words, there is a need to explore the representation of gender in videogames at a lexico-grammatical level. That is to say, visual analyses can only take research so far. There might also be a disconnect between visual representations and lexico-grammatical representations. While this is not to dismiss the important work of visual content analyses, which typically show that women are less frequently present in games, and when they are they are visually sexualised, this point is to address that representation happens on multiple levels. Given the dearth of literature which addresses lexico-grammatical representations of gender, the later chapters of analysis will seek to contribute towards bridging this gap in the research.

With the exception of Baker's (2008a) small piece of analysis to show how performativity can cross communicative modes, and my previous research (Heritage, 2020, 2021), particularly within *The Witcher* videogame series (Heritage, 2021), no work has really examined how lexis and grammar contribute towards building representations of gender within videogames. But how do we go about investigating such representations? I have already called for the use of corpus linguistic methods as corpus linguistics is not only a well-established collection of methodologies, but corpus methods are also rigorous, driven by statistics, and use representative samples to create large data sets. In the next chapter, I discuss corpus linguistics in more detail, with a focus on how corpora can be applied to the language within videogames, and the representation of gender in different media.

Ludography

Activision (2003–onwards). *Call of Duty*. Santa Monica, California: Activision.

Benzies, L., Lashley, S., Sarawr, I., Thompson, B. (1997–onward). *Grand Theft Auto*. New York City, New York: Capcom

BioWare. (2014). *Dragon age: Inquisition*. Redwood City, California: Electronic Arts.

Blizzard Entertainment. (2004–onwards). *World of Warcraft*. Irvine, California: Blizzard Entertainment.

Blizzard Entertainment. (2005–onwards). *Diablo*. Irvine, California: Blizzard Entertainment.

CD Projekt Red. (2007). *The Witcher*. Warsaw, Poland: CD Projekt Red.

CD Projekt Red. (2011). *The Witcher 2: Assassination of kings*. Warsaw, Poland: CD Projekt Red.

CD Projekt Red. (2015). *The Witcher 3: Wild Hunt*. Warsaw, Poland: CD Projekt Red.

Crystal Dynamics. (2009–onwards). *Laura Croft: Tomb Raider*. San Francisco, California: Crystal Dynamics.

EA Sports. (1993–onwards). *FIFA*. California: Redwood City, California: Electronic Arts.

Eidos Interactive. (1996–2009). *Tomb Raider*. London, United Kingdom: Eidos Interactive.

King. (2012–onwards). *Candy Crush*. Stockholm, Sweden: King.

Konami (1999–onwards). *Silent Hill*. Tokyo, Japan: Konami.

Rosedale (2003–onwards). *Second life*. San Francisco, California: Linden Lab.

Bibliography

Aarseth, E. (1997). *Cybertext: Perspectives on ergodic literature*. John Hopkins University Press.

Aarseth, E. (2004a). Quest games as post-narrative discourse. In M. Ryan (Ed.), *Narrative across Media: The languages of storytelling* (pp. 361–376). University of Nebraska Press.

Aarseth, E. (2004b). Genre trouble: Narrativism and the art of simulation. In N. Wardrip-Fruin & P. Harrigan (Eds.), *First person: New media as story, performance, and game* (pp. 45–55). Massachusetts Institute of Technology Press.

Anderson, B. (1983). *Imagined communities: Reflections on the origin and spread of nationalism*. Verso.

Anderson, B. (2006). *Imagined communities: Reflections on the origin and spread of nationalism* (2nd ed.). Verso.

Anderson, C. (2019). *Discourses of ageing and gender: The impact of public and private voices on the identity of ageing women*. Palgrave MacMillan.

Anthony, L. (2011). AntConc (3.2.4) [Computer Software]. Waseda University.

Baker, P. (2006). *Using corpora in discourse analysis*. Bloomsbury.

Baker, P. (2008a). *Sexed texts: Language, gender and sexuality*. Equinox.

Baker, P. (2008b). 'Eligible' bachelors and 'frustrated' spinsters: Corpus linguistics, gender and language. In K. Harrington, L. Litosseliti, H. Sauntson, & J. Sunderland (Eds.), *Gender and language research methodologies* (pp. 73–84). Palgrave Macmillan.

Baker, P. (2014). *Using corpora to analyse gender*. Bloomsbury.

Baker, P. (2015). Two hundred years of the American man. In T. Milani (Ed.), *Language and masculinities: Performances, intersections, dislocations* (pp. 34–53). Routledge.

Balteiro, I. (2019). Lexical and morphological devices in gamer language in Fora. In A. Ensslin & I. Balteiro (Eds.), *Approaches to videogame discourse: Lexis, interaction, textuality* (pp. 39–57). Bloomsbury.

Barrett, R. (2017). *From Drag Queens to Leathermen: Language, gender, and gay male subcultures*. Oxford University Press.

Baxter, J. (2008). Feminist post-structuralist discourse analysis: A new theoretical and methodological approach? In K. Harrington, L. Litosseliti, H. Sauntson, & J. Sunderland (Eds.), *Gender and language research methodologies* (pp. 243–255). Palgrave Macmillan.

Bergstrom, K., Fisher, S., & Jenson, J. (2016). Disavowing 'That Guy' identity construction and massively multiplayer online game players. *Convergence, 22*(3), 233–249.

Bergstrom, K., Jenson, J., & de Castell, S. (2012). What's 'choice' got to do with it? Avatar selection differences between novice and expert players or World of Warcraft and Rift. In *Proceedings of the International Conference on the Foundations of Digital Games* (pp. 97–104).

Beynon, J. (2001). *Masculinities and culture*. Open University Press.

Bakhtin, M. ([1934] 1981). *The dialogic imagination: four essays* (C. Emerson & H. Holquist, Trans.). University of Texas Press.

Bing, J., & Bergvall, V. (1996). The question of questions: Beyond binary thinking. In V. Bergvall, J. Bing, & A. Freed (Eds.), *Rethinking language and gender research: Theory and practice* (pp. 1–30). Addison Wesley Longman.

Braithwaite, A. (2014). 'Seriously, get out': Feminists on the forums and the War (craft) on women. *New Media & Society, 16*(5), 703–718.

Breuer, J., Kowert, R., Festl, R., & Quandt, T. (2015). Sexist games = sexist gamers? A longitudinal study on the relationship between video game use and sexist attitudes. *Cyberpsychology, Behavior, and Social Networking, 18*(4), 197–202.

Burgess, M., Stermer, S., & Burgess, S. R. (2007). Sex, lies, and video games: The portrayal of male and female characters on video game covers. *Sex Roles, 57*(5–6), 419–433.

Butler, J. (1990). *Gender trouble*. Routledge.

Butler, J. (1997). *Excitable speech: A politics of the performative*. Routledge.

Caldas-Coulthard, C., & Moon, R. (2010). 'Curvy, hunky, kinky': Using corpora as tools for critical analysis. *Discourse & Society, 21*(2), 99–133.

Cameron, D. (1998). Performing gender identity: Young men's talk and the construction of heterosexual masculinity. In J. Coates (Ed.), *Language and gender: A reader* (pp. 270–283). Wiley Blackwell.

Cameron, D. (2005). Language, gender, and sexuality: Current issues and new directions. *Applied Linguistics, 26*(4), 482–502.

Cameron, D. (2007). *The myth of Mars and Venus*. Oxford University Press.

Cameron, D. (2008). Gender and language ideologies. In J. Holmes & M. Meyerhoff (Eds.), *The handbook of language and gender* (pp. 447–467). Blackwell.

Cameron, D. (2009). Theoretical Issues for the study of gender and spoken interaction. In P. Pichler & E. Eppler (Eds.), *gender and spoken interaction* (pp. 1–17). Palgrave Macmillan.

Cameron, D., & Kulick, D. (2003). *Language and sexuality*. Cambridge University Press.

Campos-Pardillos, M. (2019). End-user agreements in videogames: Plain English at work in an ideal setting. In A. Ensslin & I. Balteiro (Eds.), *Approaches to videogame discourse: Lexis, interaction, textuality* (pp. 116–136). Bloomsbury.

Carrillo Masso, I. (2011). The grips of fantasy: The construction of female characters in and beyond virtual game worlds. In A. Ensslin & E. Muse (Eds.), *Creating second lives: Community, identity and spatiality as constructions of the virtual* (pp. 113–142). Routledge.

Carrillo Masso, I. (2019). *This is for the record: a case for video recording as part of a unified method of data collection for the academic study of PC games* (Doctoral dissertation, Bangor University).

Carroll, D., & Kowitz, J. (1994). Using concordancing techniques to study gender stereotyping in ELT textbook. In J. Sunderland (Ed.), *Exploring gender: Questions and implications for English language* (pp. 73–82). Prentice Hall.

Coates, J. (1996). *Women talk*. Blackwell Publishers.

Coffey-Glover, L. (2019). *Men in women's worlds: constructions of masculinity in women's magazines*. Palgrave Macmillan.

Connell, R. (2005). *Masculinities* (2nd edn.). Polity Press.

Crenshaw, K. (1991). Mapping the margins: Intersectionality, identity politics, and violence against women of color. *Stanford Law Review, 43*(6), 1241–1299.

Davis, J., Zimman, L., & Raclaw, J. (2014). Opposites attract: Retheorising binaries in language, gender, and sexuality. In L. Zimman., J. Davis., J. Raclaw (Eds.), *Queer excursions: Retheorizing binaries in language, gender, and sexuality* (pp. 1–12). Oxford University Press.

Eckert, P. (2014). The problem with binaries: Coding for gender and sexuality. *Language and Linguistics Compass, 8*(11), 529–535.

Egenfeldt-Nielsen, S., Smith, J., & Tosca, S. P. (2015). *Understanding video games: The essential introduction* (3rd edn.). Routledge.

Ensslin, A. (2012). *The language of gaming*. Palgrave.

Ensslin, A. (2015). Discourse of games. In K. Tracy, T. Sandel, & C. Illie (Eds.), The *international encyclopedia of language and social interaction*. Wiley

Ensslin, A., & Finnegan, J. (2019). Bad language and bro-up cooperation in co-sit gaming. In A. Ensslin & I. Balteiro (Eds.), *Approaches to videogame Discourse: Lexis, interaction, textuality* (pp. 139–156). Bloomsbury.

Fairclough, N., & Wodak, R. (1997). *Critical discourse analysis* (2nd edn.). Longman.

Fairclough, N. (2010). Critical discourse analysis. In T. A. van Dijk (Ed.), *Discourse as social interaction* (pp. 258–284). Sage.

Fernández Costales, A. (2012). Exploring translation strategies in video game localization. *MonTI. Monografías de Traducción E Interpretación, 4*(1), 385–408.

Fizek, S. (2012). *Pivoting the player: A methodological toolkit for player character research in offline role-playing games* (Doctoral dissertation, Bangor University).

Foucault, M. (1966). *The order of things: An archaeology of the human sciences.* Travistock.

Foucault, M. (1980). *Power/knowledge: Selected interviews and other writings* 1972–1977. Harvester.

Fox, J., & Bailenson, J. (2009). Virgins and vamps. The effects of exposure to female character's sexualized appearance and gaze in an immersive virtual environment. *Sex Roles, 61*(1), 147–157.

Gee, J. (2003). *What video games have to teach us about learning and literacy.* Palgrave Macmillan.

Gee, J. (2005). *Why video games are good for your soul: Pleasure and learning.* Common Ground.

Gee, J. (2007). *Good games and good learning.* Peter Lang Publishing.

Gee, J. (2008) Learning and games. In K. Salen (Ed.), *The ecology of games: Connecting youth, games, and learning* (pp. 21–40). Massachusetts Institute of Technology Press.

Gestos, M., Smith-Merry, J., & Campbell, A. (2018). Representation of women in videogames: A systematic review of literature in consideration of adult female wellbeing. *Cyberpsychology, Behavior, and Social Networking, 21*(9), 535–541.

Giora, R. (2002). Theorizing gender Feminist awareness and language change. In B. Baron & H. Kotthoff (Eds.), *Gender in interaction: Perspectives on femininity and masculinity in ethnography and discourse* (pp. 329–343). John Benjamins.

Goorimoorthee, T., Csipo, A., Carleton, S., & Ensslin, A. (2019). Language Ideologies in videogame discourse: Forms of sociophonetic othering in accented character speech. In A. Ennslin & I. Balteiro (Eds.), *Approaches to videogame discourse: Lexis, interaction, textuality* (pp. 269–287). Bloomsbury.

Graham, S., & Dutt, S. (2019). "Watch the potty mouth": Negotiating impoliteness in online gaming. In A. Ensslin & I. Balteiro (Eds.), *Approaches to videogame discourse: Lexis, interaction, textuality* (pp. 201–225). Bloomsbury.

Gupta, K. (2016). *Representation of the British suffrage movement*. Bloomsbury.

Heritage, F. (2020). Applying corpus linguistics to videogame data: Exploring the representation of gender in videogames at a lexical level. *Game studies, 20*(3).

Heritage, F. (2021). *Maidens and Monsters: A corpus assisted critical discourse analysis of the representation of gender in The Witcher videogame series* (Doctoral dissertation, Lancaster University).

Heritage, F., & Koller, V. (2020). Incels, in-groups, and ideologies: The representation of gendered social actors in a sexuality-based online community. *Journal of Language and Sexuality, 9*(2), 152–178.

Holoshitz, T., & Cameron, D. (2014). The linguistic representation of sexual violence in conflict settings. *Gender and Language, 8*(2), 169–184.

Hunt S. (2015). Representations of gender and agency in the Harry Potter series. In P. Baker & T. McEnery (Eds.), *Corpora and discourse studies: Integrating discourse and corpora* (pp. 266–284). Palgrave Macmillan.

Ivory, J. (2006). Still a man's game: Gender representation in online reviews of video games. *Mass Communication & Society, 9*(1), 103–114.

Jackson, S. (2012). Heterosexuality, sexuality and gender re-thinking the intersections. In M. Casey, D. Richardson, & J. McLaughlin (Eds.), *Intersections between feminist and queer theory* (2nd edn.) (pp. 38–58). Palgrave Macmillan.

Jeffries, L. (2007). *Textual construction of the female body: A critical discourse approach*. Palgrave Macmillan.

Jespersen, O. (1922). *Language its nature, development and origin*. George Allen & Unwin.

Johnson, J., & Repta, R. (2012). Sex and gender. In J. Oliffe & L. Greaves (Eds.), *Designing and conducting gender, sex, and health research* (pp. 17–37). Sage.

Juul, J. (2005). *Half-real: Video games between real rules and fictional worlds*. Massachusetts Institute of Technology Press.

Kanno, Y., & Norton, B. (2003). Imagined communities and educational possibilities: Introduction. *Journal of Language, Identity, and Education, 2*(4), 241–249.

Kiourti, E. (2019). "Shut the Fuck up Re! Plant the Bomb Fast!": Reconstructing language and identity in first-person shooter games. In A. Ensslin

& I. Balteiro (Eds.), *Approaches to videogame discourse: Lexis, interaction, textuality* (pp. 157–177). Bloomsbury.

Kirkland, E. (2009). Masculinity in video games: The gendered gameplay of silent hill. *Camera Obscura, 24*(2), 161–183.

Kirkland, E. (2015). Restless dreams and shattered memories: Psychoanalysis and Silent Hill. *Brumal: Research Journal on the Fantastic, 3*(1), 161–182.

Kirkland, E. (2016). Undead avatars: the zombie in horror video games. In D. Fischer-Hornung & M. Mueller (Eds.), *Vampires and zombies: transcultural migrations and transnational interpretations* (pp. 229–245). University of Mississippi Press.

Koller, V. (2012). How to analyse collective identity in discourse—Textual and contextual parameters. *Critical Approaches to Discourse Analysis Across Disciplines, 5*(2), 19–38.

Koller, V. (2014a). Applying social cognition research to critical discourse studies: The case of collective identities. In C. Hart & P. Cap (Eds.), *Contemporary critical discourse studies* (pp. 147–165). Bloomsbury.

Koller, V. (2014b). Cognitive linguistics and ideology. In J. Littlemore & J. Smith (Eds.), *The Bloomsbury companion to cognitive linguistics* (pp. 234–252). Bloomsbury.

Lakoff, R. (1973). Language and woman's place. *Language in Society, 2*(1), 45–80.

Lakoff, R. (1975). *Language and woman's place*. Harper and Row.

Litosseliti, L. (2006). *Gender and language: Theory and practice*. Hodder Arnold.

Macalister, J. (2011). Flower-girl and bugler-boy no more: Changing gender representation in writing for children. *Corpora, 6*(1), 25–44.

MacCallum-Stewart, E. (2014). "Take That, Bitches!" Refiguring Lara Croft in Feminist Game Narratives. *Game Studies, 14*(2).

Machin, D., & van Leeuwen, T. (2016). Sound, music and gender in mobile games. *Gender and Language, 10*(3), 412–432.

Macdonald, M. (1995). *Representing women myths of femininity in the popular media*. Bloomsbury Academic.

Mangiron, C., & O'Hagan, M. (2006). Game localisation: Unleashing imagination with 'restricted' translation. *The Journal of Specialised Translation, 6*(1), 10–21.

Martins, N., Williams, D. C., Ratan, R. A., & Harrison, K. (2011). Virtual muscularity: A content analysis of male video game characters. *Body Image, 8*(1), 43–51.

McConnell-Ginet, S. (2010). *Gender, sexuality, and meaning: Linguistic practice and politics*. Oxford University Press.

McEnery, T., & Hardie, A. (2011). *Corpus linguistics: Method, theory and practice*. Cambridge University Press.

Meyerhoff, M. (2014). Variation and gender. In S. Ehrlich, M. Meyerhoff, & J. Holmes (Eds.), *The handbook of language, gender, and sexuality* (2nd edn.) (pp. 87–102). Blackwell.

Mills, S. (2003). Third wave feminist linguistics and the analysis of sexism. *Discourse Analysis Online 1*(1).

Moon, R. (2014). From gorgeous to grumpy: Adjectives, age and gender. *Gender and Language, 8*(1), 5–41.

Newon, L. (2011). Multimodal creativity and identities of expertise in the digital ecology of a World of Warcraft guild. In C. Thurlow & K. Mroczek (Eds.), *Digital discourse: Language in the new media* (pp. 131–13). Oxford University Press.

Paaßen, B., Morgenroth, T., & Stratemeyer, M. (2017). What is a true gamer? The male gamer stereotype and the marginalization of women in video game culture. *Sex Roles, 76*(7), 421–435.

Pelurson, G. (2018). Mustaches, blood magic and interspecies sex: Navigating the non-heterosexuality of Dorian Pavus. *Game studies, 18*(1).

Potts, A. (2015). 'LOVE YOU GUYS (NO HOMO)' How gamers and fans play with sexuality, gender, and Minecraft on YouTube. *Critical Discourse Studies, 12*(2), 163–186.

Ray, A. (2019). Playing with the language of the future: The localization of science-fiction terms in videogames. In A. Ensslin & I. Balteiro (Eds.), *Approaches to videogame discourse: Lexis, interaction, textuality* (pp. 87–115). Bloomsbury.

Rivers, N. (2017). Introduction. In N. Rivers (Ed.), *Postfeminism(s) and the arrival of the fourth wave* (pp. 1–6). Palgrave Macmillan.

Rudge, L. (2019). "I cut it and I… well now what?" (Un)collaborative language in timed puzzle games. In A. Ensslin & I. Balteiro (Eds.), *Approaches to videogame discourse: Lexis, interaction, textuality* (pp. 178–200). Bloomsbury.

Sarkeesian, A. (2014). *Tropes vs. women. Feminist Frequency: Conversations with pop culture*. YouTube. https://www.youtube.com/watch?v=X6p5AZp7r_Q. Accessed February 2021.

Scharrer, E. (2004). Virtual violence: Gender and aggression in video game advertisements. *Mass Communication & Society, 7*(4), 393–412.

Schippers, M. (2007). Recovering the feminine other: Masculinity, femininity, and gender hegemony. *Theory and Society, 36*(1), 85–102.

Spender, D. (1980). *Man made language*. Routledge.

Stubbs, M. (1983). *Discourse analysis: The sociolinguistic analysis of natural language*. University of Chicago Press.

Sunderland, J. (2004). *Gendered discourses*. Palgrave Macmillan.

Tannen, D. (1990). *You just don't understand: Women and men in conversation*. Morrow.

Taylor, C. (2013). Searching for similarity using corpus-assisted discourse studies. *Corpora, 8*(1), 81–113.

Tickner, J., & Sjoberg, L. (2013). *Feminism and International Relations: Conversations about the past, present and future*. Routledge.

Toh, W. (2019). The player experience of BioShock: A theory of Ludonarrative relationships. In A. Ensslin & I. Balteiro (Eds.), *Approaches to videogame discourse: Lexis, interaction, textuality* (pp. 247–268). Bloomsbury.

Weedon, C. (1987). *Feminist practice & poststructuralist theory*. Blackwell.

Woolf, V. (1929). *A room of one's own*. Hogarth Press.

Yee, N., Ducheneaut, N., Yao, M., & Nelson, L. (2011). Do men heal more when in drag?: conflicting identity cues between user and avatar. In *Proceedings of the SIGCHI conference on Human factors in computing systems* (pp. 773–776). Association for Computing Machinery.

Zimmerman, D. H., & West, C. (1975) Sex roles, interruptions and silences in conversation. In B. Thorne, & N. Hencley (Eds.), *Language and sex: Difference and dominance* (pp. 105–129). Stanford University Press.

3

Corpus Approaches to Ludolinguistics

Armchairs Are Too Comfortable

Fillmore (1992) provides a good (albeit extreme) example of what an 'armchair' linguist is and why I typically take a negative of them:

> A caricature of the armchair linguist is something like this. He sits in a deep soft comfortable armchair, with his eyes closed and his hands clasped behind his head. Once in a while he opens his eyes, sits up abruptly shouting, "Wow, what a neat fact!", grabs his pencil, and writes something down. Then he paces around for a few hours in the excitement of having come still closer to knowing what language is really like. (Fillmore, 1992, p. 35)

Later in the same paper, he also describes a caricature of a corpus linguist who is only interested in gathering large data sets (but for the purposes of this book, we will gloss over that). Leaving aside the implications around gender (that a prototypical armchair linguist is a man), the pressing problem with armchair linguistics is that, by nature, the approach is inherently flawed. How can one accurately describe language if one does

F. Heritage, *Language, Gender and Videogames*,
https://doi.org/10.1007/978-3-030-74398-7_3

not actively look at naturally occurring language? Similarly, it is easy for armchair linguists to sit and think 'this phrase makes logical sense for the set of grammatical rules in this language', but this does not necessarily mean that the phrase will be used—and if it is, this realisation does not reveal who uses it nor why they might use it.

But just what is corpus linguistics? And why is it, in my view, a preferential method of linguistic analysis compared to armchair linguistics? That is what this chapter seeks to cover. In this chapter, I answer these two questions and discuss applications of corpus linguistic research to discourse analysis, applications to language and gender studies, and applications to videogame paratext. As I will show in this chapter, there is a huge dearth in the scholarly literature which combines corpora with the language used within videogames. Indeed, Ensslin (2015, p. 6) outlines this dearth in her review of ludolinguistics scholarship, nothing that: 'large, corpus-based studies are needed to study specific aspects of gamer language (e.g., in the world vs. in constituted play) in greater detail than has previously been achievable'.

What Is Corpus Linguistics?

As noted in Chapter 1, the word corpus (plural corpora) originates from the Latin word for 'body', and thus the field is concerned with analysing 'bodies' of texts. Corpora are collections of texts—usually full texts or representative samples of texts—which create a database that linguists can look through. Importantly, these texts are from 'the real world' (see Baker, 2014, pp. 7–14). This means that, rather than being a collection of sentences made up by armchair linguists, the texts that comprise a corpus are a 'snapshot' into how language is used within a particular genre/register of language.

Corpus linguistics is, therefore, an approach centred around the methodological tools used to analyse representative samples. It is an approach which is driven by quantitative research, but often married with qualitative analysis. That is to say, if, for example, we are interested in analysing how the modal verb *may* is used in British English, then we should not only examine how people who are 65+ years old and live in the North West of the UK use the modal verb—we would need to look at how a cross section of society use that verb. This is because not everyone in the UK is 65+ years old nor lives in the North West (see Baker & Heritage, 2021).

However, if we were particularly interested in how people of that identity were using *may* as a modal verb, then we would need to take a representative sample of those speakers. In other words, if we had only sampled two speakers with these identities and only recorded them for five minutes, then there would not be enough data, and what data we did have would not be a representative sample of people with those social identities. Those two speakers might, for example, have different identities which are influencing the ways they are using that modal verb. To overcome these problems, we would need to sample language from multiple people—and from a number of conversations that last a range of lengths of time.

When we do this and look at a representative sample, we would be able to examine the frequencies at which this modal verb occurs, and we would be able to compare the frequencies at which comparable social groups (such as people aged 0–14, 25–34, 35–44, etcetera) are using the modal verb. We could look at words which are likely to co-occur with that particular term. We could also then look at phraseological patterns at a more qualitative level, to examine how it is used in context—and it is even possible to quantify this to provide a more empirical and data-driven comparison (this example is similar to the work conducted in Baker & Heritage, 2021). Therefore, this shows a much more representative sample of how that modal verb is used and how members of certain identities are using it.

While in theory, corpus linguistic methods could be conducted by hand, running statistical tests on data sets which can exceed several million words can be painstakingly time consuming. Thus, within the field of corpus linguistics, one of the requirements of a corpus is that the texts which compile it must be digitised and must be machine-readable. In essence, computers and computer programs are used to look for patterns within these 'bodies' of texts—patterns that might not necessarily be visible without using such computer software. Therefore, this means that the computer software must be able to read the texts (so, while images might contain words, the image would need to have some sort of software extract the words on the page before it can be run through corpus software, or an analyst would have to do this manually). There is a range of computer programs which can run a number of statistical tests on corpora and have ways of visualising the data which different scholars find to be beneficial. Given the extensive number of corpus programs, I will not list them all here. However, in later chapters of analysis, I will primarily use #Lancsbox (Brezina et al., 2015) and WordSmith 7 (Scott, 2016).

At this point, as the studies mentioned in Chapter 2 have used different corpora, it is also worth making a distinction between general corpora (regularly used as a point of comparison for analysts' corpora and therefore often referred to as reference corpora) and specialised corpora (sometimes referred to as specific corpora). A general corpus will often have a range of text types that represent a broad view of how language is used in a general sense (specialised corpora are explained in the next paragraph). Although there are several general corpora, one such example of a reference corpus is the British National Corpus 2014 (BNC2014) (see Hawtin, 2019; Love, 2020). The BNC2014 contains language from a variety of text types and is divided into two sub-corpora: the written BNC2014 and the spoken BNC2014. Within this latter sub-corpus, for example, the language was sampled from speakers across Britain and accounted for a number of speakers from varying demographics—including, but not limited to age, gender, region of residence, and level of education. This kind of corpus is therefore useful if a scholar wants to investigate how language is used in a broad sense, or how members of a certain demographic use language across contexts.

A specialised corpus, by contrast, tends to contain the language from one particular context or of one particular text type. For example, Hunt (2015) created a specialised corpus of language from the Harry Potter book series. As there is a finite amount of language in this series, and the language came from one text type (novels), the corpus was specialised. Elsewhere, scholars might make specialised corpora from particular communities, in order to examine how language is specifically used within that community (see, e.g., Ensslin, 2012; Heritage & Koller, 2020). However, the relationship between reference corpus and specialised corpus is not dichotomous, but rather is a scale, as some specialised corpora can be used as a reference corpus, and some general corpora can be taken as specialised corpora. General corpora are also regularly used as reference corpora—i.e. they act as a benchmark of what 'normal' language is like. For example, imagine we had a corpus and the most frequent word was 'woman'—how do we know that it is used more in our corpus than in everyday language? How do we know that it is used in a similar way to everyday language? This is where reference corpora come in—because we can use them as a point of comparison. However, some researchers might find it more useful to use a specialised corpus as a reference corpus. For example, language on certain websites is likely to be different to language in general—and we might be interested in looking at how one community on that website uses language in comparison to the others, so in that case two specialised corpora could be constructed: one of the language across the website (which would become our reference corpus) and one of the community we are particularly interested in examining. The analysis presented later in this book typically falls closer to the side of specialised corpora—though, some could be used for points of comparison and could either be used as or form part of larger, reference corpora.

Broadly speaking, there are three primary methods which are used in corpus linguistics—though, corpus studies may choose to only look at data through the lens of just one method, or a combination of any of them. These three methods are (key)word list analysis, collocational analysis, and concordance line analysis (McEnery et al., 2006; McEnery & Hardie, 2011; Sinclair, 2001). These methods can be used in one of two approaches to data—corpus-based methods and corpus-driven methods (see Tognini-Bonelli, 2001), though the two are not mutually exclusive. I discuss all of these terms in more detail in subsequent sections. There are a number of sub-disciplines with corpus linguistics, each of which has used a combination of these methods to reveal new and interesting patterns in language in a variety of contexts. For example, previous research has used corpus software to reveal patterns of grammar use (Hunston, 2010, 2011), phraseological expressions (Hunston & Gill, 1998, 2011; Römer, 2016), and ideologies (Baker, 2014; McEnery et al., 2015). But, before we can discuss these methods of analysis, and these two analytical approaches, it is first worth discussing some of the fundamental principles in building a corpus.

Building a Corpus

As noted earlier, a corpus should be a representative sample of the subset of language under investigation. Often, it is not possible to gather all the language from a particular text type, as language is constantly being produced. Similarly, sometimes the amount of data available is a gargantuan amount. For example, it might, in theory, be possible to gather every single article published in the major British newspapers between 2010 and 2020. However, this would take an exorbitant amount of time. It is likely that the data will also hit a point of saturation. A good way to conceptualise this problem is to imagine that there are 100 boxes. You look in the first box and see that it contains a red ball. You then look in the next box and see that it contains an identical red ball. You repeat this process for 90 boxes, each of which has an identical red ball in them. What do you think the final 10 boxes will contain? Even if the final 10 boxes contained green cubes, then an analyst might say 'well, the vast majority of this data set is red balls, so let's look at those'.

However, sometimes it is not possible to get 90% of a data set—and in real life research, we can usually only get a fraction of that data. Therefore, we need a sample which is as representative as possible and a sample which adheres to the principle of total accountability. Although I have previously touched upon representativeness, it is worth bringing it back to the fore, as it is such an important concept to this whole book. The sample of language within a corpus should be a representative reflection of a particular text type. However, the size of a corpus does not necessarily equate to its representativeness. For example, in Heritage and Koller (2020), we took a sample of about 70,000 words from an online community of misogynistic men. This sample of language came from the comments across 50 different forum threads. We argued that despite the small size of the corpus, it was still a representative 'snapshot' into how members of this community were using language to construct ideologies about gendered social actors. Interestingly, when we also compared the findings from this study with data from a later study which looked at a c. 1 million-word corpus from across 200 threads, we found that the findings were still broadly similar. The kind of language used within this community was also confirmed by other studies, which looked at the same community in a different forum and which used much larger corpora (see Tranchese, 2019). One of the issues we faced in Heritage and Koller (2020) was that the community we were analysing were regularly posting and kept generating data. There was also an incredibly large backlog of data that we could have selected for analysis. With that kind of data, one must select a sample; otherwise, data collection could go on forever, and analysis would be forever changing.

However, other studies have built corpora from data sources with a finite amount of words. Although Bednarek makes the distinction that her work is not necessarily a corpus study, but that methods associated with corpus linguistics were applied to her data, she constructed a small, but still representative, corpus of three pilot episodes of British television programs (see Bednarek, 2015). Even though the corpora for each episode were relatively small (the largest specific corpus was less than 3000 words), they represent the text in its entirety. While I would argue that a corpus study could be conducted on such data, if a wider range of episodes were collected and explored, Bednarek's work demonstrates one way to gain a representative sample of data—take it in its entirety. Similarly, Oakley (2016) argues that the size of a corpus is less important than how representative it is. Oakley's corpus contained 88 texts from sex education booklets, which represented all texts of that specific text type. While more data could have been more valuable, this data simply did not exist. Both Bednarek's and Oakley's studies demonstrate that it is possible to explore the representation of gender and sexuality within specific corpora, as long as the corpus is representative of the text type.

In other studies, the data does exist but is not publicly available, nor easy to obtain. For example, Potts and Weare's (2017) analysis of 17 sentencing remarks in homicide cases, which had a female perpetrator, contained all publicly available sentencing remarks. As they note: 'the corpus is opportunistic in that it contains *all* publicly available sentencing remarks for women convicted of homicide offences in

England and Wales from a given time period, and is therefore as *representative* a sample as might conceivably be collected' (p. 25, italics in the original). Given the nature of offline videogames, there is only a finite amount of linguistic data which can be used, similar to Bednarek's (2015), Oakley's (2016), and Potts and Weare's (2017) studies.

In other studies, sometimes, there are so many texts to choose from that selecting these can be difficult. McEnery and Hardie (2011) point out, the selection of texts being analysed should adhere to the principle of total accountability, whereby the analyst does not only select texts in their corpus which will confirm a presumed theory, and that if a corpus is built on samples of language, then these samples should be taken at random where possible. This is one of the core reasons why I would argue corpus linguistic methods are preferable for analysing the representation of gender in videogames in comparison to, say, the methods implemented by those such as Sarkeesian (2014). Rather than force data into pre-established hypotheses, if we build a corpus of a number of videogames, selected at random, we can more accurately argue that we are looking at a fair and representative cross section of videogames. If we return to the earlier metaphor of the boxes with different objects, if we were take just 10 from the 100 boxes at random, the likelihood is that we will get a condensed form of the sample, or at the very least, be able to see the broader trends within the data—even if it is not a perfect method of down-sampling. However, if we take the 10 green cubes because we know that they are green cubes, we will receive a non-representative sample, and our results will be skewed.

A problem with exploring the representation of gender in videogames is that examples of sexism (or indeed examples of resisting sexism) are easy to 'cherry-pick' (a criticism lobbied against Sarkeesian, 2014 by Hoff Sommers, 2014). This could be comparable to, for example, looking at our 100 boxes and suddenly seeing that one has a blue triangle inside—or even only opening the first box to find a blue triangle, and then only analysing that one triangle instead of all the other objects. It is wholly right that we might want to say 'look at this neat thing here! This is something interesting and worth investigating', but if we do not also take a broader sample (i.e. look at the other boxes), then we might miss broader trends in the data (and noting that 90% of the data set is red balls would go amiss).

Analysing a Corpus

Now that we know how to go about building a corpus, it is worth returning to the analytical methods used in corpus linguistics, specifically: (key)word list analysis, collocation, and concordance line analysis.

(Key)Word List Analysis

Before introducing what keywords are, it is first important to differentiate them from word frequency lists. A distinction should be made between these two, as they typically are used in different ways and require different functions. Within keyword analysis, scholars explore whether or not a subset of language is statistically different to another subset of language or language in general (by comparing one corpus against a second corpus, which can act as either a reference for general language or provides some sort of other meaningful contrast with the first corpus). The statistical measures used for this comparison will be discussed in later paragraphs. By contrast, in word frequency list analyses scholars examine what terms frequently appear within a particular corpus. Typically, these terms are then separated and classified by themes (e.g. see Brookes & Baker, 2017) although this can also be applied to keyword lists.

Thus, where keyword lists differ to wordlists is that they rely on statistical comparisons. One issue does occur when deciding what should be included in wordlists, and what this means for the importance of words within a particular corpus. For example, it might be easier to generate a wordlist and look at all gendered social actors within a corpus which is less than 100,000 words, but this might not necessarily be possible in a corpus such as the spoken BNC2014 (Love, 2020) which is over 10 million words large. We might decide to implement minimum frequencies of occurrence for words, but this can often be tricky when some corpora are considerably larger than others. But how do we know whether or not proportionally a word is used more in one corpus than another?

Therefore, keyword lists can be used to show what is statistically salient within a corpus and where the language in one corpus differs to the corpus that it is being compared to. Usually, to make a meaningful comparison, the second corpus will need to be compiled of from data within the same mode, such as written or spoken. For example, if we wanted to conduct a keyword analysis on a corpus of YouTube videos (a spoken mode in an online context), then it probably would not be appropriate to select a corpus of novels written in the Regency era (a written mode in an offline context, which is considerably older). Selecting a reference corpus is never easy, and realistically speaking, there is no hard 'rule' for how to select a reference corpus.

It is worth now turning to what we mean by keywords, and how we classify what a keyword is. In order to investigate whether or not a word is considered statistically key, frequencies from corpus A are compared to corpus B. For example, if corpus A and corpus B are (roughly) the same size, and there are 100 occurrences of the word *lesbian* in corpus A and 101 occurrences of *lesbian* in corpus B, it could initially be possible to suggest that the prominence of this word is roughly even. So, we would probably see that *lesbian* would not appear as a keyword. However, if corpus A is 100,000 words and corpus B is 1 million words (i.e. 10 times bigger), and the word *lesbian* occurred 100 times in each, it would be possible to suggest that the term is more prominent in corpus A than corpus B (in theory, it is 10 times more likely to occur in corpus A than corpus B). This is where keywords can be useful: they can indicate words which are statistically more likely to occur in one corpus than another (see Brezina, 2018 for a full discussion). This example is a relatively simplified form of what happens in the statistical measures—usually, corpora are never a very neat 100,000 words, and so this means that frequencies must be adjusted to common denominators, the mean might be taken, or expected frequencies might be consdiered (though there are different statistical measures for comparing the frequencies and levels of keyness). This can often be tricky to do by hand and given that there are so many unique words to each corpus, might take a painstakingly long time to manually count and calculate.

There is a lot of debate about what the 'best' statistical test for keyness is, and realistically speaking there is no single 'best', rather ones which are most appropriate for answering research questions (see Brezina, 2018). The three most prominent measures are log-likelihood, log ratio, and BIC score (Bayesian Information Criterion). Log-likelihood is a significance test, meaning that it returns a statistic which shows whether or not there is a significant difference in how frequently a word occurs in corpus A in comparison with corpus B. In order to work this out, we take the observed frequencies of a word in two corpora (the absolute frequencies) and calculate the expected frequencies of that word. Once we have the expected frequencies of that word in each corpus, we are able to use multiple mathematical calculations to find the difference in keynes score. The mathematical calculations for the log-likelihood tests are beyond the level which this book is aimed at, and would require considerable mathematic knowledge, which I realise a number of readers may not be equipped with to fully comprehend. However, readers may choose to read Rayson (2008, pp. 527–528) or Brezina (2018, p. 84) for a full explanation of the mathematical workings of the test. For the purposes of this book, however, it is worth noting that the log-likelihood is used to show which word(s) have the most significant relative frequency difference between the two corpora. Once this test is run on every word in the corpora, the words most indicative of corpus A, as compared to corpus B, occur at the top of the keyword list (these are positive keywords, while negative keywords which are more likely to occur in corpus B will have a negative statistic and occur at the bottom of the list, though see Brezina, 2018 for a more nuanced discussion of this). However, log-likelihood has been criticised for being able to provide too many 'false hits' because low-frequency differences in small corpora can reach statistical significance when compared to large corpora (see Brezina, 2018). There is also the issue that log-likelihood is a significance measure—meaning that it tells us how much evidence we have for a difference between two corpora. However, it doesn't tell us how big nor how important a given difference is (see Hardie, 2014).

Log ratio (designed by Hardie, 2014) is an effect-size statistic, not a significance statistic. It represents how big the difference between the two corpora are for a particular keyword, which can show us how big or how important the differences are. It examines the ratio of relative frequencies, that is to say, whether or not 'x' is more likely to occur in corpus A than corpus B by normalising the frequencies of the corpora and then examining the ratios at which word 'x' occurs within both by comparing corpus A and corpus B. We could then say, for example, that *lesbian* is 10 times more likely to occur within corpus A than corpus B. *Woman*, however, might only be three times more likely to occur in corpus A than corpus B, and so we might want to give preference to examining the language around *lesbian* as opposed to the language around *woman*. This has the benefit of being able to compare multiple keywords across corpora—and effect sizes will remain comparable because they are produced as ratios.

Finally, BIC score uses the log-likelihood score and then compares this to the combined size of the two corpora, whereby the BIC equation is $BIC = LL - L(N)$ (whereby L(N) is the number of tokens in the corpora) (Wilson, 2013, pp. 5–6; Gabrielatos, 2018, p. 240). Indeed, Gabrielatos (2018) argues that BIC score is more reliable than log-likelihood, and so should be used more regularly. Again, this kind of statistical measure is quite complex, and I do not expect readers to fully comprehend the mathematical tests (which is one of the reasons why I have only superficially covered them here). However, given that there is currently such a large debate about what statistical measure is best to use, it is worth acknowledging that these three different measures can often provide different results—because they are, by nature, designed to account for the shortcomings of different tests. It is possible, however, to triangulate these tests on the data, and only examine ones which meet pre-established thresholds for each measure. This is what I do when generating keywords in Chapters 6 and 7, by using WordSmith 7 (Scott, 2016).

But moving away from the statistics behind keywords—some people might wonder why analysing keywords is important in corpus linguistic investigations. Keywords are often used as a 'way into' the data (see Baker, 2012, p. 248) because they provide a broad overview of what is salient in a corpus. Such a snapshot can both direct and shape subsequent analysis. As Baker (2004a, p. 347) argues: 'keywords will [...] not reveal discourses but will direct the researcher to important concepts in a text (in relation to other texts) that may help to highlight the existence of types of [...] ideology'. Indeed, there are a number of academic publications which have utilised keyword analyses in corpus-driven research into language, gender, and sexuality (see, e.g., Baker, 2014; Heritage & Koller, 2020). These keywords are then useful for guiding the analysis to words which are over/under-used in a corpus, and why this might be the case.

A number of studies have utilised keyword analysis to explore the kind of discourses surrounding the representation of particular groups. For example, Baker's (2004b) analysis of gay and lesbian erotic literature demonstrated that a subset of keywords related to facial expressions. Within this subset of keywords, erotica featuring and targeted at gay men used statistically key verbs like *grunted*, while verbs that were statistically key in lesbian erotica included *blushed* and *giggled*. Thus, there appears to be a difference in how masculinity and femininity were represented in different forms of erotica, varying by the sexuality of characters and target audience. Elsewhere, Baker (2005, pp. 42–52) highlights the keywords in UK parliamentary debates about lowering the age of consent for gay men. In particular, he notes that the keywords pointed to four dominant discourses: one of tolerance towards homosexuality, one which viewed homosexuality as a criminal offence, one which positioned it as an act rather than an identity, and one which positioned gay people as politically demanding.

Others have examined keywords in the discussion of gender and illness. For example, Charteris-Black and Seale's (2010) corpora consist of semi-structured interviews with men and women about health conditions. Charteris-Black and Seale note how personal pronouns which were keywords demonstrated a difference in how men and women perform gender, in so far that the men who were interviewed would use first-person plural pronouns (such as *we* or *our*), while women would use more first-person singular pronouns (such as *I*, *I'd*, and *Me*). Ultimately, this led to an analysis of what verbs collocated with the pronouns that were keywords, which revealed that men would take typically roles associated with normative masculinity and assume positions of caregivers, while women would take roles associated with normative femininity and would position themselves as in need of care. Thus, the keyword analysis revealed how the interviewees performed gender stereotypes associated with their gender identity when discussing their own health. Discovering these trends in the data—especially in terms of what was said more by interviewees of one gender over another—would have been difficult to spot without the use of corpus software, and indeed might have been overlooked because they frequently would occur in both sets of data.

Collocation

One type of pattern which corpus linguistics is particularly adept at identifying is collocation. Collocation has its roots in Firth's (1957, p. 11) notion that: 'you shall know a word by the company it keeps'. If two words collocate with each other, then they (are statistically likely to) co-occur, meaning they are more likely to appear next to or reasonably close to one another in some way than if the words in a corpus were presented in random order. As Baker et al. (2013, p. 36) note, collocates occur 'frequently within the neighbourhood of another word, normally more often than we would expect the two words to appear together because of chance'.

Before delving into previous studies which have used collocation in corpus research to explore the representation of social groups, it is first important to discuss how we can measure a collocate. For example, if a word A occurs with word B once in 1 million words, does it count as a collocate? Most scholars would agree that no, it would not be considered a collocate. What differentiates a collocate from standard co-occursion (i.e. when words might co-occur with each other but not that frequently) is the use of statistical measures to determine if a word is or is not a collocate. In order to know what collocates are worth examining in detail, it is worth understanding the statistics behind them. Although there are monographs dedicated to understanding statistics associated with collocation and keywords (see, e.g., Brezina, 2018), it is worth noting the fundamentals of the two frequently used statistical tests for collocates, MI score and T-tests.

MI is calculated using the number of times the pair together of words is observed within a set vicinity of each other against the number of times which the words would be expected to occur separately (see HarperCollins, 2008). As Hunston (2002, p. 71) argues, an MI score of 3 or more can be taken as evidence that two items are collocates (see also McEnery et al., 2006, p. 56). The MI score answers the question 'how strongly are the words attracted to each other?' (Evert, 2009, p. 1228), the higher the MI score, the greater the strength of salience between a pair of words. However, it should be noted that MI has been previously criticised for focusing on showing words that are more likely to exclusively collocate with a search term (it also does not account for directionality of collocation). But, given the aims of the current book, MI is one of many suitable statistics to answer the intended research questions.

The second test worth noting is T-score tests. T-score tests are a confidence-based test, which compares the occurrence of words against what we might expect through chance alone. Gablasova et al. (2017, p. 162) succinctly summarise the mathematical elements behind t-score tests: 'the t-score is calculated as an adjusted value of collocation frequency based on the raw frequency from which random co-occurrence frequency is subtracted. This is then divided by the square root of the raw frequency'. Typically, a T-score test of 2 or more is seen as statistically significant (see Baker, 2014, p. 136). Gablasova et al. (2017) point out a few flaws with the T-score test, for example: 'while all collocations identified by the t-score are frequent, not all frequent word combinations have a high t-score' (p. 163). Similar to the keywords, the statistics behind collocation might be above the level expected of readers of this book—and as such I will not dwell on the mathematical equations behind these statistics. However, those interested in understanding the mathematical equations behind the different statistics should see Brezina (2018).

Moving away from the statistical aspects of collocation to why collocation is important, one of the central ideas of collocation is that words can begin to take on the meaning of the words that they collocate with. As Stubbs (2003, p. 13) states: 'individual words can never be more than a starting point, since it is often collocations which create connections' (see also Stubbs, 2005). This is a phenomenon which is aptly illustrated by the concept of semantic prosody (Baker, 2015; Stubbs, 1994). Semantic prosody is when a word collocates with a set of words which belong to either a specific semantic group or appears in the vicinity of words (or phrases) which indicate positive or negative effect and thus we associate that first word with the semantics of the collocates. For example, McEnery et al. (2015) argue that, in a specialised corpus of tweets about the murder of Lee Rigby, words such as *radical*, *leader*, and *condemn* collocate with the lemma MUSLIM. McEnery et al. argue that this collocation was used in an attempt to (dis)associate the actions of the individuals with the belief system of the religion. In other words, ideologies about Islam were portrayed through the use of collocation, and the lemma *Muslim* was imbued with meaning from the surrounding words.

With regard to gender, studies have demonstrated the prevalence of semantic prosody in the media. For example, in a corpus of newspaper articles, Caldas-Coulthard and Moon (2010, 2016) found the word *woman* collocated with words such as *sexy* and *busty* (this study was touched upon in Chapter 2). As Caldas-Coulthard and Moon (2016, pp. 116–117) note: 'many adjectives signify sexuality, including the size collocate *busty*, and all evaluate positively. The broadsheet data is more mixed, though here too most adjectives are positive and often sexualised: appearance is commented on far more than with [*man*]'. In this example of research which explores semantic prosody, the adjectives which the lemma *woman* collocates with give more weight for the idea that women are sexualised in the British media. One of the strengths of Caldas-Coulthard and Moon's research was the corpus they used: The Bank of English, which is a corpus of five million words of language taken from the British tabloids between 2002 and 2003. This corpus was representative of the language used in the British Tabloid newspapers. In a similar investigation using the same data set, Moon (2014) suggests that as women age they are more likely to be described with collocational adjectives such as *frail* or *bitter*. Similarly, Caldas-Coulthard and Moon, (2016) note that the de facto label for middle-aged or older women is that of a grandmother. The findings of Moon (2014) and Caldas-Coulthard and Moon (2016) echo Crenshaw's (1991) call for intersectional analyses of gender—i.e. that we should analyse how the representation and perception of gender roles are impacted by other social identities (in this instance, particularly paying attention to both age and gender).

Other scholars have used the 1990s BNC to examine collocates of the lemmas MAN and WOMAN (see Pearce, 2008). Pearce (2008) found that WOMAN collocated with and tended to take the object position of verbs which denoted sexual violence such as *rape* and that WOMAN collocated with and was the object of verbs which positioned them as recipients of powerful actions by others (such as *coerce* or *marginalize*). Certain verb collocates also positioned WOMAN as the 'recipients' of the sexual actions of others (e.g. *ravish* and *shag*). Furthermore, Pearce found that a subset of adjectival collocates related to appearance (e.g. MAN collocated with adjectives such as *broad-shouldered*, while WOMAN collocated with adjectives such as *plump* and *slender*). Thus, Pearce's study was able to use collocational analysis to demonstrate how gender was represented within British English in a more general sense.

Baker (2005) used collocational analysis to examine how gay men were represented in the British newspapers *The Daily Mail* and *The Mirror*. In particular, the adjectives which collocated with the term *gay* typically suggested a number of discourses, including ones which drew on the notions: that gay people were transient with transient relationships, that being gay was a behaviour rather than an identity, that they were linked to crime and violence (as both perpetrators and victims), that they were perceived as shameful and secretive, but also that they were shameless—in particularly flamboyant, that they were promiscuous, that they would influence children to also *become* gay, and that they were political lobbyists. One of the benefits to Baker's research is that he cross compares the collocates with concordance lines, in order to see how the term was used and to garner a better understanding of the kinds of discourse prosodies at play—and to confirm that the lexical semantics held true in context.

Concordance Line Analysis

The final major method in corpus linguistics which I would like to draw attention to is concordance line analysis/close reading of concordance lines. When a particular word or phrase is searched in a corpus, the context in which it is used can be examined. A large amount of corpus research utilises concordance line analysis: ultimately, it represents the fundamental aspect of corpus linguistics—which is to examine language in context. Unlike keywords and collocates, concordance line analysis does not necessarily require complex statistical models. One of the benefits of concordance line analysis is that it allows the researcher to move beyond lexical semantics—for example, the word *fuck* might be used as a swear word, but in a particular context may be used more frequently to refer to the act of having sex. This distinction could potentially reshape an analysis and should be considered.

One of the benefits of checking concordance lines is that they can allow researchers to examine different prosodies around a word. For example, adjectives such as *shitty*, *awful*, *crap*, and *abysmal* would all suggest a generally negative view of a word. However, it may be the case that they do not occur as collocates (as there may be many near-synonyms). Indeed, Baker's (2015) analysis of the change in how men are represented in COHA (the Corpus of Historical American English) started with statistically key collocates of *man*, which lead to a concordance line analysis. The concordance line analysis demonstrated what kind of words positioned men in a positive way and what as seen as a positive value for men to have at different periods in American history. This utilised the notion of prosodies, by looking at positive words which co-occurred with *man*. For example, *honest* was a collocate of *man* in 1810–1859. The concordance lines which this occurred with language that also showed that *man* was modified by adjectives such as *good* (such as in the line *he was a good, honest man*), suggesting that *honest*(y) was a positive virtue.

Concordance line analysis can also be used in tandem with other methodological frameworks, such as keyword analyses. For example, an analyst may choose to inspect all concordance lines of a specific list of words, such as each word within a keyword list. Aull and Brown (2013) examined the concordance lines for terms which occurred within the top 25 keywords within a data set of news reports covering major events within women's professional sports. They note that this was useful for examining words in different contexts of use. Similarly, in Heritage and Koller (2020), we found that social actors were particularly salient within the top 25 keywords, which lead to a quantification of all social actors within the corpus. The terms *man/woman* and *he/she* were particularly salient, and so an appraisal analysis (see Martin & White, 2005) was conducted on a random sample of 50 concordance lines for each term. Ultimately, this revealed that although the terms (and collocates of the terms) were relatively innocuous, men were spoken about as being incapable victims of women, while women were positioned as only having the capability to judge and torment men. Furthermore, there was a preoccupation with the aesthetic qualities of both men and women, which would not have necessarily been shown through keyword or collocational analysis.

However, one issue with concordance line analysis is the analyst must manually search the concordance lines to analyse the data. In some case (when there are only a small number of concordance lines) this is a viable method (such as in Heritage & Koller, 2020). However, in larger data sets, applying a framework to the concordance lines for every single instance of a word might be too time-consuming and less viable. In these cases, it is often worth checking a subset of concordance lines (see, Potts, 2015). Nevertheless, at least checking the concordance lines for how a term is typically used is a key aspect to corpus research. Moving beyond simple lexical semantics allows for a deeper understanding of how keywords, collocates, and search terms are used.

Corpus-Based and Corpus-Driven Studies

Earlier, I noted that corpus studies can broadly be differentiated by whether they are corpus-based or corpus-driven. In corpus-based studies, the researcher has a hypothesis in mind and uses the corpus to test that hypothesis. Similarly, the researcher might have a particular phrase (or set of phrases) that they want to investigate within a corpus. For example, we might want to look at the representation of gender in a particular reference corpus, and so we might use terms we know are ostensibly gendered. For example, Taylor's (2013) study looking at how the terms GIRL and BOY were represented in three general corpora—all of which were built around British national broadsheet newspapers. These corpora were 'SiBol 93 (about 95-million words), SiBol 05 (about 113-million words) and Port 2010 (about 125 million words)' (p. 94). In her case study, Taylor takes these pre-established terms and uses a variety of corpus methods to see how girls and boys are represented. She was then able to note similarities and differences across times, particularly focusing on collocates and how they represented gender in such ways. Taylor's work is particularly in line with a particular analytical approach called Corpus-Assisted (Critical) Discourse Analysis (CADS) (see also Partington et al., 2013). The reason for this is that once Taylor had managed to uncover some interesting findings with her corpus methodology, she then took the analysis a step further by applying a discursive analytical framework (in particular, looking at the different process types of verbs—see Chapter 5 for a discussion of process types).

Other studies might be considered corpus-driven. In corpus-driven research, the analyst assumes no hypothesis and lets the data 'speak for itself'. For example, we might generate keywords and then analyse these keywords more extensively, using such keywords to guide our analysis. In other words, this kind of analysis 'is more inductive' (see Biber, 2015, p. 196). For example, Baker (2014, pp. 19–44) takes a corpus-driven approach to looking at the language used by male and female speakers in the British National Corpus (1994 edition). Baker looked at the statistically significant keywords used by male and female speakers and examined differences in the language they used. The conclusions were therefore gained more inductively than taking pre-established terms. In his analysis, Baker notes that while there were some differences, once more variables were considered (such as participant roles in conversation) these differences decreased somewhat.

Important in the distinction between corpus-based and corpus-driven studies is that the difference is one of gradience—and viewing the two approaches as wholly mutually exclusive can be problematic. Similarly, viewing CADS and what is sometimes called corpus-based discourse analysis (see Baker, 2006) (i.e. using a combination of other corpus methodologies to critically examine discourse—which can be conducted from a corpus-based or corpus-assisted perspective) as diametrically opposed is problematic. CADS can add an additional layer of analysis and can give us an additional lens through which to look at data, but inductive categorisation systems from analysts (e.g. grouping into broad semantic categories) can also reveal interesting patterns in the data. This does not mean one is inherently 'better' than the other, rather they are just different ways to approach a corpus analysis.

Corpora and Videogame Studies

In previous sections, I have drawn attention to some studies of videogame paratext which use corpus methods to explore how players interact with each other, with a particular focus on studies which look at how gender and sexuality are constructed in these interactions (see, e.g., Carrillo Masso, 2011; Ensslin, 2012; Potts, 2015). What appears to be less common, however, is research which take either a corpus— or computational—approach to the language used within videogames. Broadly speaking, there are three notable studies, all of which demonstrate that videogames could be a fruitful site for corpus linguistic analyses but are problematic in ways which show why a dedicated monograph is needed.

The first of these studies was conducted by Ray (2019), who analysed translated science-fiction terminology within videogames. Although Ray writes that her methodology is 'corpus-based' (p. 92), no information is provided on the size of the corpus used or the corpus tools used to analyse the translated lexemes. The most information, with regard to corpus creation, that a reader is provided with is that 'each lexical creation was manually noted in a table with its French equivalent' (p. 92). Therefore, it appears as though the games analysed by Ray were collected in their entirety, although this cannot be confirmed from the way that it is reported. It is wholly possible that 'corpus' has been used as synonymous with 'collection of data' in this sense, though this can often be confusing for corpus linguists. The way Ray collected her data can be considered useful as it allows an analyst to become very familiar with a corpus. Although this kind of research is useful to those interested in translation, it is perhaps less useful for those who wish to look at how societal values and identities are (re)produced through videogames as a form of mass media.

In a similar vein to the research methods employed by Ray (2019), Fekete and Porkoláb (2019) have used computational methods to examine the linguistic features of place names in *The Elder Scrolls* series. In this study, Fekete and Porkoláb extracted over 1000 place names from the videogame series' wiki page and examined the morphological and onomastic aspects of fictional toponyms (names of the fictional locations). The researchers attempted to use mathematical modelling to examine how different place names could be grouped and where there were similarities. While an interesting study which demonstrates how different elements of worlds are built within videogames, this kind of method is arguably somewhat different from the methods employed in corpus linguistics. In terms of data size, Fekete and Porkoláb (2019, p. 32) note: 'the sample contained 1042 toponyms, and during the compilation of the database, our intention was to represent every place-name of the game's universe'. While this is not to say that this is a small data sample, it is arguably too small to be considered a corpus that is suitable for a corpus linguistic study. Similarly, in corpus linguistic studies, scholars would normally be interested in examining other linguistic elements—such as how those place names are used, how they are evaluated, or what they collocate with. Thus, although this sample might be representative, the methods implemented by Fekete and Porkoláb (2019) are much more computational-focused, as opposed to corpus-focused. That is to say, they do not explore elements such as lexico-grammar, nor how ideologies are (re)produced within the text.

The final study I wish to draw attention to is my own. In Heritage (2020), I presented initial findings of a corpus of c.330,000 words built around 10 videogames—I discuss this corpus and use it in different ways in Chapter 5. In this study, which helped lay the foundations for this book, I primarily tried to justify that corpora could be used to examine the representation of gender within videogames. I generated a keyword list of the top 50 keywords and demonstrated that about 15% related to gender. I then examined how *he* and *she* were used by looking at collocates and concordance lines, arguing that women were more likely to be seen with regard to their knowledge and wisdom, while men were more likely to be discussed in relation to violent actions. Indeed, I build on these findings in Chapter 5 by taking a wholly corpus-assisted approach to the data, categorising the collocates in different ways, and examining a greater number of collocates to reveal a greater range of representations in more detail. The study I presented in Heritage (2020) was only designed to serve as a starting point—and indeed, I could not demonstrate everything that can be done with corpus linguistic methods. There is a difficult and fine line to strike in these kinds of papers: introducing a new concept to a well-established field can take time and space, which I hope this book is able to provide. There are still several ways to conduct a corpus study and still a number of videogames which could be examined in more detail, and this book seeks to demonstrate some of these with a greater range of videogames.

Conclusions

This chapter has hopefully highlighted the underlying principles of corpus linguistics and shown how they can be applied to the study of language and gender. I have also touched upon previous applications of the method to ludolinguistics.

While in this chapter I have touched upon the mathematical theory which underpins the different quantitative methods implemented in corpus linguistics, I have attempted to do so in a way which does not require readers to spend months understanding advanced mathematical theory. There are currently a number of debates within the research into corpus statistics (see, e.g., Brezina, 2018). However, what I have tried to present in this chapter is a broad overview of <u>why</u> those statistics are used and give rough guidance on <u>how</u> they are used.

Obviously, there are a number of different methods in corpus linguistics, and these move beyond just (key)word list analysis, collocation, and concordance line analysis. For example, Scott (1997) has argued for the use of key-key words, which are keywords that are shared across corpora. Baker et al. (2008) have argued for the use of consistent collocates—to examine what collocates are salient across corpora. Elsewhere, Brezina et al. (2015) have argued for the use of collocational networks, which show shared collocates and collocational associations. There are also additional methods for analysis, such as using certain types of taggers (i.e.

running a corpus through additional software to identify part of speech or the semantic domains of words) or combining the data generated by applying these methods with discursive analytical frameworks. I have not delved into the vast breadth of additional methods in this section—simply because, with the possible exception of methods of tagging, most corpus methods rely on an aspect of keyword, collocational, or concordance line analysis. I have also not delved into the different discursive frameworks because to do so would be beyond the scope of this book. However, when they are used in later chapters, I will discuss them in detail as and when appropriate. In sum, these methods are not an exhaustive list, and the field of corpus linguistics is ever-growing. What I hope this chapter has been able to do, however, is to provide a broad overview of the very fundamental methods used and show how they can be applied to the study of gender and identity.

When this background review on the fundamental notions of corpus linguistics is combined with the discussion in Chapter 2 (in which I discussed the related to research into gender and identity), and when these findings are viewed with the review of the previous ludolinguistics research, a number of gaps emerge within the literature. Although the review of the background literature provided above is not exhaustive, at least three primary trends can be seen:

1. Ludolinguistic research tends to focus on videogame paratext
2. When ludolinguistics research does examine the language used within videogames (rather than in videogame paratext or player interactions) from a critical perspective, there is not a focus on language as a communicative mode
3. To date, little work has been done to combine fully-fledged corpus linguistic methods to explore the representation of identity within videogames.

Throughout the following chapters, I attempt to demonstrate the validity of researching the representation of gender within videogames through corpus methods, drawing in particular on keyword analysis, collocates, and concordance line analysis.

Bibliography

Aull, L., & Brown, D. (2013). Fighting words: a corpus analysis of gender representations in sports reportage. *Corpora, 8*(1), 27–52.

Baker, P. (2004a). Querying keywords: Questions of difference, frequency and sense in keywords analysis. *Journal of English Linguistics, 32*(4), 346–359.

Baker, P. (2004b). "Unnatural acts": Discourses of homosexuality within the House of Lords debates on gay male law reform. *Sociolinguistics, 8*(1), 88–106.

Baker, P. (2005). *Public discourses of gay men.* Routledge.

Baker, P. (2006). *Using corpora in discourse analysis.* Bloomsbury.

Baker, P. (2012). Acceptable bias? Using corpus linguistics methods with critical discourse analysis. *Critical Discourse Studies, 9*(3), 247–256.

Baker, P. (2014). *Using corpora to analyse gender.* Bloomsbury.

Baker, P. (2015). Two hundred years of the American man. In T. Milani (Ed.), *Language and masculinities: Performances, intersections, dislocations* (pp. 34–53). Routledge.

Baker, P., & Heritage, F. (2021). How to use corpus linguistics in sociolinguistics: A case study of modal verb use, age and change over time. In A. Okeeffe & M. McCarthy (Eds.), *The Routledge handbook of corpus linguistics* (2nd edn.). Routledge.

Baker, P., Gabrielatos, C., & McEnery, T. (2013). Sketching Muslims: A corpus-driven analysis of representations around the word "Muslim" in the British press 1998–2009. *Applied Linguistics, 34*(3), 3255–3278.

Baker, P., Gabrielatos, C., KhosraviNik, M., Krzyżanowski, M. ł., McEnery, T., & Wodak, R. (2008). A useful methodological synergy? Combining critical discourse analysis and corpus linguistics to examine discourses of refugees and asylum seekers in the UK press. *Discourse & Society, 19*(3), 273–306.

Bednarek, M. (2015). "Wicked" women in contemporary pop culture: "Bad" language and gender in Weeds, Nurse Jackie, and Saving Grace. *Text & Talk, 35*(4), 431–451.

Biber, D. (2015). Corpus-based and corpus-driven analyses of language variation and use. In B. Heine &d H. Narrog (Eds.), The Oxford handbook of linguistic analysis (2nd edn.) (pp. 193–22). Oxford University Press.

Brezina, V. (2018). *Statistics in corpus linguistics: A practical guide.* Cambridge University Press.

Brezina, V., McEnery, T., & Wattam, S. (2015). Collocations in context: A new perspective on collocation networks. *International Journal of Corpus Linguistics, 20*(2), 139–173.

Brookes, G., & Baker, P. (2017). What does patient feedback reveal about the NHS? A mixed methods study of comments posted to the NHS Choices online service. *BMJ Open, 7*(4).

Caldas-Coulthard, C. R., & Moon, R. (2010). 'Curvy, hunky, kinky': Using corpora as tools for critical analysis. *Discourse & Society, 21*(2), 99–133.

Caldas-Coulthard, C. R., & Moon, R. (2016). Grandmother, gran, gangsta granny semiotic representations of grandmotherhood. *Gender and Language, 10*(3), 309–339.

Carrillo Masso, I. (2011). The grips of fantasy: The construction of female characters in and beyond virtual game worlds. In A. Ensslin. & E. Muse (Eds.), *Creating second lives: Community, identity and spatiality as constructions of the virtual* (pp. 113–142). Routledge.

Charteris-Black, J., & Seale, C. (2010). *Gender and the language of illness.* Palgrave Macmillan.

Crenshaw, K. (1991). Mapping the margins: Intersectionality, identity politics, and violence against women of color. *Stanford Law Review, 43*(6), 1241–1299.

Ensslin, A. (2012). *The language of gaming*. Palgrave.

Ensslin, A. (2015). Discourse of games. In K. Tracy, T. Sandel, & C. Illie (Eds.), The *international encyclopedia of language and social interaction*. Wiley.

Evert, S. (2009). Corpora and collocations. In A. Lüdeling & M. Kytö (Eds.), *Corpus linguistics: An international handbook* (pp. 121–148). Walter de Gruyter.

Fekete, T., & Porkoláb, Á. (2019). From Arkngthand to wretched squalor: Fictional place-names in the elder scrolls Universe. *ICAME Journal, 43*(1), 23–58.

Fillmore, C. (1992). Corpus linguistics or computer-aided armchair linguistics. In J. Svartvik (Ed.), *Directions in corpus linguistics: proceedings of Nobel Symposium 82* (pp. 35–60). De Gruyter Mouton.

Firth, J. (1957). *A synopsis of linguistic theory. Studies in linguistic analysis.* Blackwell.

Gablasova, D., Brezina, V., & McEnery, A. (2017). Collocations in corpus-based language learning research: Identifying, comparing and interpreting the evidence. *Language Learning, 67*(1), 155–179.

Gabrielatos, C. (2018). Keyness analysis. In C. Taylor & A. Marchi (Eds.), *Corpus approaches to discourse: A critical review*. Routledge.

Hardie, A. (2014). *Log ratio—An informal introduction.* Lancaster University. http://cass.lancs.ac.uk/log-ratio-an-informal-introduction. Accessed February 2021.

HarperCollins. (2008). *A guide to statistics: T-score and mutual information.* Harper Collins. https://wordbanks.harpercollins.co.uk/other_doc/statistics.html. Accessed February 2021.

Hawtin, A. (2019). *The written British national corpus 2014: Design, compilation and analysis* (Doctoral dissertation, Lancaster University).

Heritage, F. (2020). Applying corpus linguistics to videogame data: Exploring the representation of gender in videogames at a lexical level. *Game studies, 20*(3).

Heritage, F., & Koller, V. (2020). Incels, in-groups, and ideologies: The representation of gendered social actors in a sexuality-based online community. *Journal of Language and Sexuality, 9*(2), 152–178.

Hoff Sommers, C. (2014). *Factual feminist*. American Enterprise Institute.

Hunston, S. (2002). *Corpora in applied linguistics*. Cambridge University Press.

Hunston, S. (2010). How can a corpus be used to explore patterns?. In A. O'Keeffe & M. McCarthy (Eds.), *The Routledge handbook of corpus linguistics* (pp. 152–166). Routledge.

Hunston, S. (2011) *Corpus approaches to evaluation: Phraseology and evaluative language*. Routledge.

Hunston, S., & Gill, F. (1998). Verbs Observed: A corpus-driven pedagogic grammar. *Applied Linguistics, 19*(1), 45–72.

Hunt S. (2015). Representations of gender and agency in the Harry Potter series. In P. Baker & T. McEnery (Eds.), *Corpora and discourse studies: Integrating discourse and corpora* (pp. 266–284). Palgrave Macmillan.

Love, R. (2020). *Overcoming challenges in corpus construction: The spoken British national corpus 2014*. Routledge.

Martin, J. R., & White, P. R. R. (2005). *The evaluation of language: Appraisal in English.* Palgrave Macmillan.

McEnery, T., Xiao, R. & Tono, Y. (2006). *Corpus-based language studies: An advanced resource book.* Routledge.

McEnery, T., & Hardie, A. (2011). *Corpus linguistics: Method, theory and practice*. Cambridge University Press.

McEnery, T., McGlashan, M., & Love, R. (2015). Press and social media reaction to ideologically inspired murder: The case of Lee Rigby. *Discourse & Communication, 9*(2), 237–259.

Moon, R. (2014). From gorgeous to grumpy: Adjectives, age and gender. *Gender and Language, 8*(1), 5–41.

Oakley, L. (2016). *An investigation into the representations of sexuality in sex education manuals for British teenagers, 1950–2014* (Doctoral dissertation, The University of Birmingham).

Partington, A., Duguid, A., & Taylor, C. (2013). *Patterns and meanings in discourse: Theory and practice in corpus-assisted discourse studies (CADS)*. John Benjamins.

Pearce, M. (2008). Investigating the collocational behaviour of MAN and WOMAN in the BNC using Sketch Engine. *Corpora, 3*(1), 1–29.

Potts, A. (2015). 'LOVE YOU GUYS (NO HOMO)' How gamers and fans play with sexuality, gender, and Minecraft on YouTube. *Critical Discourse Studies, 12*(2), 163–186.

Potts, A., & Weare, S. (2017). Mother, Monster, Mrs, I: A critical evaluation of gendered naming strategies in English sentencing remarks of women who kill. *International Journal for the Semiotics of Law-Revue Internationale de Sémiotique Juridique, 31*(4), 1–32.

Ray, A. (2019). Playing with the language of the future: The localization of science-fiction terms in videogames. In A. Ensslin & I. Balteiro (Eds.), *Approaches to videogame discourse: Lexis, interaction, textuality* (pp. 87–115). Bloomsbury.

Rayson, P. (2008). From key words to key semantic domains. *International Journal of Corpus Linguistics, 13*(4), 519–549.

Römer, U. (2016). Teaming up and mixing methods: Collaborative and cross-disciplinary work in corpus research on phraseology. *Corpora, 11*(1), 113–129.

Sarkeesian, A. (2014). *Tropes vs. women. Feminist frequency: Conversations with pop culture*. YouTube. https://www.youtube.com/watch?v=X6p5AZp7r_Q. Accessed February 2021.

Scott, M. (1997). Pc analysis of key words—And key key words. *System, 25*(2), 233–1245.

Scott, M. (2016). *WordSmith tools version 7*. Lexical Analysis Software.

Sinclair, J. (2001). *Corpus concordance and* collocation. Oxford University Press.

Stubbs, M. (1994). Grammar, text and ideology. *Applied Linguistics, 15*(2), 201–223.

Stubbs, M. (2003). Conrad, concordance, collocation: Heart of darkness or light at the end of the tunnel? Talk presented at *The Third Sinclair Open Lecture*. The University of Birmingham.

Stubbs, M. (2005). Conrad in the computer: Examples of quantitative stylistic methods. *Language and Literature, 14*(1), 5–24.

Taylor, C. (2013). Searching for similarity using corpus-assisted discourse studies. *Corpora, 8*(1), 81–113.

The Bank of English Corpus. (2003). Copyright HarperCollins.

Tognini-Bonelli, E. (2001). *Corpus linguistics at work*. John Benjamins.

Tranchese, A. (2019). Using corpus analysis to investigate "extreme" Incel misogyny online. Talk presented at *12th BAAL LGaS SIG event: Intersections of language, gender and sexuality in media and technology*. Birmingham City University.

Wilson, A. (2013). Embracing Bayes factors for key item analysis in corpus linguistics. In M. Bieswanger & Ko.-S. Amei (Eds.), *New approaches to the study of linguistic variability: Language competence and language awareness in Europe* (pp. 3–11). Peter Lang.

4

Building a Corpus of Language from Videogames

How Do We Get the Data?

In the previous chapter, I discussed some of the fundamental principles in building corpora—namely adhering to the principle of total accountability and ensuring that a corpus is a representative sample of a subset of language. However, it seems odd that there has been a lack of research which has used corpora to explore the language within videogames, especially given the prevalence of this text type. I would argue that one reason for this might be because collecting data from videogames can be difficult. This chapter is designed to give an overview of different methods that researchers might wish to employ in collecting data from videogames and outlines the different methods of data collection which are used throughout this book. Rather than dispersing this chapter among other chapters, I wanted to give readers an opportunity to understand the complexities involved in creating videogame corpora and provide them with some ideas on how they might go about building one for themselves. This therefore means that in later chapters of analysis, readers will hopefully understand why certain choices were made while constructing the videogame corpora used within those chapters.

F. Heritage, *Language, Gender and Videogames*,
https://doi.org/10.1007/978-3-030-74398-7_4

Corpus construction is a complex area—there are many ways that people might want to 'tag' their corpus, and to delve into such complex systems would not be feasible within this book. However, when we build a corpus, we must ask whether or not the data will be able to answer our research question (see Reppen, 2010). Now that we know we are interested in looking at the representation of gender within videogames, it is worth explicitly stating that the overarching research question is 'how is gender represented in fantasy videogames?'. This could be realised in different ways—for example, in Chapter 5 it is realised through asking 'how is gender represented in a general corpus of videogames?', while in Chapter 6 it is 'how is gender represented within a specific corpus of *The Witcher* videogames?', and in Chapter 7 it is 'what do different gendered characters say in *World of Warcraft*?'. I have deliberately left the overarching question as broad because sometimes getting information about who says what in videogames can be difficult (I will demonstrate this later in the chapter), and so by looking at representations (which can involve character speech), we are able to take a slightly broader approach to the text type. With this research question (and the sub-questions for future chapters of analysis) in mind, it is worth turning to discuss some of the ways that videogame corpora can be built. As I demonstrate in this chapter, there are several ways to build videogame corpora, so a good understanding of the different approaches can be beneficial when deciding how to best collect the data.

Language Around Videogames

Before I discuss the methods used to gather data from videogames, I wish to draw attention to an argument from research which has looked at the representation of gender in videogame paratext. Some scholars have argued that the language used in videogame paratext is a 'window' into how language is used within that videogame (see Carrillo Masso, 2011; Miller & Summers, 2007; Summers & Miller, 2014). For example, Summers and Miller (2014) analysed the representation of female videogame characters in magazines and found that female characters were typically over-sexualised. In their conclusion, they argue: 'if female characters are portrayed in this fashion merely in advertising the game, then one can only imagine how they are depicted in the actual game' (ibid., p. 1038). Thus, some scholars believe that by looking at the language (or representations in other communicative modes) around a videogame, we are able to uncover a glimpse into how gender is represented within that videogame. However, I only agree with Summers and Miller's argument to an extent because I disagree with the implicature of their argument. In other words, I agree that we can **only** imagine about something we have not actually investigated. To assume that the representation of gender in a videogame will be the same as in articles about that game makes a dangerous presupposition—especially given that the producers of magazine articles about videogames are not the same as people who produce the game.

The genre of the texts analysed by Summers and Miller is also important. Summer and Miller analysed magazines (i.e. printed materials that do not move). In some videogames, players are able to select what outfits they, and other characters, wear. This means that the images may have been put in the magazine to give a sensationalised depiction of the games. As I have previously argued, representation can cross communicative modes (see Heritage, 2020). Even if the characters in the magazines are represented as scantily clad, or are represented in problematic ways on a visual level, this is not to say that the representation will be the same at a linguistic level in either the magazine articles or the videogames themselves. Thus, this work is positioned against this presupposition that poor representation in paratext equates to poor representation within the text itself.

Language Within Videogames

As I noted in Chapter 2, this book is specifically designed to look at the language within videogames, not around videogames. As such (and because I view them as different texts which will represent gender in different ways), this chapter seeks to discuss the methods by which we can build corpora to look at the representation of gender within videogames.

There are a number of reasons why collecting corpora from videogames might be difficult, one of the most obvious of which is that players are often given a degree of choice in how they play a number of games. This might be a simple choice, such as 'does the player talk to this character or not?'—if the player chooses to talk to that character, they would be given dialogue that they may not see if they choose not to talk to them. However, this kind of choice could be more complex, such as when players are given choices on what they can say. In games such as *Dragon Age* (Bioware, 2009), players are given up to, and including, 8 options of what they can say (though this may be more/less depending on the game). Each option can lead to different dialogue with more permutations, and therefore gathering all of the language which occurs as a result of these choices can be difficult. These permutations can branch out and have further sections, creating incredibly complex webs of choices for players to engage with.

This chapter seeks to problematise data collection methods in investigations which have looked at the language used within videogames. Specifically, I note that a number of videogames will not present players with every possible piece of language and that a number of videogames allow players to 'shape their own narrative'. These games thus contain multilinear narratives where narratives can change depending on player choice. All of these choices have some degree of language, whether that be a quest description, an interaction between a non-playing character and the player, or an item description. Depending on what option a player chooses, different permutations are provided, and an analyst may be provided with a range of different data. This kind of narrative structure is outlined in Fig. 4.1.

In Fig. 4.1, a single choice may lead to multiple different uses of language. It should be noted that this is not limited to two options—though the limited number of options included here have been used as an example. These choices will trigger different dialogue options with non-playing characters (characters whose language is pre-scripted). The player will then have a chance to explore these dialogues further with more choices. Although Fig. 4.1 stops after two different choices, there may be many more (and this is dependent on the videogame). It should also be noted that some of the language from some dialogue choices may

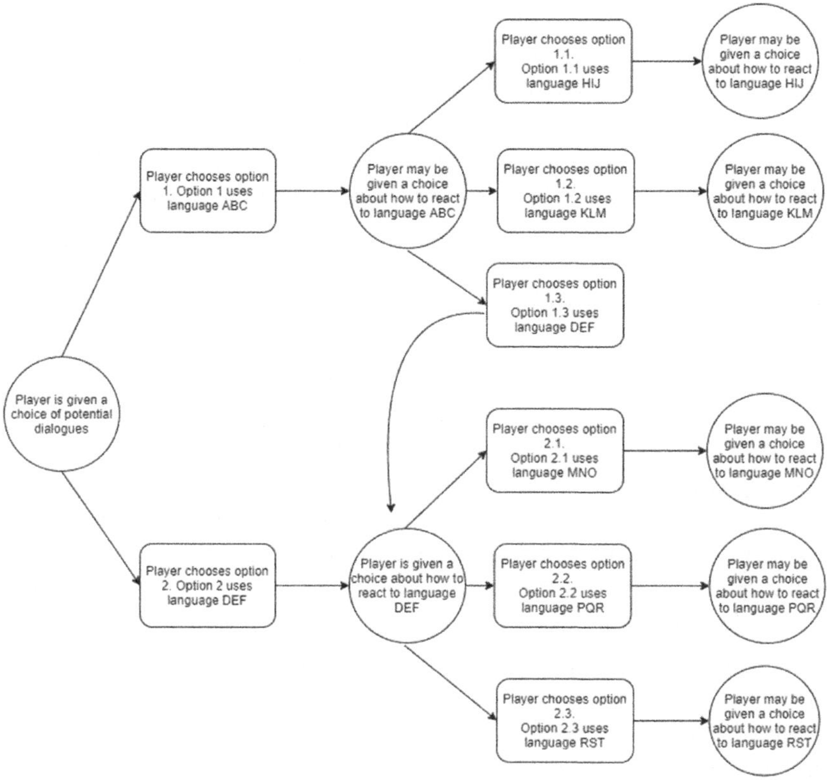

Fig. 4.1 Example of how players' choices can generate different forms of language

overlap (hence, the inclusion of acronyms such as PQ**R** and **R**ST). Similarly, some instances might lead players on to narrative 'paths' which they would have originally started on if they would have selected a different previous option (see, e.g., the link between Option 1.3 using language DEF).

Therefore, when building corpora of videogames, an analyst must be cautious and ensure that what is collected is a representative sample of both (a) all possible routes and permutations that a player may take or (b) a specific route or series of options that a player may take. This may make building the corpora difficult when attempting to adhere to the principle of total accountability (McEnery & Hardie, 2011). In this case, deciding what permutations are random (and indeed obtaining random permutations) may prove difficult.

Indeed, although not a corpus study, Goorimoorthee et al. (2019) appear to have fallen into this difficult bind. They examined differences in the representation of accents and how this impacts a player's experience in a *Dragon Age: Origins* (*DAO*) (Bioware, 2009). With regard to the sampling of data, the authors claim they: 'collect[ed] and label[ed] character speech data to map the distribution of accents throughout a typical playthrough of DAO' (p. 274). However, *DAO* is a videogame where the player is able to choose what permutation(s) to follow. This thus raises questions about how a play through of games like this can ever be 'typical'. While the study by Goorimoorthee et al. (2019) was able to fill many gaps in ludolinguistic literature and was genuinely innovative, it appears as though the analysts faced issues regarding player choice. This issue is one of the reasons why building representative corpora of videogames can be so difficult.

Therefore, I would argue that we need to take a representative sample of these different permutations. It would be no good, for example, only taking the first possible choice, and it would similarly be no good only taking all of one section but not another. But, how do we gather all these permutations? I would argue that there are 4 potential methods:

1. Use computer coding or software to extract all the language
2. Play through all possible permutations and transcribe them
3. Use fan transcripts and collate these
4. Use websites which have documented the language via one of the three processes above.

In this short chapter, I outline these methods and discuss the benefits and drawbacks to each.

Using Computer Coding: Generating Text Dumps

When a videogame (which is not hosted on online servers) is downloaded or installed on a computer, it must include a file of language upon which the videogame software will draw the data to be shown on screen. In other words, if software must read a file in order to show a player language, that language must already be within the program files. This language may be encrypted but is nevertheless present in the game files. A quoted snippet of this, demonstrated below, is the encrypted version of the videogame *The Witcher 2: Assassination of Kings* (CD Projekt Red, 2011). The default file location for this file is Users > Program files (x86) > Steam > Steamapps > Common > The Witcher 2. Please note, this is because the game was downloaded via the digital distribution service *Steam* (Valve, 2003–onwards) and was done on a Windows computer. The same results may differ if a Mac computer is used, and cannot be done on a games console, such as a Play Station or Nintendo Switch.

¼&žM□›Ó7□o□ß°¿ú□Iÿ"þ0y[ú y?ˆ

$"*□UÐ«£W¡¯¨_˜¿¼□›ÿ0 á □tÜ

?Ü*□Už«ˆW¡¯²_Û¿©□Ôÿ= ç e

tÞ

9□*'UŸ«ŽWà¯µ_Ö¿ì□€ÿ, í 05Ú

;Ü*™Už«„Wà¯¨_×¿ì□‡ÿ! í 0$Ø

?'*□Už«"W³¯ü_Ì¿¤□†ÿ+ ý wtß

1□*"Uƒ«ÎW0y0*–«,øY ³wggÎxœ,8²pMá&Â°„" Ã%~KG– ¾,ðY³`gcÎ□œi8æpKáhÂñ,' Í%• KG–¯,èY³bgeÎgœi8ðp]áhÂö„>
(The Witcher 2, 2011)

By using a computer program—in this case, one called Gibbed Red Tools (Gibbed, 2015), or alternatively coding in a program such as Python, the file can be converted so as it is readable by humans. This file can then be saved in a format which is readable by corpus software (such as by saving the file extension as .TXT). Below, I demonstrate a snippet from the same text file, which has undergone this process. Please note, I cannot say for certain whether the snippet is an identical replication of the above quote, given that the above quote must be decoded and there is no way to see what symbols match to words.

> Your Highnes... Witcher Geralt. What a pleasure. Would you like to experience with your toung tastes of my wonderful soup? A bit, just a zip. I don't want to take the pleasure from you, Sire. So you would like to. Splendid. How much, witcher? Witcher Geralt, what a pleasure. Would you mind if I cut you into pieces? And you could use a bath. Oh, you know, stuff. You could use a bath. Any Scoia'tael scouts in the area heard the sounds of the fighting. They won't miss that hole we dropped through either... Nothing, sorry. We need to find another way out. And to think, these drunkards protect people from the Scoia'tael. [PL] Nie? No cóż... Drunkards... Iorveth could take them singlehanded. Peasants in uniforms... Indeed. [PL] Pękam ze śmiechu, Geralt. [PL] Musiałbym się zastanowić. I could open a teleport... (The Witcher 2, 2011)

The file which contains the encoded language is called a 'text dump' or 'string file'. While these files provide all the language within a game, there are still a number of issues with a decrypted string file. A practical issue with gathering the data in this way is that it can often be hard to find the right software to use if one does not already know how to use code to extract the language from the files. For those who do not know how to code, this can lead to questions of knowing what software to use for what game and what the reliability of particular software is. Unfortunately, there is no single resolution to this because no single piece of software can decode all videogames, and it must be done on a game-by-game basis. Although there have been some attempts to create open-sources of code for researchers to get the data without having to find such pieces of software (see, Roberts & Rennick, 2020).

Moving away from software to generate this readable file, it is worth discussing the quality of the data which this method yields. The language is placed in an order which is only logical to a certain degree. In text dump files, sentences may be placed next to each other, even though they may be from different narrative paths. This mismatch of where dialogue is placed means that the text does not read in the same way as prose. For example, there might be three lines as such:

The witcher ran into the farm and ate the chicken
The bandit decided he had enough of talking
The witcher thought the chicken tasted delicious

These snippets of language occur as entire sentences and, although the language may be split up at points, it is still legible and presented as both complete and grammatically 'correct'. It is not presented as having words placed in any random location in a sentence, for example:

The Witcher bandit farm decided chicken ate.

Therefore, while the structuring of text dump files may contain enough information to understand what discourses are present and to run a collocational analysis, it can be difficult to explore interaction and changes in the narrative.

An additional aspect to consider is that some games, such as *The Witcher 2*, contain translators' notes in the text dump files. In *The Witcher 2*, these translator notes are in Polish and marked by a preceding [PL] (these are visible and included in the quote provided earlier). These notes would need to be removed before the corpus can be accurately analysed without skewing the results (as translators' notes do not appear in the videogame) unless the analyst is interested in examining the translators' notes as a corpus. Although the games have been localised—meaning that not only were they translated, but they were rephrased and edited to appear as though they were made in American English, by someone who was raised with both Polish and American influences, this removal of the translators' notes can be an arduous task for single analysts.

Although the text dump files have some problematic aspects for corpus linguists, they offer a resolution to the lack of videogame corpora while still adhering to the principles of total accountability. As this method gathers all of the language which is contained within a videogame, there is no need to ensure that all files are random, and the files are as representative of the videogames as possible. Furthermore, the language contained within the text dump files is accurate. That is to say, even though the language from certain permutations may appear next to the language from other permutations, what is written in the file will be the exact same as what the player reads. Thus, text dumps offer a viable source of data for building a corpus of videogames: they contain all the language used within a videogame, they are accurate transcriptions of the language, and they can be extracted and cleaned relatively quickly.

Transcribing Narrative Permutations

The second method I now focus on is the most laborious method and time-consuming method for the analyst: playing through the videogame multiple times, transcribing different narrative permutations of the dialogue, and manually transcribing item descriptions or other bits of language that may not appear as dialogue. However, this method does come with the benefit of being able to include tags in certain locations and structure the corpus in a way which is logical to the researcher. That is to say that analysts can use their own tagging system, such as XML tags, to indicate what language belongs to which permutation. Some corpora, and various ways of coding, allow an analyst to only look at the language presented by 'x' within a corpus—if 'x' is marked. For example, we might mark the beginning of a stretch of text with '<speaker = "m">' and the end of that stretch of text with </speaker > . This would indicate that the speaker is 'm'—which might be male (depending on the coding system the analyst uses). Doing this would allow us to conduct analyses on who says what within our corpus. Similarly, different permutations (or the language from specific characters) could be saved as different files.

In order to collect these, a practical method while running these permutations is to create a number of save files of each section within the videogame where the language may branch off into further permutations. For example, an analyst may save their game as a single file before each scene of dialogue (and finish collecting data with several files). This allows the analyst to return to a specified point and transcribe all potential outcomes from those points. One may also have to play through a number of times to see if any other potential dialogue is opened through a series of particular choices. Another practical way around this might be to watch a number of 'play throughs' on websites such as YouTube and use these videos to see what is said in other dialogue permutations (this is discussed in the next subsection).

For larger videogames, such as *Skyrim* (Bethesda, 2011), this can be incredibly time-consuming, as a single permutation may contain entirely different language from other permutations. Indeed, anecdotally, to gather 6,000 words of data from one particular narrative within *The Witcher 3* took in excess of 35 hours' worth of gameplay to reach the required point in the videogame and another 40 hours to play through all permutations and transcribe the data (see Heritage, 2021). Although the data were well-annotated, it took so long to gather (and ended up being so rich) that a corpus of multiple narratives and scenes could not be collected.

Although the focus of my previous work has been to look at the impact player choice has on the language provided in dialogue permutations, I have previously provided the following steps for conducting this kind of analysis (see Heritage, 2021, p. 287). These steps are as follows:

1. Create a 'metadata' quest file—this should contain the names of the characters, the quest title, and any quests which must be completed as a pre-requisite for this quest to be played. N.B., this can also indicate if the text from the quest is given from an object instead.
2. Play through every single possible narrative permutation. Transcribe the data for each narrative path and cross-compare this data with transcripts from other narrative paths.
3. Mark the first stretch of text as compulsory—this is the first introduction to a quest, which even though players may abandon, they must be presented with.
4. Mark when the player is given a choice and on-screen options.
5. Mark which of these options the player must press in order to progress to the next scene and which of these options are not compulsory for progression.
6. Play through all options. If there are additional options within these choices, mark these as a secondary layer of options.

7. Mark any text which is wholly compulsory to the story (i.e. regardless of choices, the player must see that data).
8. Tag where the dialogue changes from the dialogue presented to players significantly (especially where relevant to social issues).
9. Tag lists and other content that occurs in a suggested sequence (e.g. in a suggested order on the screen)—these should be tagged with sequential numbers.
10. Tag any points where the player is able to automatically end the quest and the dialogue that is included in this.

This kind of tagging allowed for an in-depth discussion of a single quest from *The Witcher 3*, though this method is also applicable to other videogames where a player is given dialogue options.

In sum, although this method yields the least amount of data for the time it takes to gather, it is arguably the highest quality, as the researcher is able to ensure it meets their individual needs.

Text from Fans

Similar to the methodological challenges faced by Bednarek (2018) in building her corpora of television transcripts, transcribing a videogame can be a laborious task (see the above subsection). Bednarek (2018) notes that one potential method of creating a corpus of language from televisions shows could be to take transcripts which fans have created. However, one issue with this is that fans may misspell words, could add in screen directions, or may mistranscribe aspects that could be vital to the analysts' investigation. The same problems arise when using fan transcripts of videogames.

Recently, researchers have used several texts from fan websites in order to start to account for player choice in games such as in the *Final Fantasy* series (Roberts & Rennick, 2020). Roberts and Rennick followed several permutations placed on fan websites for the *Final Fantasy* series with a view of coding the differences choices create into their corpus. In order to do this, permutations were 'nested' within broader dialogues, which indicated when a choice had occurred. However, the choice structures presented in *Final Fantasy* were relatively simplistic—usually, there was only one 'level' of choice (i.e. a choice would only affect the language immediately after the choice was made, but all would lead back to the same language after). This is not always the case, and in the case of some games like *The Witcher 3*, there can be several 'levels' of choice that can have much greater impacts on the storylines.

However, this is not to say that all text from fans are the same, nor have the same problems. One thing some fans do is upload their play throughs to various video hosting websites. Returning to the data presented in Potts' (2015) study, 'Let's Play' videos are a common feature on websites such as YouTube. If an analyst wanted to transcribe data from a game that they did not have access to, they would be able to transcribe the data that by watching these play throughs (Though, one must bear in mind copyright issues around having 'lawful access' to the data). This is also particularly useful when comparing how different choices impact the narrative. For example, if there are multiple choices in a videogame, the analyst would have to play through all, record their own play through and transcribe that data. Videos uploaded to YouTube, or other similar platforms, which depict people playing a particular videogame, would allow the analyst to reduce the amount of time spent between interactions or working out puzzles and different permutations for themselves. Though the process would still be lengthy, and the recording quality of the data may vary from video to video, it still presents a possible viable option. However, sometimes, these kinds of transcripts or uploaded data do not contain additional information—such as the language used to describe an item. Thus, it may be the case that the corpora are less representative than some text dump files.

Ultimately, while data directly gathered from fans can be a time-saving method, analysts run the risk of using skewed data which is not necessarily subject to the same levels of rigour that they themselves employ. However, sometimes, depending on how large data samples are, texts from fans may be one of the few ways to actually gather the data. Should this method be used, however, the analyst must check for various spelling and grammatical mistakes, additions, and elements which would not normally be included in a transcript. One such way to do this, on larger data sets, might be to take a representative sample of data from the game transcript and compare that to data generated through the second method discussed in this chapter (following and transcribing all narrative permutations).

Using Websites

While I have discussed data explicitly generated by fans (such as where fans of videogames have transcribed the data), there are some websites which are run by fans of the videogames. These websites can sometimes yield highly accurate data from videogames. For example, the website *WoWhead*, a website dedicated to data from *World of Warcraft* (*WoW*), asks players to install an add-on to their computer (an add-on is a piece of software that only runs with *WoW*). When playing the game, this add-on scrapes the data a player interacts with, such as the language in quests, the descriptions of items, and the names of non-playing characters. In other words, in order to get a representative view of the massively multiplayer online role-playing game, *WoWhead* crowdsources the data. This data is then stored on the website for others to access.

Elsewhere, some websites are used to upload text dump files. For example, text dumps for *The Legend of Zelda* series (Miyamoto & Tezuka 1986–onwards) have been made available on websites such as *Gamespot* (GameSpot, 2019). This website allows for the text dump files from multiple games across the series to be accessed by researchers and can provide a valuable tool for examining the language within that series.

In sum, while the kind of data afforded from fans may not always be a fully accurate reflection of the language used within the videogame, it is often plentiful and a quick to obtain. When implementing this method to collect data, an analyst may be limited by what websites are dedicated to what games, and if fans are willing to post data. Similar to issues faced by using software to extract the language from within videogames, this must be considered on a game-by-game basis.

Summary

This very short chapter has been written to highlight the different ways in which videogame corpora can be gathered. Rather than focusing on elements such as discursive analytical techniques, I have attempted to do two things in this chapter. First, I have attempted to provide an overview of different data collection methods, with the hopes that these might help future researchers in their replication of the methods I employ in this book. Second, I have attempted to demonstrate some of the data collection methods used for the three corpora presented in the later chapters, with the hopes that the discussion of these data collection methods helps better contextualise what is, and is not, currently feasible and/or preferred.

I have argued that using paratext of videogames does not accurately reflect the language within videogames (see Carrillo Masso, 2011; Summers & Miller, 2014), and so this kind of method should not be used as a substitute for collecting data from with videogames. I have also argued that we cannot take a 'typical playthrough' as a form of data collection (as argued by scholars such as Goorimoorthee et al., 2019, p. 274)—because there are so many choices that 'typical' becomes highly subjective and does not necessarily reflect the kind of data that players might encounter.

I have demonstrated that there are four main ways to gather data from videogames—using computer programs, transcribing the data by hand, using fan transcripts, and using websites to get one of the former three data types. These former three data types can be put on three interconnected clines: one for how accurate the data is, one for how long the data takes to gather, and one for how the data is structured. For example, computer programs are the fastest and most accurate way to gather the data, but often the data is placed in structures which are hard to fix and need cleaning (meaning that it is sometimes not tagged for what the researcher wants). By contrast, transcribing the data allows the analyst to tag the file for what they are analysing and structure the files how they like, but this often takes the most time. In the next few chapters, I collect data using a variety of these methods and apply corpus analytical techniques in tandem with discursive analytical techniques.

Ludography

Bethesda. (2011). *Skyrim*. Rockville, Maryland: Bethesda Softworks.

Bioware. (2009–onwards). *Dragon Age*. Redwood City, California: Electronic Arts.

Blizzard Entertainment. (2004–onwards). *World of Warcraft*. Irvine, California: Blizzard Entertainment.

CD Projekt Red. (2011). *The Witcher 2: Assassination of Kings*. Warsaw, Poland: CD Projekt Red.

Miyamoto, S., & Tezuka, T. (1987–onwards). *The Legend of Zelda*. Tokyo, Japan: Nintendo; Capcom.

Bibliography

Bednarek, M. (2018). *Language and television series. A linguistic approach to TV dialogue*. Cambridge University Press.

Carrillo Masso, I. (2011). The grips of fantasy: The construction of female characters in and beyond virtual game worlds. In A. Ensslin & E. Muse (Eds.), *Creating second lives: Community, identity and spatiality as constructions of the virtual* (pp. 113–142). Routledge.

GameSpot. (2019). *GameFaqs*. GameSpot. www.gamefaqs.gamespot.com. Accessed February 2021.

Gibbed. (2015) *Gibbed red tools*. Nexus Mods. https://www.nexusmods.com/witcher2/mods/768/. Accessed February 2021.

Goorimoorthee, T., Csipo, A., Carleton, S., & Ensslin, A. (2019). Language ideologies in videogame discourse: Forms of sociophonetic othering in accented character speech. In A. Ennslin & I. Balteiro (Eds.), *Approaches to videogame discourse: Lexis, interaction, textuality* (pp. 269–287). Bloomsbury.

Heritage, F. (2020). Applying corpus linguistics to videogame data: Exploring the representation of gender in videogames at a lexical level. *Game studies, 20*(3).

Heritage, F. (2021). *Maidens and monsters: A corpus assisted critical discourse Analysis of the representation of Gender in The Witcher videogame series* (Doctoral dissertation, Lancaster University).

McEnery, T., & Hardie, A. (2011). *Corpus linguistics: Method, theory and practice*. Cambridge University Press.

Miller, M., & Summers, A. (2007). Gender differences in video game characters' roles, appearances, and attire as portrayed in video game magazines. *Sex Roles, 57*(9–10), 733–742.

Potts, A. (2015). 'LOVE YOU GUYS (NO HOMO)' How gamers and fans play with sexuality, gender, and Minecraft on YouTube. *Critical Discourse Studies, 12*(2), 163–186.

Reppen, R. (2010). Building a corpus: What are the key considerations?. In A. O'keefee & M. McCarthy (Eds.), *The Routledge Handbook of corpus linguistics* (pp. 31–37). Routledge.

Roberts, S. G., & Rennick, S. (2020). Building a corpus of RPG dialogue to study the representation of women in video games. Talk given at *The CLCR Research Seminar Series, School of English Communication and Philosophy*. Cardiff University.

Summers, A., & Miller, M. (2014). From damsels in distress to sexy superheroes: How the portrayal of sexism in video game magazines has changed in the last twenty years. *Feminist Media Studies, 14*(6), 1028–1040.

Valve. (2003-onwards) *Steam*. [computer software]. Steam. https://store.steampowered.com/. Accessed February 2021.

5

Gender in a General Corpus of Videogames

What Data to Look At

The previous chapters were concerned with laying the foundations for understanding three central concepts:

1. why it is important to look at the representation of gender within videogames
2. why it is important to use corpus methods to look at such representations
3. how we might go about building a corpus of videogames.

This chapter, and the subsequent two chapters, diverge from simply laying the foundational arguments and apply these concepts to authentic data. Similarly, the analysis presented in this chapter and subsequent chapters all use various corpus methods in different ways to highlight the wide array of corpus linguistic methods and how these can also be applied to discursive analytical frameworks.

In this chapter, I employ a corpus-assisted analysis on a general corpus of 10 different videogames. The samples taken from the videogames

F. Heritage, *Language, Gender and Videogames*,
https://doi.org/10.1007/978-3-030-74398-7_5

total approximately 330,000 words. Although this is a small number of videogames, this corpus is meant to illustrate a 'snapshot' of how gender was represented in some of the most critically acclaimed games between 2012 and 2016 (when work on building this corpus began). However, there was a second reason for choosing these years. #Gamergate, the online movement which generated considerable heated online debate about the representation of gender in videogames, happened in 2014 (see Massanari, 2017). Thus, the corpus analysed in this chapter also provides a snapshot into the kinds of discourses drawn on to represent gender when feminist media critics were highlighting problematic visual representations of women in games.

In this chapter, I take a corpus-assisted approach to the data, choosing to examine how two gendered pronouns (*he* and *she*) and two gendered nouns (*man* and *woman*) are used to construct representations of gender. Keyword analysis and subsequent concordance line analysis revealed that pronouns such as *they* and *their* were only ever used as third-person plural pronouns (as opposed to third-person singular pronouns). This use of plural pronouns as opposed to singular pronouns suggested a lack of representation of non-binary characters (see Heritage, 2020). Similarly, an analysis of the keywords of this corpus in comparison to the GLoWBE corpus (Davies, 2017) revealed that no terms in the top 500 keywords were lexis for non-binary gender identities. For example, terms such as 'two-spirited', a label used in Native American cultures which denotes an identity outside of the Western gender-binary, did not appear in the keyword list (for a discussion on how this term is used, see Davis, 2014, 2019).

The gendered terms might seem to go against the tenants of post-structuralist feminist perspectives—which see gender as a fluid social construct (meaning there are multiple gender identities). Eckert (2014) draws attention to what she calls **fractal recursivity**. She argues that:

> the danger that the binary presents in the study of language and gender is the reliance on fractals for getting at what underlies it, since fractals offer a magnification of the ideology that maintains the binary rather than a glimpse at the broader dynamics that constitute gender. (p. 50)

In other words, there is a danger of only examining, say, the representation of men and women, as opposed to the whole spectrum that gender identities. However, this notion of fractal recursively can be problematic when only certain types of gender identity are represented as normative in texts. Unfortunately, this data appears to represent gender in relatively binary ways (i.e. only men and women). Therefore, while the data presented only allows for an examination of fractals, I will still discuss the findings in relation to 'types' of masculinity and femininity and performances.

Selection Criteria

Before I discuss the different games that compile the corpus, it is first important to point to a possible tension between theories relating to total accountability and the effect of genre and register. While in previous chapters, I have noted that, when compiling a corpus, researchers should choose samples of language at random, this does not necessarily mean that we should not also account for obvious variation caused by genre and/or register. For example, if we were to take a game such as *Grand Theft Auto* (DMA Design, 1997), which several feminist scholars have critiqued for the representation of gender (see, e.g., Arbuckle et al., 2019, pp. 5–6; Jenson & de Castell, 2015), we would see a very different kind of representation of gender in comparison to a game such as *Barbie As The Island Princess* (Human Soft and Ivolgamus, 2007). Under various international laws, certain elements can only be shown to players of certain ages. For example, *Grand Theft Auto* contains violence, sex, and discrimination (so it is given a rating to indicate that it is only suitable for those aged 18+). By contrast, *Barbie As The Island Princess* contains none of these (so is suitable for all ages). We might therefore assume that words related to violence, sex, and discrimination would appear in *Grand Theft Auto*, but not in *Barbie As The Island Princess*. If we were to build a corpus which contained 10 games like *Barbie As The Island Princess* and one like *Grand Theft Auto*, we might be surprised to see some keywords related to topics such as sex—and we might see odd representations of gender in other searches.

Within register studies, there are three central elements to consider: field, tenor, and mode (Halliday, 1978). These three elements of register can create very noticeable differences in the language used within texts and should be accounted for. Although there is a wealth of literature on register studies and the different elements related to register, given the limitations of space, I will primarily focus on these three. Field relates to the subject matter of the text (e.g. the difference between language used in videogames to entertain and ones specifically designed for teaching or high-fantasy RPGs in comparison to football simulators). Tenor relates to the relationship between the creator of the text(s) and the audience (e.g. has the game been made by a developer specifically for a pre-selected and limited target audience? Similarly, who is the intended target audience and why might this matter?). Mode relates to how the text is constructed (e.g. the difference between text-based games such as *Colossal Cave Adventure* discussed in Chapter 1 and visual-heavy games. Outside of videogames, this could also be the difference between an email and a hand-written letter).

This kind of variation means that while we could, in theory, compile a corpus of all videogames from a variety of genres and registers to examine how language is used across games, we might end up with a corpus that does not tell us anything of interest—because intra-group differences within videogames might not necessarily appear as easily. All the games analysed in this chapter have been selected based on several criteria. These criteria are as follows:

1. The videogame had to be rated at least 16+ (or equivalent)
2. The videogame had to be narrative-driven fantasy games (i.e. not games like *Fifa* or *Call of Duty*)
3. The videogame had to be one which can be played offline
4. The videogame had to contain language (so silent games such as *Journey* (Thatgamecompany, 2012) were excluded)
5. The videogames had to be released between 2012 and 2016 inclusive.

There were various reasons for these criteria—(1) accounts for variation caused by what representations can legally be included due to age restrictions, (2) accounts for differences caused by genre, (3) was included because a lot of online games rely on the language used by players in chat boxes (though, see Chapter 7 for an analysis of the pre-scripted language in an MMORPG), (4) was included to ensure that there was actually something to analyse in the corpus, and (5) was to account for variation caused by the time at which the text was produced (see Chapters 1 and 2).

Once these selection criteria had been decided, I retrieved five different lists from the website *Metro*. Every year, *Metro* releases a 'top 100' videogames list (see, e.g., GameCentral, 2013), and these were used as an indication of the most popular game released in any given year. I extrapolated all the games in the lists for 2012–2016 inclusive into an excel file. Once this was done, I then checked each game for the selection criteria listed above. If a game did not meet any of the criteria, it was removed from the list. I then numbered the remaining games in sequential order and used a random number generator to select 10 games at random. I then purchased a digital copy of these games (where possible; in some cases, I had to purchase a physical copy), for two reasons: first, it made it possible to run computer programs on some of the games. Second, thinking about ethics and copyright of the data, I followed the UK government's Intellectual Property Office (2014) advice about copyright with respect to data mining and manipulation—specifically that it is a requirement to have 'lawful access' to the data (i.e. I had to purchase a copy, rather than use an illegal copy). Thus, even if I could not extract the data from the videogame using computer code, I still had lawful access to the data and could use a different method. Nevertheless, the data reported in this monograph is limited and does not offer a replacement for playing the actual game.

While collecting the data for these games, I found very quickly that some games were considerably larger than others—for example, *The Witcher 3: Wild Hunt* (CD Projekt Red, 2015) contained c. 300,000 words, while *Bayonetta 2* (PlatinumGames, 2014) contained only c. 10,000 words. In order to ensure that a small number of games did not disproportionately influence the analysis, I limited all game's data collection to c. 55,500 words. The games, their word counts, and the methods used to collect the data (discussed in Chapter 4) are listed in Table 5.1. Note, while it was preferential to use computer software to

Table 5.1 Information about VG2014

Videogame name (year of release)	Word count in each file	Method used
Bayonetta 2 (2014)	9,592	Play through
Bioshock Infinite (2013)	17,307	Fan transcript
Dark Souls 3 (2016)	42,165	Computer software
Dragon Age: Inquisition (2014)	52,523	Play through
Dying Light (2015)	19,580	Play through
Fallout 4 (2015)	54,529	Computer software
Final Fantasy 15 (2016)	36,270	Fan transcript
Mass Effect 3 (2012)	23,233	Computer software
Metal Gear Solid V: The Phantom Pain (2015)	16,397	Play through
The Witcher 3: Wild Hunt (2015)	55,425	Computer software
TOTAL	**327,027**	–

extract the data from the games, this was not always possible. While I wanted to avoid using fan transcripts as much as possible, I found that for two videogames, this was all I was able to obtain (I had purchased these as physical copies, which made it impossible to extract the data with computer code). For these transcripts, I played through the videogames and cross-referenced what was said in the transcript to what was actually said in the videogame. I then corrected any mistakes before including the file in the corpus. Throughout, I refer to the collective corpus as VG2014 (2014 as this is the middle point for years of data collection).

To start the analysis, and to show that gender was a salient factor in the corpus, I started by running a keyword analysis against GLoWBE (Davies, 2017). The findings of this keyword analysis are presented in Heritage (2020) and so I do not duplicate the results here. However, broadly speaking, I found that gendered keywords were present in the top 50 keywords for this corpus, and this keyword list included the gendered pronouns *he* and *she*.

Looking at *He*

First, I ran a collocational analysis on the pronouns *he* and *she*, in order to see what words these pronouns were most likely to be used with. As mentioned previously, although I examined the pronouns *they* and *their*, these pronouns were only ever used as third-person plural pronouns (indicating that they referred to collectives, rather than non-binary characters).

Therefore, I start the analysis below by discussing the collocates of *he* and how this pronoun is used in the representation of men and masculinity. I started by generating a list of the top 50 collocates, using MI score for collocates and setting a minimum frequency of occurrence at ≤ 5. (Collocates were also checked to see if they were statistically significant by T-score, and they all were). Broadly speaking, this list of collocates could be categorised into one of four grammatical categories: nouns (including pronouns), verbs, adverbs, and prepositions. The latter of these two categories, however, only had one collocate in each. For the purposes of this chapter, I will not discuss the adverbial or prepositional collocates of *he*. Instead, given the vast number of noun and verb collocates, this chapter focuses on these instead. Within this list of collocates, the lowest MI score was 5.775 (the collocate *he*) and the highest was 7.973 (the collocate *answered*). The collocates are presented below in Table 5.2, as organised by their grammatical category.

Table 5.2 Collocates of *he*

Grammatical category	**Collocates**
Nouns	ben-hassrath; detainee; Geralt's; himself; his; horse; Kai; Letho; Radovid; rifle; sniper
Verbs	agreed; answered; asked; changed; convinced; couldn't; decided; decides; departed; discovered; doesn't; faced; felt; finished; fool; he's; hears; investigate; knew; knows; link; meant; mentioned; murdered; needs; proved; promised; ran; reached; row; sees; showed; tracks; turns; uses; wants; wishes
Adverbs	slowly
Prepositions	across

With regard to nouns, there were three types used: concrete nouns, namely *ben-hassrath*, *detainee*, *horse*, *rifle*, and *sniper*; proper nouns, namely *Geralt's*, *Kai*, *Letho*, and *Radovid*; and the pronouns *himself* and *his*. At this point, it is worth drawing attention to the first four concrete nouns—*ben-hassrath*, *detainee*, *rifle*, and *sniper*. These collocates denote some form of violence or are associated with violence. *Ben-hassrath* are comparable to secret police, *detainees* typically denote prisoners of war, and both *rifle* and *sniper* are guns—typically used in warfare. This point about collocates being associated with violence and war is important because it could be linked to the idea of physical masculinity (see Connell, 2005) and position idealised masculine traits as associated with violence (see also McAllister et al., 2019). Indeed, this idea that men are associated with violence is a recurring theme (see also Heritage, 2020 for evidence of this in a close reading of concordance lines).

Elsewhere within the noun collocates, there were three male names (*Geralt*, *Kai*, and *Radovid*,) and two male pronouns (*himself* and *his*). To some degree, this is unsurprising, given that a number of instances of *he* were used to refer back to male characters. However, the lack of female character's names is quite important as it shows that potentially male characters and their actions are discussed by themselves, rather than in relation to female characters (this is something discussed in more detail in a later section). Nevertheless, the noun collocates appear to be broadly divisible by nouns that denote violence and nouns which denote male characters.

By far the biggest category of collocate for the pronoun *he* was verb collocates. By themselves, these collocates cannot reveal too much—other than some being in a broad semantic domain of war and violence, such as *murdered*. As such, a process type analysis was conducted by analysing all instances of these verb collocates. Before exploring the different process types of the verbs, for readers who may not be familiar with the concept, it is worth explaining what verb process types are. There are six process types—three major and three minor (there are a number of sub-types within the major and minor process types, but that is beyond the scope of discussion here) (see Darics & Koller, 2019; Halliday & Matthiessen, 2014; Lischinsky, 2018).

The three major process types are material (which involves acting upon someone/something), mental (which relates to cognitive processes, perceiving something, or feelings), and relational (which relates to attributes and assigning an identity to a concept). The three minor process types are: behavioural (which is usually associated with either material and mental processes and which lexicalise inner behaviours as outward actions); verbal (which typically relate to the act of saying or communicating); and existential (which prove states of being, existing, and happening) (see Bartley, 2018; Ezzina, 2015; Halliday & Matthiessen, 2014; Lischinsky, 2018; Thompson, 2013, pp. 95–110). Using verbs with different process types can allow for different kinds of representations—as these verbs demonstrate the kind of transformative actions we see social actors (in this case, characters) performing. I have summarised the labels associated with different process types, the participants within those clauses, and provided worked examples in Table 5.3 below. For this section, I will only focus on the different processes (i.e. the kind of words associated with each process type verb), rather than those under the agent/patient labels (though I will discuss these later in the chapter).

Decisions on process type categories were made by reading the concordance lines for each verb collocate and then categorising them depending on most frequent usages. A summary of the verb collocates and their process types is displayed below in Table 5.4. Importantly, because several collocates can be used in polysemous ways (and could be used as a verb, rather than seemingly a noun), these collocates were categorised after reading concordance lines for context.

Of note within Table 5.4 is that two of the five material processes (where the actor is making a physical change in the world) also relate to aggression and violence (*murdered* and *faced*—note, *face* here is used as in *faced in battle*).

Furthermore, in the mental process type verbs, all verb collocates are either past tense or present perfect—meaning that the discussion about what male characters are thinking or mentally processing relates to either what they previously thought or what they are thinking in the exact moment they are discussed. This also means that there is a lack of collocates which relate to how male characters might think or feel in the

Table 5.3 Process types and labels used within them

Process type	Agent	Verb process	Patient (optional for intransitive)	Optional (sometimes also patient)	Example
Material	Actor	Process	Goal	Recipient	Jane **[actor]** gave **[process]** the ball **[goal]** to John **[recipient]**
Mental	Senser	Process	Phenomenon		Dave **[senser]** wanted **[process]** his husband **[phenomenon]**
Relational	Carrier	Process	Attribute	Intensive or possessive (e.g. is vs has)	Mary **[carrier]** is **[process - intensive]** a chef **[attribute]** Mary **[carrier]** has **[process-possessive]** a mole **[attribute]**
	Token	Process	Identity		Sam **[token]** is **[process – intensive]** the teacher **[identity]** The car **[identity – possessive]** is **[process]** Sam's **[token]**
Behavioural	Behaver	Process	Range/ Circumstance		Charlie **[behaver]** was waiting **[process]** for the train **[circumstance]**
Verbal	Sayer	Process	Verbage	Receiver	Carrie **[sayer]** spoke **[process]** about end-of-life care **[verbiage]** to Billy **[receiver]**

(continued)

Table 5.3 (continued)

Process type	Agent	Verb process	Patient (optional for intransitive)	Optional (sometimes also patient)	Example
Existential	Existent	Process		Circumstance	There was **[process]** a friendly troll **[existent]** in the forest **[circumstance]**

Table 5.4 Verb process types for the verbal collocates of *he*

Process type	**Collocates**
Material	discovered; faced; investigate; murdered; showed
Mental	changed; convinced; decided; decides; felt; knew; knows; needs; sees; wants; wishes
Relational	(he)'s
Behavioural	departed; finished; fool; hears; link (up/with); meant; proved; ran; reached; row; tracks; turns; uses
Verbal	agreed; answered; asked; mentioned; promised
Existential	couldn't; doesn't

future. Collocates that could have been used to indicate possible future outcomes could have included *decide*, *feel*, and *want*, all of which could be pre-modified with a modal verb such as *will*. However, a concordance line analysis revealed that this was uncommon. Therefore, there appears to be a lack of discussion about male character's future mental states and a focus on either how they are currently reacting or have previously reacted.

There are also a number of behavioural verb collocates—many related to physical behaviours—such as *depart*(ing), *track*(ing), and *us*(ing). There are a number of these processes which indicate some form of directionality, which suggests that rather than being stuck in one position, the male characters appear to be active in their movement. Therefore, this brings into question what it means to be a man and the kind of physical requirements associated with masculinity across videogames. An earlier paragraph drew attention to the collocates which indicated the centrality of men's ability to fight and engage in physical violence within games (collocates such as *murdered*), but these verbs suggest that men are typically represented as moving between locations—or at least having the ability to do so. Thus, there appears to be an intersection of identities in these kinds of verbs: that most men are represented as able-bodied across these videogames, and that this able-bodiedness is required in order for them to physically fight and enact ideals of normalised masculinity.

While these collocates give an indication of how male characters are represented—i.e. as people that create physically dangerous environments, or who are not thought about in terms of what future emotions they will have, they do not necessarily reveal the whole picture. Thus, in order to gain a better understanding of how *he* was used, a close reading of 100 concordance lines was conducted.

In order to conduct such an analysis, WordSmtih 7 (Scott, 2016) was used, as it has a function to randomise what concordance lines are presented to an analyst. The sample of 100 random concordance lines revealed that the pronoun *he* was regularly used in tandem with language which denoted violence (30 out of 100 concordance lines). For example:

> one day **he** awoke and began to **murder and destroy** (The Witcher 3)
> [The] [d]etainee asked why **he murdered** Ben-Hassrath, responded that he had only defended himself. (Dragon Age: Inquisition)
> When Sir Yorgh faced Sinh, the slumbering dragon, **he drew blood** with a flash of his steel, but Sinh responded by spewing forth the poison (Dark Souls 3).

Importantly, in all 30 instances, the pronoun was used in an agentive way—that is to say, it was the male character who was conducting the violent act(s). In other words, there could have been constructions such as 'the detainee defended himself before he was murdered', but this passivisation did not occur. (Although passivation like this does not necessarily account for grammatical change, see the analysis of *man* and *woman* in a later subsection). This concordance line analysis thus provides a window into the kind of discourse(s) being drawn on in the characterisation of male characters across these 10 videogames. However, what these concordance lines also demonstrate is that there is a good amount of variation in the way the kinds of physically violent acts which men enact are lexicalised (this idea of agency is discussed in more detail later in this chapter).

Looking at *She*

Having now discussed how male characters were represented through looking at the pronoun *he*, I turn the attention to examining the representation of female characters through the pronoun *she*. Similar to the discussion of the findings from *he*, I start by discussing the collocates for this pronoun. The same measures were implemented in generating the collocate list for *she*. The lowest MI score of a collocate was MI $\geq$ 4.7 (*where*) while the highest MI was $\leq$ 7.2 (*thinks*). The collocates are organised by their grammatical categories and reproduced below in Table 5.5.

There is an instantly recognisable difference in the collocates of *he* and *she*. This noticeable difference comes in the form of adjectives. Within the top 50 collocates of *he* there were no adjectives. When looking at the adjectival collocates of *she*, the use of *pretty* demonstrates issues around how important facial aesthetics are to the characterisation and representation of women (see, e.g., Gill, 2008, 2009; Wood, 2017)—this is something that male characters were not subjected to. While this is not to say that they are not visually sexualised (indeed, players might be 'shown' this sexualisation rather than have male characters discussed in

Table 5.5 Collocates of *she*

Grammatical category	**Collocates**
Nouns	anything; Brecken; child; Ciri; Comstock; her; herself; Kazuhira; Lady; life; Lunafreya; Rosalind; she; woman; Yennefer
Verbs	ask; asked; did; didn't; died; does; doesn't; gave; gets; gone; had; knew; knows; learned; made; meet; needed; returned; say; says; stay; thinks; told; took; wanted; wants; was
Adjectives	alive; divine; hard; pretty; tough
Adverbs	when; where
Quantifiers	both

such a way), at a linguistic level, this collocate provides some evidence of how writers focus on the physical aesthetics of female characters in a way which they do not for male characters.

However, there are also a number of other differences within the grammatical categories. Given the limitations of space, I will not dwell on the adjectives, adverbs, or quantifiers, rather primarily discuss the nouns and verbs that this pronoun collocates with. This is for two reasons: first, there are only a small number of collocates in these categories. Second, I only examined nouns and verbs for *he*, and so by only focusing on these in this section, this allows for a more equal comparison.

In terms of noun collocates, 3 were concrete nouns: *child*, *lady*, and *woman*; 7 were proper nouns: *Brecken*, *Ciri*, *Comstock*, *Kazuhira*, *Lunafreya*, *Rosalind*, and *Yennefer*; and one abstract noun: *life*. Compared to the kind of nouns that collocated with *he*, there appear to be more proper nouns, and these proper nouns refer to a variety of gendered characters. While *he* only collocated with male characters names, *she* collocated with four female character names (*Ciri*, *Lunafreya*, *Rosalind*, and *Yennefer*) and three male character names (*Brecken*, *Comstock*, and *Kazuhira*). Potentially, this could link back to Woolf's (1929) commentary (mentioned in Chapter 2), about how female characters are regularly seen in relation to male characters.

In a similar vein, when examining the concrete nouns further—*child* and *lady* both demonstrate some relation to other characters. While *child* demonstrates an obvious familial relation, the use of *lady* typically occurs as an honorific, such as in *lady Comstock* (Bioshock: Infinite). In this game, *Comstock* is the name of the main male antagonist. Thus, a large portion of the noun collocates demonstrate the female character's relations to other characters—both familial and romantic. Ultimately, this could contribute towards a negative representation of women, in that they may be seen as less capable in their own right, and less like fully formed independent characters.

More differences can be seen when examining the verb collocates of *she* and their process types. The verb collocates of *she* and their process types are reproduced below in Table 5.6. Similar to the analysis of *he*, decision on process type were made by analysing how the verbs were used in context.

Table 5.6 Verb process types for the verbal collocates of *she*

Process type	**Collocates**
Material	gave; made; meet; took
Mental	knew; knows; learned; needed; thinks; wanted; wants
Relational	had; was
Behavioural	did; didn't; died; gets; gone; returned; stay
Verbal	ask; asked; say; says; told
Existential	does; doesn't

Importantly in these process types, there are fewer mental and behavioural verb processes than there were for collocates of *he*. This is owing to the fact that of the 50 collocates for *he*, 37 were verbs, while only 27 of the 50 collocates for *she* were verbs.

In terms of the material verbs, there are none which directly relate to violence nor war. However, the material processes typically relate to items, such as *gave* (an object), *took* (an object), or *made* (an object). Thus, while material process verbs for dealing with humans appear as collocates of, *he*, material process verb collocates of *she* tend to be actions done towards objects instead. This could suggest an unequal representation (because male characters are more likely to directly influence other characters). However, it should be noted that the fact that the female characters are mainly influencing and dealing with objects does not necessarily equate to a negative representation—just an unequal one.

In the mental process verbs collocates of *she*, like the verb collocates of *he*, the collocates are all either past tense or present perfect tense. Thus, this could indicate that while both pronouns occur with verbs, they are more likely used to discuss male and female characters in terms of what they are thinking or what they have thought—not what they will think or feel. Taylor (2013) argues that we should look beyond differences in representations, and that we should also look for similarities. In particular, her work examines similarities in the ways that male and female social actors are represented, and indeed, the findings presented here appear to resonate with her call to 'look [...] in both directions' (Taylor, 2013, p. 84).

When quantifying these processes types, there are some differences across collocates. Because there were differences in the number of verb collocates for *he* and *she*, the frequencies at which the verb process types occur (within the verb collocates for each gendered noun) were normalised for comparison. Figure 5.1 below demonstrates these frequencies in a bar chart.

In terms of normalised frequencies, we can see that *she* is more likely to occur with material, relational, verbal, and existential verb processes, while *he* is more likely to occur with mental and behavioural verb processes. Of particular note are the frequencies at which *he* is likely to occur with mental and behavioural verbs, and the frequencies at which *she* is more likely to occur with verbal and existential verbs. This difference could indicate some unintentional biases on the writer's behalf: that writers associate male characters more with thinking or with enacting some sort of task, while they might associate female characters more with talking or just existing.

However, similar to the arguments I made while analysing *he*, these collocates alone do not provide a full insight into how female characters are represented within the corpus. Thus, similar to the work conducted for *he*, a random sample of 100 concordance lines were examined for *she*.

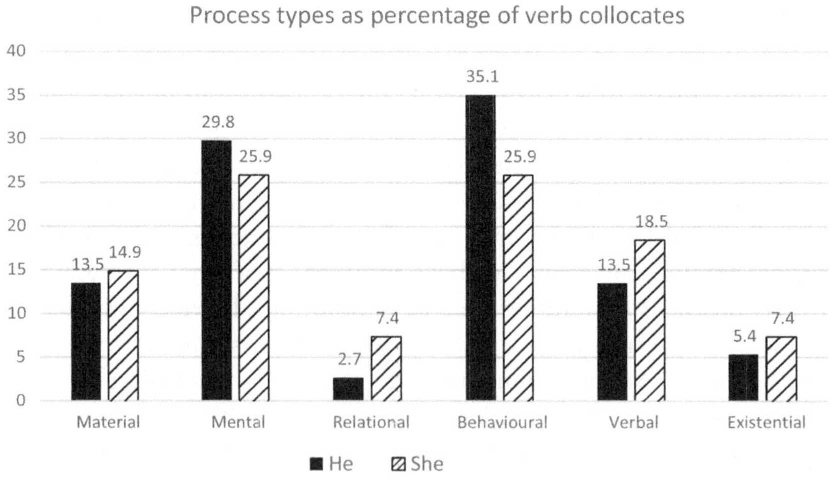

Fig. 5.1 Comparative frequencies of verb process types

The close reading of the concordance lines revealed that, typically, female characters were discussed in terms of their relationships (38 instances in 100 concordance lines). For example:

> Haven't seen her in ages. Besides, even if I knew, **she** and **I have a special relationship.** (Bayonetta 2)
> While Daisy Fitzroy has murdered my beloved, **she** shall not **have the child**! (Bioshock Infinite)
> After **giving birth to Ocelotte, her youngest**, she quietly disappeared. (Dark Souls 3)

Ultimately, it appears as though women are primarily discussed in relation to other characters who are either friends and/or family—for male characters, this only occurred three times in the sample of 100 concordance lines.

This has a number of implications for the roles of women: they are seen as mothers, children, and friends, but rarely represented as, say, a videogame's main antagonist. They are rarely discussed in terms of their leadership roles, but their relational roles are brought to the fore. While women—as well as men and those outside the gender binary—do tend to have relations with others, these relationships are not reported as such for male characters, and so this might suggest that there are unequal representations and thus there might be different expectations for female characters. These kinds of representations could reflect and/or manifest in offline contexts. A report from the UK charity 'Working Families' (a charity dedicated to work-life balance and equality) reports that the labour division in families has historically been viewed as fathers who work long full-time hours, while mothers stay at home with children and conduct housework (see Working Families and Bright Horizons, 2019). While there is evidence that this is changing in more recent years, a stereotype of mothers as caregivers and focused on familial relations might still exist—and by enforcing the stereotype of women as mothers and caregivers, this might reinforce social expectations for women fulfil these familial roles.

A Discourse Shared Across Both Pronouns

I want to now turn to something which is often overlooked in critical discourse analyses: positive representations which are resistant to stereotypes. The nature of CDS (i.e. challenging and critiquing power structures) can often lead to researchers approaching data with an emancipatory agenda—and often discourses which do not fit an agenda can easily be overlooked if they do not show why a particular representation is problematic. In other words, sometimes it is easier to focus on negative representations than positive representations. In a similar vein, Taylor (2013) has drawn attention to the fact that similarities between gendered terms (such as *boy* and *girl*) are often overlooked (this point was raised in the previous subsection). This section now turns to one small subset of collocates and concordance lines which shows a positive representation of female characters, and which is also shared with how male characters are represented.

When analysing the collocates of *she*, the concordance lines of one collocate (*hard*) suggested that there might be a potential 'counter' discourse (see Sunderland, 2004; Terdiman, 2018). In these concordance lines, female characters were discussed in terms of their physical hardiness. However, given that this was not always related to a characteristic of the woman, and there was only other collocate (*tough*) which would suggest the presence of such a discourse—which only occurred 6 times, I initially decided not to report it. However, an examination of the random sample of 100 concordance lines confirmed that this discourse was lexicalised in different ways across the corpus (8 instances in 100 concordance lines). For example:

> She's been around a long time, she's everywhere, and **she hits hard** or she hits light, but the choosing isn't up to you (Dragon Age: Inquisition)
> **She's tough**, but I'd feel better if we got this over with and got back on the road (Final Fantasy 15)

As can be seen from the above excerpts, women are not only discussed in terms of their physical strength but also are discussed in terms of their ability to enact physical violence (similar to the physical violence *he* was associated with).

Given the wide array of literature which has demonstrated that men are typically associated with violence, and that this is also prevalent in videogame discourse, these examples could possibly be the writers trying to enact some form of counter-discourse—i.e. they may be acknowledging that these ways of representing women exist and may be trying to break them. This finding thus illustrates the need to check the concordance lines for infrequent lexical usages which build up a broader picture of how a particular set of (gendered) characters are represented. While it may not be the case that this kind of representation occurs often, this kind of prosody suggests that female characters are, at times, the ones who can be physically strong and/or violent.

However, we should also remember how much more frequently this kind of representation occurs for male characters in comparison to female characters—over three times as much in the concordance lines, with many more collocates suggesting this. So, while we could argue that there is some overlap in how these gendered pronouns are used, we could still argue that there are differences.

Man and *Woman*

One issue with the above analysis of *he* and *she* is that while we are able to discuss things like the process type verbs that collocate with these pronouns, a corpus approach using these search terms does not really allow us to fully look at agency roles of male and female characters. Agency roles are important in linguistic analysis because they are able to demonstrate 'the extent to which a character is the passive "victim" of circumstance, or [whether they are] actively in control of the environment, making decisions and taking action' (Mills, 1995, p. 111). In short, an analysis of agency examines who does what verbs and who has verbs done upon them.

Before I go on to discuss agency roles of gendered characters in more detail, it is first important to make a distinction between formal grammar and systemic functional grammar. While I have demonstrated some of the labels associated with systemic functional grammar and process types in Table 5.3, it is worth turning to look at the difference between labels used in systemic functional grammatical analyses and formal grammatical analyses. In formal grammar, scholars are concerned with analysing rigid formalist grammatical structures—such as subjects, objects, and verbs. The examples below demonstrate two different sentences as parsed for the subject, object, and verb:

John [subject] kicked [verb] the ball [object]
The ball [subject] was kicked [verb] by John [prepositional phrase].

However, in systemic functional linguistics (SFL), different labels are used, because SFL is concerned with the meaning-making potential of grammatical constructions (see Halliday, 1994). In SFL terms, the same constructions would be labelled as follows:

John [actor] kicked [process] the ball [goal]
The ball [goal] was kicked [process] by John [actor].

Note, despite moving places within the sentence, *John* remains the actor (because he is the one doing the kicking), and *the ball* remains the goal (because it is the thing being kicked). In formal grammatical terms, both these phrases change grammatical categories (i.e. *the ball* changes from the object to the subject, while *John* changes from the subject to part of a prepositional phrase). Therefore, analysing constructions with a formalist approach might reveal less about relationships between social actors than if we were to approach agency from a functional perspective.

Two particularly important roles within this approach to agency are that of the 'agent' and the 'patient' (note, 'agents' are labelled differently depending on the process type of the verb—see Table 5.3). As Darics and Koller (2019, p. 217) summarise, the actions within these verbs are 'a transformation of state operated by an agent' (see also Cooren, 2004, p. 376). Consequently, an agent is someone—or something—bringing about the said transformation (Darics & Koller, 2019: 218). Although the most obvious agents are humans, this is not always the case (see Cooren, 2010; Koschmann & McDonald, 2015). Sometimes, agents of verbs can also be institutions, texts, or anything which enables some form of transformation to social reality. The opposite participant of this, i.e. the person or thing acted upon, is called the patient.[1]

While I touched upon this a little bit earlier with the analysis of *he*, commenting that *he* was always agentive, sometimes the passivised constructions (where *he* would be the person having things done upon them) might seem unnaturalistic. Take, for example, the following three sentences:

He murdered everyone who was in the hall
He was murdered by an ex-lover
An ex-lover murdered him

These examples demonstrate some issues with different forms of agency and the use of a lexical approach to examine such agency roles. While the first example is prototypical, as *he* is the subject and the agent, the second example demonstrates a passive construct. Here, *he* is both the subject (in formalist terms) and patient (in SFL terms) of the verb—*he* is the person who has undergone the transformative action (being murdered). The third example demonstrates two points—the male character is in the object position and the patient position. However, this third example also shows why it is so difficult to take a lexical-based corpus approach to transitivity. In this instance, the pronoun *he* has changed lexical forms to the pronoun *him*. In other words, constructions like 'an ex-lover murdered he' appear to be incongruent because *him* is typically used in the object position of formalist structures. Despite denoting the same concept (the man for whom the pronoun refers to), the lexical form has changed, and thus this complicates searching for all instances of either *he* or *him*.

[1] Although the concept does not appear in the analysis presented in this chapter, Darics and Koller (2019) also draw attention to what they call 'semantic agency' (pp. 218–219). They state that grammatical action is a binary category—someone or something is either grammatically active or passive. In contrast, semantic agency is a graded category, in that agents can be more or less agentive. Two examples of the examples they provide succinctly demonstrate this difference: 'He took the helm of the department' and 'Yang himself became CEO'. Both 'he' and 'Yang' are agents, but 'took' suggests a greater level of semantic agency than 'became'.

One such way to circumvent this issue, while still examining how gendered characters enact agency roles, is to use gendered nouns, such as *man* and/or *woman*. Take the following examples:

The man murdered everyone who was in the hall
The man was murdered by an ex-lover
An ex-lover murdered the man.

In all three examples, although *man* must occur with an article—I have used 'the' here, but this could equally be 'a(n (+adjective))'—it still use the same lexical form regardless of formalist grammatical position or semantic grammatical position. Note, 'a(n)' could be used in conjunction with an adjective, such as 'an idiotic man murdered'.

While other gendered nouns such as *boy* or *girl* could have been selected, I have chosen to examine *man* and *woman* primarily because of the well-documented corpus research into the impact of ageing and representation of gender (see, e.g., Anderson, 2019; Caldas-Coulthard & Moon, 2010, 2016; Moon, 2014). A number of scholars have demonstrated that as people get older, the ways they are represented change (see Anderson, 2019; Taylor, 2013). For example, *boy(s)* and *girl(s)* tend to be used to refer to young children; these kinds of social actors are typically represented as innocent, but this changes when they start being called *men* and *women*. In the corpus, *boy(s)* and *girl(s)* were less frequent than *man* and *woman*, and so I focused on these nouns denoting older gendered social actors.

In order to analyse the functional agency roles of *man* and *woman*, I first extracted all instances where these nouns co-occur with a verb. This differs from the previous methods used earlier within this chapter—where I started by looking at verb collocates and then examined concordance lines for these collocates. While the analysing verb collocates can be useful, there are several problems with it for examining agency across the series. First, collocates are words which are statistically likely to co-occur with a word and must meet pre-established cut-offs (e.g. MI $\geq$ 3 and/or have a minimum frequency of 5). This means that verbs that occur outside of these established parameters might not be counted—and there could be a lot of different verbs that are infrequent, but all could position gendered social actors in a similar way. Second, if we were to look at every single instance where *man* or *woman* occurred, we would need to analyse thousands of concordance lines—and so it is just not practical.

In order to circumnavigate these issues, I used WordSmith7 (Scott, 2016). I started by tagging the corpus using the CLAWS tagging tool (Garside, 1987). CLAWS is a conventional system of grammatical tagging, which is highly reliable (see Fligelstone et al., 1997; Garside, 1987; Leech et al., 1994). As Rayson (n.d.) explains, the tool 'consistently achieve[s] 96–97% accuracy [...] judged in terms of major categories, the system has an error-rate of only 1.5%, with c.3.3% ambiguities unresolved, within the BNC' (see also Leech et al., 1994). In sum, CLAWS is able to identify the grammatical category of most words in a corpus and places a tag at the end of these words. Hence, this allows scholars to examine collocation between either certain grammatical tags or a word and the particular grammatical categories of words that it co-occurs with (this is also referred to as colligation). This therefore allows for a search of the terms *man* and *woman* with every verb that occurs within a 5L-5R window.

While there were 387 occurrences of *man* and 153 occurrences of woman within the corpus, there were 298 instances of transitive verbs occurring with the term *man* and only 85 which occurred with the term *woman*. In the subsequent analysis, I did not include intransitive verbs—for example, 'piss off, old man' because 'old man' is not the object/goal of the verb.

The frequencies at which *man* and *woman* occurred as the agent/patient of a transitive clause are demonstrated below in Table 5.7. Something to be considerate of, in terms of transitivity, is that sometimes, subordinate clauses could contain transitive verbs, but the actor

Table 5.7 Frequency of *man* and *woman* as agents and patients in transitive verbs

	Agent (percentage)	Patient (percentage)
Man	219 (73.5%)	79 (26.5%)
Woman	31 (36.5%)	54 (63.5%)

within that subordinate clause could be the patient of the main clause. For example: 'I saw a woman lying there all quiet' was coded as having the *woman* in the patient position, as the *woman* is the patient of the main clause but is the agent of the subordinate clause. That is to say, she is the patient being 'seen', while also the agent of the 'lying there' (note, she also has a low degree of semantic agency within the subordinate claws, see Darics & Koller, 2019). Thus, as the *woman* is part of the main clause (i.e. the clause in which she is an agent is not independent), this example was coded as the *woman* in the patient position.

This data reveals that women appear less frequently within transitive verb constructions, and when they do appear, they are statistically more likely to be referred to as having something done to them. This bears a resemblance to the work of Heritage (2021), on the verb *kidnapped* which co-occurred with *woman* in *The Witcher* videogame series. In that research, I argued that this suggests reproduced a damsel in distress trope. Importantly, I argued that this trope was revealed by analysing the data, rather than starting with this trope and explicitly looking for it within videogame(s), as others such as Sarkeesian (2014) have previously done. Thus, while my previous research and the results presented above support the arguments made by Sarkeesian, they do so by allowing the data to 'speak' for itself. This finding appears to support the previous finding from within *The Witcher* videogame series and suggests that women are linguistically objectified among a variety of games. This quantification also gives weight to Sarkeesian's argument that women in videogames are not agents, insofar as women across videogames are linguistically more likely to be patients of transitive verbs (note, Sarkeesian discusses agency with relation to physical actions in videogames, not linguistic agency).

A chi-square test revealed that this difference in frequency was statistically significant ($x^2 = 14.1077$; $p \leq .001$). This shows that there are some issues regarding the representation of gender in terms of whether or not women are agents or patients within transitive clauses. There are two primary issues here: the first is the low frequency at which women occur in comparison to men (and because of this, *woman* is less likely to occur with a transitive verb). The second is that they are more likely to be the ones acted upon (see also Heritage, 2020). It is interesting to note, however, the percentages at which men are represented as agents or patients: men are much more likely to be the ones conducting actions, rather than having actions done upon them.

This finding in isolation does provide some deeper insight which might be useful for ludolinguistics scholars, particularly for those who are interested in visual representations of gender—as work on visual representations could be triangulated with this kind of research. However, in a broader context, this finding does not necessarily reveal that much additional information. Yes, women are seen to be passivised more regularly, but what are the different verbs occurring with *man* and *woman*? This is important because different verb-processes can create different representations. For example, if one reads that the woman was *hit*, it is arguably a more problematic representation than if a woman was *thought about*. Therefore, we need to dig deeper and examine the different process types for the verbs and the frequencies at which *man* and *woman* is the agent/patient of particular process types.

The process types as a percentage of all transitive verbs that colligate with *man* and *woman* (within the sample I took) are outlined below in Table 5.8 (note, although both agency and action roles can also be analysed for intransitive verbs, particularly with behavioural and some material processes, here I only focus on transitive cases). Table 5.8 demonstrates that typically, material and mental processes are more likely to occur with *man* and *woman*. However, there are some differences, with *man* being more likely to occur with relational, behavioural, and existential verbs than *woman*, while *woman* is more likely to appear with verbal processes.

Table 5.8 Percentages of verb processes for *man* and *woman*

	Percentage of process type occurring with *man*	Percentage of process type occurring with *woman*
Material	30.2	32.9
Mental	17.8	24.8
Relational	16.4	8.2
Behavioural	14.8	9.4
Verbal	7.4	17.6
Existential	13.4	7.1

The frequencies at which *man* and *woman* occur with different process types show a difference in their representation. Broadly speaking, the most noticeable difference occurs within verbal process types, where *woman* is more likely to co-occur with a verbal process than *man*. In turn, this could possibly reflect a sexist ideology relating to how much women talk (see Cameron, 2007 for a discussion of this myth). This kind of difference could also suggest that even if it is not women doing the talking, they are seen as more likely to be spoken to/about than male characters. Interestingly, male characters are also more likely to occur with relational process type verbs—meaning that they are also more likely to be described in terms of their identity and/or their characteristics.

It is also possible to analyse how frequently *man* and *woman* occur in the agent/patient position of these transitive clauses. Figure 5.2 below demonstrates what percentage of the process types positioned *man* and *woman* as either the agent or patient.

One of the most striking points of data from Fig. 5.2 is the frequencies at which *man* is positioned as the agent of material processes, while *woman* is positioned as the patient of such process types. While male characters are thus represented as enacting physical changes in the

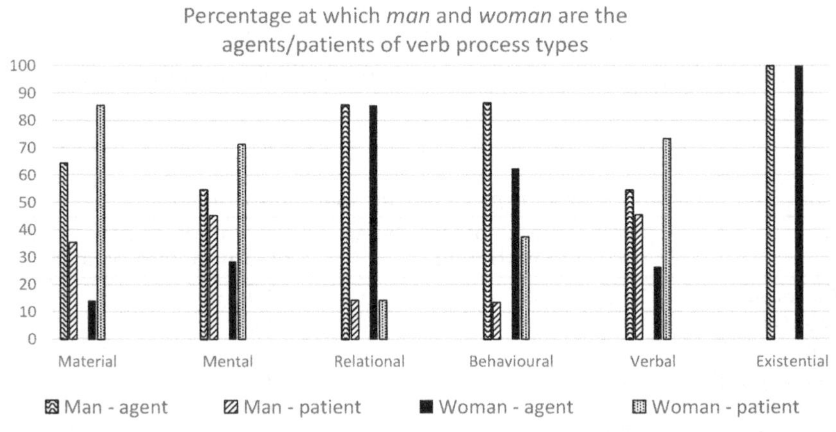

Fig. 5.2 Frequency at which *man* and *woman* are agents or patients of each process type

world, female characters are the ones who have physical changes enacted upon them. Similarly, there are disproportionate frequencies at which *man* is discussed as the agent of a mental process, while *woman* is the patient of such verbs. Typically, this kind of process relates to mental perception—such as 'I'm looking for a young woman' (in the transitivity framework, perception is a sub-group of mental processes, see Halliday & Matthiessen, 2014).

Another point of note is the frequency at which women are the patients of verbal process types (in SFL terms, they are the 'receiver')—meaning that they are spoken to, rather than doing the speaking. This could possibly suggest that while female characters may play important roles in videogames, as they may hold power or be able to progress the storyline in some way, they ultimately are not represented as doing the speaking, but having others speak to them.

A different, but nonetheless important, point to make with the data presented in Fig. 5.2 is that *man* is never more likely to occur as a patient of a particular process type. While I have discussed that *man* occurs as the agent of a transitive verb in 73.5% of transitive clauses, this did not necessarily reveal the percentages at which different process types positioned *man* as the agent/patient. It could have been the case that, for example, *man* was always the patient of material verbs. However, this is not the case, and *man* is always more likely to be the agent than the patient. The same cannot be said about *woman*—*woman* was more likely to be the agent in half of the process type categories, and more likely to be the patient in the other half.

It is also important to note how frequently *man* and *woman* occur as either an agent or patient within/across process types. For *woman*, there appear to be extreme differences between the frequencies at which they are agents or patients—with the minimum difference being 25% (behavioural process type verbs). For *man*, this is different, with the minimum difference being 9% (verbal and mental process type verbs). For *woman*, a difference of 40%+ is seen across 5 out of 6 process types, while a difference of this size is only seen in 3 process types of men. The other 2 process types have quite similar frequencies at which *man* is either the agent or the patient. The differences at which these process types position the *man* as either the agent or patient thus possibly construct male characters as more complex and more well-rounded (i.e. they tend to do things and have things done to them in roughly even amounts in 2/6 process type verbs).

Returning to Taylor's (2013) call to examine similarities between gendered terms in CADS, in terms of the percentage of clauses which are material process types, one might initially suggest that there is some similarity between *man* and *woman*. *Man* occurs with material process verbs in 30.2% of transitive clauses, while *woman* occurs in 32.9%. In terms of percentages at which these kinds of process type verbs occur, one might initially have argued that there is a similar representation. However, when we move beyond just frequency at which this process type occurs and examine agency roles within those verbs, there is a gargantuan difference, in that *man* is only the patient of material verbs 37% of the time, but *woman* is the patient 87% of the time. Therefore, it is important to 'look [...] in both directions' (Taylor, 2013, p. 84), and while there may be some similarities, within the similarities there also appear to be differences.

While I also conducted an analysis on the collocation between *man* and *woman* within a 10L-10R window, in order to examine who did what to whom, these terms only collocated with each other 14 times across the corpus. Within these occurrences, there were no cases of *man* or *woman* acting upon the other. Typically, when these occurred with each other, they were used to either discuss men and women together or occurred where the gender of the playing character could be pre-selected. In this latter group, the language was identical for both *man* and *woman*, which could suggest a move towards positive representation: that players are able to construct their own gendered realities.

Discussions and Conclusions

This chapter has used what might be best considered a 'corpus-assisted' approach to the data (see Baker, 2006). In other words, in this chapter, I took pre-established words (*he*, *she*, *man*, and *woman*) and then used corpus methods to analyse them. In addition, I applied a critical discursive framework (verb process types) to the corpus findings. I argued that the pronoun *he* was more likely to occur with particular nouns and verbs that denoted violence. The concordance line analysis of this pronoun revealed that it was always the male character inciting the violence. By contrast, I argued that *she* was more likely to occur with social actors and language denoting familial and platonic relationships. I demonstrated within the analysis of the collocates for these pronouns that there was also a focus on the physical aesthetics of women. This kind of representation did not occur for the pronoun *he*. For *man* and *woman*, I examined the kind of verbs that these nouns occurred with and I argued that *man* was much more likely to be the agent of transitive verbs, while *woman* was more likely to be the patient of transitive verbs. I demonstrated the need to look at the different process types of verbs for transitivity, as there were differences in how frequently *man* and *woman* occurred as either the agent or patient depending on the process type of the verb.

While previous research has examined the visual representation of gender (see, e.g., Martins et al., 2011; Matthews et al., 2016), less has examined how this is lexicalised in the language—that is to say, while we are regularly shown how attractive someone is in a videogame, are we always told it? Corpora could thus be triangulated with other methods, such as multimodal analysis, to examine how gender is represented across communicative modes. Nevertheless, this analysis demonstrated that there was some gender bias—and one way to uncover such bias was through the analysis of collocates.

This analysis has also looked specifically at agency across a number of videogames. While it may be easy to say that women are objectified (visually) through analysis of concepts such as 'the male gaze' (see, e.g., Sarkeesian, 2014), the analysis presented in this chapter goes beyond that—it looks specifically at grammatical constructions and the data suggests that men are much more likely to be the characters doing verbs, while women are much more likely to have verbs done upon them. Therefore, future research might consider triangulating analyses to examine whether visual agency matches reported linguistic agency.

Elsewhere, this chapter has demonstrated the need to consider both similarities and differences, but also differences within overarching similarities (see Taylor, 2013). I was able to demonstrate that in about 30% of clauses *man* and *woman* were likely to occur with a material process (a similarity), within these clauses *man* and *woman* took on different agency roles (a difference). Thus, while on one level there may appear to be some similarities, it is vital to look deeper at features such as agency within these similarities, as these can often reveal some problematic aspects to the representation of gender.

In this chapter, I also drew attention to a more progressive discourse, as revealed through concordance line analysis. I argued that a number of concordance lines demonstrated that some women were beginning to be represented as physically strong and could enact physical violence. This kind of representation is a bit of a double-edged sword. On the one hand, it is good that female characters are beginning to share some characteristics of male characters—that they can be characterised as physically capable. However, it is also negative in the sense that violence, in a general sense, can be considered problematic, especially if this is normalised through the media. But is violence avoidable in these kinds of games? The fantasy genre tends to be associated with various acts of violence—slaying dragons, defending villages, etc. If we removed this entirely, a good number of the underpinning themes of the genre might be removed all-together. Although I welcome the change to also have violent women, there will undoubtedly be some media critics who take issue with any form of violence within games.

Something missing in this chapter is a full discussion on how non-binary gender identities are lexicalised if they are present at all. While there has been a good amount of queer scholarship into gender in videogames (see, e.g., Ruberg, 2015; Ruberg & Phillips, 2018; Youngblood, 2018), the data typically positioned gender in binary terms, i.e. only men/women. While this is not to say that transgender characters did not exist in these games (in fact, previous scholarship has praised the representation of transgender characters in some of these games, see, e.g., Youngblood, 2018), these transgender characters were likely positioned as either transgender men or transgender women. Thus, one must question what can really be said about the fluidity of gender in these kinds of games. Gender is something preformed, and representations are a kind of performance, but players are left with only fractals of the gender spectrum, which we might consider problematic.

In this chapter, I elected to primarily focus on a small number of discursive analytical techniques: namely examination of process types, agency, and transitivity. There are, of course, a number of different discursive analytical techniques which could have been employed. Indeed, there are a number of different ways that corpus methods could also have been employed—such as analysing keywords, word frequencies, or even collocational networks. However, in this chapter, I wanted to show just some of the ways that corpus methods could contribute to studying how gender is represented within videogames. Future chapters shall take different corpus methods and different discursive analytical frameworks in order to examine the representation of gender in different games. However, what I hope this chapter has done is demonstrated fruitful synergies between videogame data, corpus methods, and discursive frameworks in analysing the representation of gender.

Furthermore, this chapter analysed these videogames as a 'snapshot' of the kind of representations presented within some of the bestselling videogames in a period of time around when videogames were being heavily criticised by media critics. Therefore, this chapter has looked across videogames, rather than at a specific videogame or videogame series. It could be the case, for example, that one videogame in this corpus demonstrated some really positive representations of gender, while some might have been truly awful. For this, a different analysis of singular videogame series is needed. Indeed, this is what is what I analyse in the next chapter.

Ludography

Bethesda. (2015). *Fallout 4*. Rockville, Maryland: Bethesda Softworks.

BioWare. (2012). *Mass effect* 3. Redwood City, California: Electronic Arts.

Bioware. (2014). *Dragon age: Inquisition*. Redwood City, California: Electronic Arts.

CD Projekt Red. (2015). *The Witcher 3: Wild Hunt*. Warsaw, Poland: CD Projekt Red.

DMA Design. (1997). *Grand Theft Auto*. Edinburgh, United Kingdom: DMA Design.

FromSoftware. (2016). *Dark Souls 3*. Tokyo, Japan: Bandai Namco Entertainment.
Human Soft and Ivolgamus. (2007). *Barbie as the island princess*. Santa Monica, California: Activision.
Irrational Games. (2014). *Bioshock: Infinite3*. Novato, California: 2 K Games.
Kojima Productions. (2015). *Metal Gear Solid V: The Phantom Pain*. Tokyo, Japan: Konami.
PlatinumGames. (2014). *Bayonetta 2*. Tokyo, Japan: Nintendo.
Square Enix. (2016). *Final Fantasy XV*. Tokyo, Japan: Enix.
Techland Publishing. (2015). *Dying light*. Burbank, California: Warner Brothers.
Thatgamecompany. (2012). *Journey*. San Mateo, California: Sony.

Bibliography

Anderson, C. (2019). *Discourses of ageing and gender: The impact of public and private voices on the identity of Ageing women*. Palgrave MacMillian.
Arbuckle, A., Saklofske, J., & Bath, J. (2019). The implementing new knowledge environment partnership: Mechanisms of war, feminist values, and interventional games. In J. Saklofske, A. Arbuckle, & J. Bath (Eds.), *Feminist war games? Mechanisms of war, feminist values, and interventional games* (pp. 3–11). Routledge.
Baker, P. (2006). *Using corpora in discourse analysis*. Bloomsbury.
Bartley, L. V. (2018). Putting transitivity to the test: A review of the Sydney and Cardiff models. *Functional Linguistics, 5*(4), 1–24.
Caldas-Coulthard, C. R., & Moon, R. (2010). 'Curvy, hunky, kinky': Using corpora as tools for critical analysis. *Discourse & Society, 21*(2), 99–133.
Caldas-Coulthard, C. R., & Moon, R. (2016). Grandmother, gran, gangsta granny semiotic representations of grandmotherhood. *Gender and Language, 10*(3), 309–339.
Cameron, D. (2007). *The myth of Mars and Venus*. Oxford University Press.
Connell, R. (2005). *Masculinities* (2nd edn.). Polity Press.
Cooren, F. (2004). Textual agency: How texts do things in organizational settings. *Organization, 11*(3), 373–393.
Cooren, F. (2010). *Action and agency in dialogue: Passion, incarnation and ventriloquism*. John Benjamins.

Darics, E., & Koller, V. (2019). Social actors "to go": An analytical toolkit to explore agency in business discourse and communication. *Business and Professional Communication Quarterly, 82*(2), 214–238.

Davies, M. (2017) *The corpus of global web-based English.* English-corpora. https://www.english-corpora.org/glowbe/. Accessed February 2021.

Davis, J. (2014). "More than just 'gay Indian'": Intersecting articulations of two-spirit gender, sexuality, and indigenousness. In L. Zimman., J. Davis., & J. Raclaw (Eds.), *Queer excursions: Retheorizing binaries in language, gender, and sexuality* (pp. 62–80). Oxford University Press.

Davis, J. (2019). Refusing (Mis) recognition: Navigating multiple marginalization in the US two spirit movement. *Review of International American Studies, 12*(1), 65–86.

Eckert, P. (2014). The problem with binaries: Coding for gender and sexuality. *Language and Linguistics Compass, 8*(11), 529–535.

Ezzina, R. (2015). Transitivity analysis of "The crying lot of 49" by Thomas Pynchon [Sic]. *International Journal of Humanities and Cultural Studies, 2*(3), 283–292.

Fligelstone, S., Pacey, M., & Rayson, P. (1997). How to generalize the task of annotation. In R. Garside., G. Leech, G., & A. McEnery (Eds.), *Corpus annotation: Linguistic information from computer text corpora* (pp. 122–136). Longman.

GameCentral. (2013). 100 best-selling video games of 2012 revealed. *Metro.* https://metro.co.uk/2013/01/14/100-best-selling-games-of-2012-revealed-3351774/. Accessed February 2021.

Garside, R. (1987). The CLAWS Word-tagging System. In R. Garside, G. Leech & G. Sampson (Eds.), *The computational analysis of English: A Corpus-based Approach* (pp. 30–41). Longman.

Gill, R. (2008). Empowerment/sexism: Figuring female sexual agency in contemporary advertising. *Feminism & Psychology, 18*(1), 35–60.

Gill, R. (2009). Beyond the 'sexualization of culture' thesis: An intersectional analysis of 'sixpacks', 'midriffs' and 'hot lesbians' in advertising. *Sexualities, 12*(2), 137–160.

Halliday, M. A. K. (1978). *Language as social semiotic, the social interpretation of language and meaning*. Edward Arnold.

Halliday, M. A. K. (1994). *Introduction to functional grammar* (2nd edn.). Edward Arnold.

Halliday, M. A. K., & Matthiessen, C. (2014). *Halliday's introduction to functional grammar* (4th edn.). Routledge.

Heritage, F. (2020). Using corpora to analyse the representation of gender in videogames. *Game studies, 20*(3).

Heritage, F. (2021). *Maidens and monsters: A corpus assisted critical discourse analysis of the representation of gender in The Witcher videogame series* (Doctoral dissertation, Lancaster University).

Jenson, J., & de Castell, S. (2015). Online games, gender and feminism in. In *The international encyclopedia of digital communication and society* (pp. 1–5). Wiley.

Koschmann, M. A., & McDonald, J. (2015). Organizational rituals, communication, and the question of agency. *Management Communication Quarterly, 29*(1), 229–256.

Leech, G., Garside, R., & Bryant, M. (1994). CLAWS4: The tagging of the British National Corpus. In *Proceedings of the 15th International Conference on Computational Linguistics (COLING 94)* (pp. 622–628). Kyoto, Japan.

Lischinsky, A. (2018). Doing the naughty or having it done to you? Agent roles in erotic writing. *Porn Studies, 5*(2), 156–174.

Martins, N., Williams, D. C., Ratan, R. A., & Harrison, K. (2011). Virtual muscularity: A content analysis of male video game characters. *Body Image, 8*(1), 43–51.

Massanari, A. (2017). #Gamergate and the fappening: How Reddit's algorithm, governance, and culture support toxic technocultures. *New Media & Society, 19*(3), 329–346.

Matthews, N. L., Lynch, T., & Martins, N. (2016). Real ideal: Investigating how ideal and hyper-ideal video game bodies affect men and women. *Computers in Human Behavior, 59*(1), 155–164.

McAllister, L., Callaghan, J. E., & Fellin, L. C. (2019). Masculinities and emotional expression in UK servicemen: 'Big boys don't cry'? *Journal of Gender Studies, 2 8*(3), 257–270.

Mills, S. (1995). *Feminist stylistics.* Routledge.

Moon, R. (2014). From gorgeous to grumpy: Adjectives, age and gender. *Gender and Language, 8*(1), 5–41.

Rayson, P. (n.d.). *CLAWS part-of-speech tagger for English.* Lancaster University. http://ucrel.lancs.ac.uk/claws/. Accessed February 2021.

Ruberg, B. (2015). No fun: The queer potential of video games that annoy, anger, disappoint, sadden, and hurt. *QED: A Journal in GLBTQ Worldmaking, 2*(2), 108–124.

Ruberg, B., & Phillips, A., (2018). Not Gay as in happy: Queer resistance and video games (Introduction). *Game Studies, 18*(3).

Sarkeesian, A. (2014). *Tropes vs. women. Feminist frequency: Conversations with pop culture*. YouTube. https://www.youtube.com/watch?v=X6p5AZp7r_Q. Accessed February 2021.

Scott, M. (2016). *WordSmith tools version 7*. Lexical Analysis Software.

Sunderland, J. (2004). *Gendered discourses*. Palgrave Macmillan.

Taylor, C. (2013). Searching for similarity using corpus-assisted discourse studies. *Corpora, 8*(1), 81–113.

Terdiman, R. (2018). *Discourse/Counter-discourse: The theory and practice of symbolic resistance in nineteenth-century France*. Cornell University Press.

Thompson, G. (2013). *Introducing functional grammar* (3rd edn.). Routledge.

United Kingdom Government's Intellectual Property Office. (2014). *Exceptions to copyright: Research*. United Kingdom Government.

Wood, R. (2017). *Consumer sexualities: Women and sex shopping*. Routledge.

Woolf, V. (1929). *A room of one's own*. Hogarth Press.

Working Families and Bright Horizons. (2019). *Modern families index, 2019*. Working Families.

Youngblood, J. (2018). When (and What) Queerness counts: Homonationalism and militarism in the mass Effect series. *Game Studies, 18*(3).

6

Gendered Language in *The Witcher* Videogame Series

Magic in the Book

The previous chapter examined how gender was represented across a number of videogames. While this kind of research can be useful, because it can provide a 'snapshot' into how the genre as a whole represents gender, it does not quite examine how gender is represented in individual games—or, indeed, in an individual series of games. This chapter seeks to address some of these issues by using *The Witcher* videogame series as a case study. *The Witcher* videogame series is based on a book series by Andrezj Sapkowski (1992, 1993, 1994, 1995, 1996, 1997, 1999). Gender in *The Witcher* books is represented in interesting ways. Take, for example, how Sapkowski (1996) wrote about the gender-based ideologies held by the leader of a group of sorceresses: '"Dear ladies", Sheala said, having remained silent for some time. "Remember that you are **the dominant sex**. So don't behave like little girls, fighting over a bowl of sweetmeats"' (Sapkowski, 1996, p. 39). This poignant excerpt demonstrates several gender roles within the fantasy world of *The Witcher*. Ideologies within the book series may also bleed into the videogame series, and so it is important to acknowledge additional materials outside

F. Heritage, *Language, Gender and Videogames*,
https://doi.org/10.1007/978-3-030-74398-7_6

of one data set (corpus) which may have an influence on the language used (see Partington et al., 2013).

Background to *The Witcher*

The Witcher videogame series was developed by CD Projekt Red and is comprised of three different instalments: *The Witcher 1* (2007), *The Witcher 2: Assassination of Kings* (2011), and *The Witcher 3: Wild Hunt* (2015). The entire videogame series has sold over 50 million copies worldwide as of June 2019 (Brown, 2020). More recently, the videogame (and the novels which the videogame are based on) were adapted into a television show for Netflix. This adaptation quickly became the second most popular show on Netflix in the United States of America, and the most popular in both the UK and Australia (see Clark, 2019). The Netflix adaptation has also boosted sales of the videogames, as sales have increased by over 550%, while sales of the book series increased by 560% (see Grubb, 2020). Clearly, the TV show, videogames, and the book series have reached a large number of people—which means that many people may have engaged with these representations, and possibly adopted them into their sociocultural models of how gender 'should' be enacted.

The Witcher, as a series, is set in a fictional universe where technology is roughly similar to that of the Medieval era, magic exists, and there is a range of nonhuman races and monsters. The main character (controlled by the player in the game series) is Geralt, the eponymous witcher—a professional monster hunter who travels around an unnamed world taking on jobs killing monsters and getting drawn into political conflicts. While the TV series starts by showing the events that happen in the first few books, the videogames depart from these storylines. Although the videogames show some of the events through cut-scenes (small movies) at the beginning of *The Witcher 1*, generally they tell stories which occur after the main story of the book series. Therefore, any characters that are included or excluded from the series (with the exception of Geralt) are the result of choices made by the developers of the videogame series.

Overall, there is a dearth of literature which examines how gender is represented within the series as a whole, and even less which examines how it is represented within the videogames (though, see Heritage, 2021). In my previous work, which is drawn upon this chapter, I have argued that gender is often represented in complex but problematic ways in *The Witcher*. In other studies outside of corpus approaches, some scholars have examined how players interact with the first few areas of the videogame (see, e.g., Toh, 2015). However, in general, there is a lack of literature which has critically examined this series through the lens of (critical) discourse analysis.

Aims of This Chapter

In this chapter, I aim to utilise a corpus-driven approach to the language used in *The Witcher 1*, *The Witcher 2*, and *The Witcher 3*. Throughout this chapter, I aim to answer the primary research question: 'what does a corpus-driven approach to the data reveal about the representation of gender in *The Witcher* series?'. However, there is also a secondary research question which this chapter aims to address. Given that there is an 8-year difference between when the games were released, I also aim to answer the question 'has there been any diachronic change in the language used to represent gender, and if so, what is this?'.

In order to answer these questions, I approach the data by first generating keywords lists. I present the top 150 keywords for each individual game as well as a keyword list which contains the top 150 keywords for the corpus as a whole. I note that the keywords were grouped into one of seven categories based on how they represent gender: words which denote a male social actor but are not a name (such as *king*), words which denote a female social actor but are not a name (such as *queen*), male names (such as *Geralt*), female names (such as *Triss*), gender-neutral words (such as *bandit*), and non-gendered words (such as *armor*), and pronouns (such as *you*).

I also explore what the frequencies of the keywords reveal about the representation of gender within the series. I argue that there appear to be unequal representations on a quantitative level, but that it is still important to also go beyond lexical semantic analysis based on keywords and that the representation of gender should also be examined on a qualitative level (see Heritage & Koller, 2020; Milani, 2013). Indeed, considering words at a quantitative level before analysing the word at a qualitative level is a common practice within academic research on corpus approaches to the representation of gender and sexuality (see, e.g., Baker, 2014; Heritage & Koller, 2020; Milani, 2013). Therefore, this chapter focuses on the quantitative features in the data, and these quantitative analyses are supported by qualitative analyses.

Furthermore, I argue that while explicitly gendered words provide an indication of how gender is represented within the games, it does not provide the full story, and both gender-neutral and non-gendered terms should also be investigated. This leads to an analysis of the collocates and collocational networks for the term *trophy* (a non-gendered keyword). I argue that although *trophy* is non-gendered in terms of lexical semantics, collocates and collocational networks suggest that it is used to maintain gender biases.

Collecting (and Analysing) the Data

Before I discuss how the data were analysed and the findings this analysis presents, it is first worth drawing attention to how the data were gathered. In the previous chapter, one of the limitations I implemented on all the data for VG2014 was that no file could exceed approximately 55,500 words, in order to prevent certain files skewing the corpus. *The Witcher 3* was one such file.

The three corpora were collected using fan-made computer software. This fan-made software produced text dump files (see Chapter 4). In order to decrypt the files for each game (called string files), different software was required for each game. As noted in Chapter 4, these text dumps are located within the game files, which are available when a videogame is downloaded on to a computer using software such as *Steam*. (The location would be similar to as follows: Users > Program files (x86) > Steam > Steamapps > Common > The Witcher 2; see Chapter 4). For *The Witcher 1*, the string file was stored within a 'bin' sub-folder of 'the Witcher' folder. The string file used the '.BIF' file extension, which encrypted all the language in the game, but it was accompanied by a '.KEY file', which gave the decryption instructions. I used the tool UnBIF (Csimbi, 2012) to decrypt the language and change the files into .xml (which required the .KEY file to be uploaded in addition to the .BIF file). This .xml file was then turned into a .txt file for corpus software by changing the file extension.

For *The Witcher 2*, the string file was located in the 'cooked PC' sub-folder and was coded as a '.W2strings file'. To decode this file type, I used Gibbed Red Tools (Gibbed, 2015). In order to use this tool, the windows command prompt was run. In the command screen, the following was written:

C:\Program Files (x86)\Gibbed's RED Tools\Gibbed.RED.Strings.exe

Once Enter was hit, the following message appeared on the screen:

Usage: Gibbed.RED.Strings.exe [OPTIONS] + input [output]

Options:

-d, --decode strings file

-e, --encode strings file

-h, --help show this message and exit

From this, a space followed by '-d' was added along with another space. The whole file location of the .W2string files was then copied into the command prompt. This 'unzipped' all the files and allowed the .W2string files to be converted to a .txt file via changing the file extension.

The process for gathering the data from *The Witcher 3* was identical to *The Witcher 2*, with three exceptions. First, the files were stored under the 'content' sub-folder, rather than the 'bin' or 'cooked PC' sub-folder. Second, the files were stored as '.W3string files'. This meant that Gibbed Red Tools could not read nor process these files, which led to the third difference: Lua Utis Tools (Zaitsev, 2015) was used to run the same process that Gibbed Red Tools ran for *The Witcher 2*.

Once I had the three text dumps, I read through each line and removed any computer macros which were accidentally transferred over, along with any translators'/localisation notes. This produced three separate corpora, the size of which are outlined in Table 6.1 below.

Once these corpora had been compiled, WordSmith 7 (Scott, 2016) was used in order to generate the keyword lists. One of the reasons why

Table 6.1 Size of *The Witcher* corpora

Videogame	Number of tokens
The Witcher 1	149,716
The Witcher 2	255,763
The Witcher 3	294,285
Total	699,764

WordSmith 7 was selected over other corpus software was because it triangulates various statistical measures of keyness before presenting an analyst with a keyword list. In order to be presented as a keyword, a word must be statistically significant by log-likelihood, log ratio, and BIC score (discussed in Chapter 3). While it is possible to adjust the statistical requirements cut-off points in WordSmith 7, I used the default cut-off points (log-likelihood p-value of 0.01, a log ratio of 0.01, and a BIC score of 4). Once these lists were generated, I categorised the keywords into one of the seven categories mentioned earlier.

Words which denote a male/female social actor could be words such as *king* or *princess*—words which typically denote the gender identity of the being referred to (this also included words marked for grammatical gender, such as gendered demonstratives). Names were listed separately due to their function. When a person is named, that person has typically undergone a process of individualisation. Hand in hand with individualisation is the idea that the media are able to individualise those whom the writers find to be the most important (see van Leeuwen, 2008). van Leeuwen argues that middle-class newspapers (i.e. broadsheets) would use individualisation more frequently for specific politicians and assimilate the working class, while papers aimed at the working class (i.e. tabloids) would do the inverse of this—both of which used individualisation to place prominence on the person/people being individualised. To highlight individualisation and the difference between individualisation and assimilation, take, for example, the following headline from *The Guardian* (a UK newspaper): 'Boris Johnson's message to the working class: good luck out there' (Jones, 2020). In this example, 'Boris Johnson' is individualised, while 'the working class' (i.e. working-class people) are assimilated—and the focus of this article indicates that 'Boris Johnson' will take prominence, and that as an individual he is responsible for what happens to the assimilated group.

The categories non-gendered and gender-neutral words have a subtle but important distinction between them: gender-neutral terms are terms which could be associated with any gender (e.g. *bandits*), while non-gendered terms are words which are typically associated with no gender (e.g. *gold*). In order to best make a distinction between these terms, I draw on the idea of socially gendered lexemes (see Coffey-Glover, 2019, pp. 87–88). Socially gendered lexemes are typically 'common nouns such as *soldier*, *mechanic* or *truck driver* [...] because although they are technically gender-neutral, in reality they have connotations of male reference'. This idea of these terms being 'technically gender-neutral' underpins the distinction I make. I argue that while their connotative meanings might indicate one gender, people from different genders might also fill that role (e.g. while one might think of soldiers as men, there are several female soldiers—both in real life and within the data).

One way I differentiated between if a common noun was socially gendered was to test whether the noun could be pre-modified with a lexically gendered noun (i.e. a noun which includes the semantic feature [+male] or [+female] in their denotative meanings; see Coffey-Glover, 2019, p. 87). If a noun could be pre-modified with a gendered term such as 'female', for example 'female bandits', then it was considered gender-neutral. Important in the application the way gender-neutral terms were identified above is that these nouns also denote living/autonomous beings (see Buss, 2005; Holroyd, 2009; for overviews of feminist autonomy). While non-living nouns may have gendered connotations (e.g. we might associate the word *battle* with 'men' because we associate the 'soldiers' who fight in the battle with men), I was only interested in looking at how living social actors were gendered. Thus, I define gender-neutral terms as typically common nouns (usually signifying professional roles or identity labels) which denoting living beings. These living beings might have associations with gender norms, but the word could also refer to someone of a different gender. Importantly, my definition of a gender-neutral term means that they can only be nouns or male/female third-person pronouns.

By contrast, non-gendered terms included grammatical categories, for example, adjectives (such as *grand*), verbs (such as *rain*), adverbs (such as *flaming*), and interjections—including both noises made by characters (such as *argh*) or greetings (such as *hey*). One slight area of overlap between these terms and terms classified as 'gender-neutral' is the inclusion of some nouns, such as *battle* (a nominalisation) and *coin.* Importantly, in the non-gendered category, the nouns do not denote living beings (nor professions/identities). While they may have some gendered connotations (such as assuming that only men participated in a battle), the words themselves do not refer to animate social actors. This is not to say, however, that this category should be ignored for how it represents gender and the gendered associations found with links to non-living beings (as will be shown later in this chapter).

One exception in the categorisation system was made, due to familiarity with the corpora. The word *witcher* has been categorised as a male social actor because, in both Sapkowski's (1992, 1993, 1994, 1995, 1996, 1997, 1999) original books and the videogames, only young boys are taken to be trained as witchers.[1] Therefore, it is an exclusively gendered profession. However, all concordance lines for the keywords were examined, in order to ensure that they were placed in their appropriate categories.

Finally, pronouns other than gendered third person pronouns (such as *I*, *we*, or *they*) have been placed in their own category, as there is no indication of what gender the character is, or what gender the character being spoken about is. This also includes pronominal contractions such as *we'll*.

[1] In the novels, Ciri is sometimes referred to as the 'witcher girl', I have not included this when categorising this word because in the novels she is marked as being unique as the only girl to have gone through the training. She did not, however, undergo the final test and mutations to become a full witcher. Therefore, this job role has been classified as denoting male social actors.

Keyword Lists for Individual Games

In order to start analysing the keywords, I took the top 150 keywords from each game, analysed the concordance lines for each term and categorised them by the groups noted in the previous section. All keywords occurred $\geq$ 10 times, and all were significant by the statistical measures discussed in Chapter 3.

The Witcher 1: Keywords

The categorisation of keywords from *The Witcher 1*, based on the groups mentioned above, is presented below in Table 6.2.

Table 6.2 The top 150 keywords in *The Witcher 1*

Category	Words
Male names	Alvin; Berengar; Dandelion; Foltest; Geralt; Javed; Kalkstein; Leuvaarden; Siegfried; Velerad; Yaevinn; Zoltan
Female names	Adda; Alina; Shani; Triss
Male social actors	bastard; king; lords; master; witcher; witchers; witcher's
Female social actors	princess; sorceress
Gender-neutral words	bandit; beasts; dh'oine; dwarves; drowners; elves; humans; griggs; knights; mage; monster; monsters; nonhumans; reverend; salamandara; salamander; salamander; scoia'tael; striga; vodyanoi; wolf
Non-gendered words	ah; argh; armor; begone; can't; coin; come; curse; dice; die; do; don't; drink; elven; eternal; farewell; fight; find; fire; flaming; follow; get; go; gold; grand; greetings; ha; haven't; help; here; here's; hmm; hurry; interesting; kill; killed; know; leave; let's; magic; mercy; mhm; must; need; no; nothing; order; orens; plague; please; potion; rain; raining; return; reward; Rivia; see; shove; sniff; speak; stop; swamp; sword; take; talk; tell; thank; thanks; there's; tower; Vizima; want; wait; weather; wett; what; what's; where's; who's; why; won't; yes
Pronouns	I; I'd; I'll; I'm; it's; I've; me; my; they'll; we'll; we're; you; you'd; you'll; you're; you've; your; yourself

Initially, there appears to be more words which denote male social actors in comparison to female social actors, and there appears to be more male names than female names (there are 12 male names compared to 4 female names and 8 terms denoting non-named male social actors and 2 for female social actors). This could give some weight to previous content analyses which found that male characters were up to more likely to occur than female characters—sometimes up to four times more likely (see Beasley & Collins Standley, 2002; Burgess et al., 2007; Ivory, 2006; Gestos et al., 2018; Scharrer, 2004; Paaßen et al., 2017). However, the number of names does not necessarily provide full information about the representation of gender (see Baker, 2006). For example, all the male names could only occur one hundred times, while all the female names could occur four hundred times (which would suggest that although there are a smaller number of female characters, this smaller number might take more prominence). In order to begin to address this, the raw frequencies for the terms denoting gendered social actors and gendered names in *The Witcher 1* are presented below in Table 6.3.

One of the issues with the data presented above is that the perceived sample sizes are too small for standard non-parametric significance tests,

Table 6.3 Raw frequencies of male/female names and male/female social actors in *The Witcher 1*

Male name	Freq.	Female name	Freq.	Male social actor	Freq.	Female social actor	Freq.
Alvin	102	Adda	43	bastard	61	princess	57
Berengar	45	Alina	83	king	133	sorceress	48
Dandelion	72	Shani	93	lords	62		
Foltest	108	Triss	137	master	106		
Geralt	358			witcher	459		
Javed	51			witchers	119		
Kalkstein	54			witcher's	39		
Leuvaarden	37						
Siegfried	65						
Velerad	37						
Yaevinn	61						
Zoltan	38						
Total	1,028		356		979		105

such as a t-test[2] (so it is not possible to claim that one set is statistically more likely to occur than another set). Rather than report the results of a statistical test, which will not be statistically significant due to the sample sizes, the following sections compare the raw frequencies at which these terms occur. The frequencies of the words which denoted male social actors occurred 9.8 times more frequently than words for female social actors. Additionally, male names occurred 2.9 times more frequently than female names. Thus, in terms of raw frequencies of gendered words, there appears to be a gender bias, and the data suggests that words associated with men and masculinity are disproportionately represented in the data. Importantly, this finding moves us away from equating the number of gendered characters and/or gendered social actors in the game with the frequency at which such representations occur.

This difference is especially useful to videogame researchers. One of the key studies which discusses the frequency at which men appear in comparison to women was conducted around the time *The Witcher 1* was released (Miller & Summer, 2007). By using this approach, I have been able to highlight what characters were given the most attention and examine the gender of the characters which were given the most attention. This shows that, while there may be more male names in comparison to female names in this game, male characters are also spoken about more frequently than female characters—so it is not a case that a small number of female characters occur very regularly.

The Witcher 2: Keywords

Table 6.4 below demonstrates how the top 150 keywords of *The Witcher 2* were categorised.

Similar to the results from *The Witcher 1*, there are more keywords for male social actors in comparison to words which denote female social actors. There are 18 keywords which denote a male name (if possessives are removed this is reduced to 16) and 10 for female (without possessives this is 9). There are also 8 terms for male social actors (which are

[2] This test is different from the T-score used for collocational analysis.

Table 6.4 The top 150 keywords in *The Witcher 2*

Category	Words
Male names	Cedric; Demavend; Dethmold; Foltest; Foltest's; Geralt; Henselt; Henselt's; Iorveth; Letho; Loredo; Radovid; Roche; Shilard; Stennis; Valette; Vernon; Zoltan
Female names	Anais; Eilhart; Merigold; Philippa; Sabrina; Saskia; Saskia's; Síle; Triss; Ves
Male social actors	he's; king; kings; prince; sire; witcher; witchers; witcher's
Female social actors	she's; sorceress; sorceresses
Gender-neutral words	commandant; dh'oine; dragon; dwarf; dwarves; elf; elves; gods; guards; Kaedweni; kingslayer; mages; majesty; monster; monsters; Nilfgaardian; nonhumans; scoia'tael; soldier; soldiers; Temerian; thief; troll; wraiths
Non-gendered words	Aedirn; ah; armor; arse; battle; blood; bloody; camp; can't; coin; curse; death; defeat; dice; die; do; don't; eh; elven; fight; find; Flotsam; get; go; got; greetings; ha; happy; heard; heh; help; here; hey; hm; Kayran; kill; know; La; leave; let; let's; loc; magic; mist; Muinne; need; Nilfgaard; oh; orens; ploughing; Pontar; Redania; reward; right; see; sword; take; talk; tell; Temeria; thanks; Valette; Vergen; wait; want; what's; who's; why; won't
Pronouns	I'll; I'm; I've; me; that's; they'll; they're; we'll; we're; you; you'd; you're; you've; your

not names) and 3 for female social actors. Thus, again, it is possible to suggest that there is some bias in *The Witcher 2*: that there are more male characters and more male social actors within this videogame.

Similar to the previous section, the raw frequencies of both the social actors and names are presented below in Table 6.5.

Similar to the findings from *The Witcher 1*, in *The Witcher 2* male names were 2.5 times more likely to occur than female names within the game. Male social actor references were 5.8 times more likely to occur in comparison to female social actor references. In terms of diachronic change, this shows a slight shift as there are more references to named female characters and more terms for female social actors. However, this difference is still problematic because there are large quantifiable differences in the frequencies at which such concepts occur. Thus, while it

Table 6.5 Raw frequencies of male/female names and male/female social actors in *The Witcher 2*

Male name	Freq.	Female name	Freq.	Male social actors	Freq.	Female social actors	Freq.
Demavend	73	Anais	69	he's	294	she's	124
Dethmold	146	Eilhart	68	king	485	sorceress	186
Foltest	108	Merigold	67	kings	89	sorceresses	92
Foltest's	108	Philippa	184	prince	107		
Geralt	1,010	Sabrina	94	sire	79		
Henselt	367	Saskia	261	witcher	1,079		
Henselt's	126	Saskia's	80	witchers	98		
Iorveth	353	Síle	146	witcher's	113		
Letho	182	Triss	357	he's	294		
Loredo	181	Ves	64	king	485		
Radovid	117						
Roche	236						
Shilard	62						
Stennis	87						
Valette	88						
Vernon	141						
Zoltan	110						
Total	3,495		1,390		2,344		402

might be possible to say that there is a step towards equal representation at a quantitative level between *The Witcher 1* and *The Witcher 2*, this does not mean that this step has made the representation equal.

Both the forenames and surnames of some characters appear as keywords, as exemplified by *Triss*, whose surname is *Merigold*. Sometimes, her entire name is referenced, but sometimes she is referred to only by her first name or surname. There are only two female characters with both forename and surname as keywords in *The Witcher 2*—*Triss Merigold* and *Philippa Eilhart*. With regard to the male names, this only happens in the case of *Vernon Roche*. This coupling of first name and surname further shows that even more male characters' names are considered key than female characters (if surnames are considered, 14 individual male characters occur within the top 150 keywords, while only 7 individual female characters occur). Therefore, while these characters are clearly central to this videogame, we could argue that male characters are a) more likely to be included in the game (there are more male names as keywords than female names), and b) that they are likely to be referenced more than female characters (they are referenced more frequently than female names).

In addition to knowing that *witcher* should be categorised as a male social actor, the above point relating to the occurrence of both forenames and surnames within the top 150 keywords can only be made due to familiarity with the corpora. There is a debate within the CADS literature about whether or not analysts should be familiar with their corpora or approach the data without any prior knowledge of the data in the corpus (see Partington et al., 2013). Sinclair (2004, pp. 188–189) argued that we should view a corpus as a 'black box', a data set that we have never encountered before because if we have familiarity with the texts within a corpus, that might guide our analysis. While Partington et al. go on to argue that we should be familiar with the texts in our corpus, they succinctly summarise some other scholar's approach to this problem:

> Corpus linguistics proper has also frequently been characterised by the treatment of the corpus as a 'black box', that is, the analyst is not always encouraged to familiarise him/herself with particular texts within the corpus in case the special features these texts may possess should distort his or her conceptions of the corpus as a whole. (2013, p. 12)

I would argue that familiarity with the corpus has benefited the analysis and has allowed for a slightly deeper understanding of how gender is represented within the data.

The Witcher 3: Keywords

This section discusses what the keywords for *The Witcher 3* reveal about the representation of gender. The top 150 keywords, as categorised into the groups previously used, are presented below in Table 6.6.

In comparison to previous games, the ratio of male to female social actors appears to still be unequal, with more words for male social actors than female social actors: there are 13 keywords denoting male names and 7 for female names. There are also 11 keywords for male social actors

Table 6.6 The top 150 keywords in *The Witcher 3*

Category	Words
Male names	Avallac'h; Crach; Craite; Dijkstra; Emhyr; Eredin; Geralt; Geralt's; Hjalmar; Lambert; Lugos; Radovid; Zoltan
Female names	Cerys; Ciri; Ciri's; Freya; Keira; Triss; Yennefer
Male social actors	'im; baron; baron's; jarl; king; man's' emperor; whoreson; witcher; witchers; witcher's
Female social actors	crones; sorceress; sorceresses; witch
Gender-neutral words	bandits; beast; elves; folk; gods; guard; griffin; hunters; inhabitants; mage; mages; manager; merchant; monster; monsters; Nilfgaardian; pellar; pesant; Redanian; Temerian; warriors
Non-gendered words	aen; akh; alchemy; Ard; armor; arse; attack; battle; blade; blood; bog; card; cards; chance; clan; coin; color; contract; crossbow; curse; damage; death; decided; decoction; defeat; diagram; eh; elder; elven; enhanced; Eredin; eternal; fate; fight; find; fire; found; gui; gwent; gwint; help; hunt; increases; isle; isles; kaer; kill; letter; magic; manuscript; morhen; mutagen; mysterious; near; Nilfgaard; Novigrad; once; orchard; Oxenfurt; perch; potion; Redania; return; reward; ruins; runestone; sadly; search; select; senses; sign; silver; Skellig; Skellige; stamina; strength; superior; sword; talk; Temeria; temple; treasure; Trolde; trophy; Undvik; using; var; Velen; village; vitality; wild; woods
Pronouns	I'll; ye; your

and 4 for female social actors. Similarly, the raw frequencies of terms for gendered names and male/female social actors are presented below in Table 6.7.

The frequencies at which male and female names occur suggest that only a small amount of progress has been made. In the top 150 keywords for *The Witcher 1*, there were 9 male names and 4 female names. In the top 150 keywords for *The Witcher 2*, there were 17 male names and 10 female names. However, in the top 150 keywords for *The Witcher 3*, there are 13 male names and 7 female names. When calculating the ratios at which male names occur in comparison to female names in each keyword list, male names were 2.25 times more likely to occur in the top 150 keywords in *The Witcher 1*, 1.7 times more likely to occur in

Table 6.7 Raw frequencies of male/female names and male/female social actors *The Witcher 3*

Male name	Freq.	Female name	Freq.	Male social actors	Freq.	Female social actors	Freq.
Avallac'h	50	Cerys	61	'im	73	crones	62
Crach	52	Ciri	338	baron	109	sorceress	111
Craite	64	Ciri's	57	baron's	53	sorceresses	62
Dijkstra	62	Freya	73	jarl	78	witch	135
Emhyr	73	Keira	97	king	224		
Eredin	54	Triss	137	man's	61		
Geralt	1,431	Yennefer	174	emperor	66		
Geralt's	125			whoreson	95		
Hjalmar	72			witcher	941		
Lambert	55			witchers	155		
Lugos	55			witcher's	87		
Radovid	137						
Zoltan	53						
Total	2,283		937				

the keyword list for *The Witcher 2*, and 1.85 times more likely to occur in the top 150 keywords for *The Witcher 3*. Therefore, there is certainly some progress towards a point of equal representation in terms of the number of male to female characters in *The Witcher 3* in comparison to *The Witcher 1*. However, *The Witcher 3* also appears to have taken a slight step backwards towards less equal quantifiable representations in terms of how many male/female characters were keywords in comparison to *The Witcher 2*.

The number of words for male and female social actors within the top 150 keywords suggests that there has been a change in the representation of gender. In the top 150 keywords lists for *The Witcher 1*, there were 8 words denoting male social actors and 2 denoting female social actors, while in *The Witcher 2* there were 8 words denoting male social actors and 3 denoting female social actors. In the keyword list for *The Witcher 3*, there were 11 terms for male social actors and 4 for female social actors, suggesting a slight decrease in the ratio of male social actors to female social actors within the top 150 keywords. Although there has been a decrease in the number of keywords which denote male social actors compared to those which denote female social actors, there is still a disproportionately higher number of keywords in *The Witcher 3* which denote male social actors.

In terms of the ratios at which the raw frequencies of male/female names occur within the games, the difference is only slightly lower than those presented in the data from *The Witcher 1* (2.9 times greater) and *The Witcher 2* (2.5 times). In the keyword list for *The Witcher 3*, the frequency of male names occurring within the data was 2.4 times higher than female names. With regard to raw frequencies of the words for gendered social actors, keywords denoting male social actors were 5.2 times more likely to occur in the top 150 keywords than terms for female social actors. This appears to suggest progress towards equal representation of gender within *The Witcher 3*, as in *The Witcher 1* words for male social actors were 9.8 times more likely to occur, and in *The Witcher 2*, they were 5.8 times more likely to occur. Thus, in terms of the number of keywords denoting male social actors and the frequencies at which those keywords appear in the corpus, it is possible to suggest that there has been some diachronic change in terms of visibility of female characters. However, this is not to suggest that these frequencies are now equal nor that there has made a massive change in the representation of gender at a quantifiable level, and in *The Witcher 3* there are still a disproportionately high number of terms for male social actors used compared to words for female social actors. The diachronic change in the ratios of these frequencies is summarised below in Table 6.8.

Table 6.8 Ratios of male to female words and names across the corpora

Game	Ratio of male names to female names (how many in the top 150 keywords)	Ratio of frequency at which male to female names occur (frequencies)	Ratio of male to female social actors (how many in the top 150 keywords)	Ratio of frequency at which male to female social actors occur (frequencies)
The Witcher 1	2.25:1	2.9:1	4:1	9.8:1
The Witcher 2	1.7:1	2.5:1	2.6:1	5.8:1
The Witcher 3	1.85:1	2.4:1	2.75:1	5.2:1

Therefore, at a quantitative level, it is possible to suggest that there are biases both in terms of the number of words that occur for male/female characters and the number of named male/female characters.[3] Indeed, these ratios appear to resonate with previous content analyses which suggested that in some games the ratio of male to female characters could be as high as 4:1 (see Burgess et al., 2007; Paaßen et al., 2017; Scharrer, 2004). However, in terms of the ratio at which these terms occur (i.e. their raw frequency), the representation appears to be worse than what background literature would suggest, and as though male characters are referred to considerably more than female characters. Although there appears to be some diachronic change in the frequency of these words, the ratios repeatedly suggest that female characters are under-represented in comparison to male characters.

Keywords from the Three Games Combined

While the previous section discussed the representation of gender in all three games individually, this section now turns to discuss the keywords for the series as a whole. Analysing the corpora combined is important: not only does it give an indication of how gender is represented in the series as a whole, but words which might not have occurred as statistically key in any three games might be considered key when the games are combined. In terms of the former reason for why analysing the series as a whole is important, a number of online services now sell all three games in a single bundle, meaning that players might be tempted to play all three games consecutively, and this could affect their cognitive representations of gender. In terms of the latter point, by doing an analysis of the games combined, it is possible to get a view of what is relevant to the series as a whole.

I combined the corpora for *The Witcher 1*, *2*, and *3*, and then generated the top 150 keywords. These were then grouped using the categories

[3] Although terms like *witcher* and *Geralt* are somewhat predictable male terms as this is the central character's name and profession (which may increase the difference in the ratio of male to female words), there are a number of choices that the writers have made to deemphasise the role of female characters.

established earlier. The categorised keywords are presented in Table 6.9 below.

In terms of frequency of male/female character names and words for male/female social actors, as was the case with every game individually, in this keyword list there are more words for male characters than female characters and more words for male social actors than female social actors (15 male names; 6 female names; 7 words for male social actors; 2 for female social actors). The raw frequencies at which these occur are presented below in Table 6.10

Even though the smallest difference in frequency of male names occurring in a keyword list in comparison to female names was 1.7 in *The Witcher 2*, when *The Witcher* corpus as a whole is examined, male names were 2.3 times more frequent in the keyword list than female names

Table 6.9 The top 150 keywords in the corpus as a whole

Category	Words
Male names	Dandelion; Dethmold; Foltest; Foltest's; Geralt; Geralt's; Henselt; Henselt's Iorveth; Letho; Loredo; Radovid; Roche; Vernon; Zoltan
Female names	Ciri; Philippa; Saskia; Síle; Triss; Yennefer
Male social actors	he'll; he's; king; master; witcher; witchers; witcher's
Female social actors	sorceress; sorceresses
Gender-neutral words	bandits; beast; dwarves; dh'oine; elf; elves; folk; gods; guard; guards; humans; kaedweni; knights; mage; mages; monster; monsters; Nilfgaadian; nonhumans; peasants; Redanian; scoia'teal; soldier; Temerian; troll; wolf
Non-gendered words	Aedirn; ah; armor; arse; attack; battle; blood; bloody; camp; can't; coin; curse; death; decided; dead; defeat; diagram; dice; die; don't; elven; eternal; farewell; fight; find; fire; Flotsam; greetings; heard; help; here; hm; hunt; isle; kaer; kaedwen; kill; killed; know; leave; let's; magic; morhen; Muinne; must; need; Nilfgaard; Novigrad; oh; order; orens; Oxenfurt; Pontar; Redania; return; reward; Rivia; senses; silver; Skellige; swamp; sword; talk; tell; thanks; tower; treasure; Velen; Vergen; village; Vizima; wait; what's; wild; won't
Pronouns	I'll; I'm; I've; me; they'll; they're; we'll; we're; ye; you; you'd; you'll; you're; you've; your

Table 6.10 Raw frequencies of male and female social actors in the corpus as a whole

Male name	Frequency	Female name	Frequency	Male social actors	Frequency	Female social actors
Dandelion	164	Ciri	340	he'll	163	sorceress
Dethmold	147	Phillippa	238	he's	535	sorceresses
Foltest	345	Saskia	263	king	842	
Foltest's	125	Síle	156	master	278	
Geralt	2,799	Triss	631	witcher	2,479	
Geralt's	177	Yennefer	213	witchers	372	
Henselt	371			witcher's	239	
Henselt's	128					
Iorveth	359					
Letho	215					
Loredo	181					
Radovid	274					
Roche	280					
Vernon	158					
Total	5,723		1,841	4,908		518

(there were 14 male names and 6 female names). Character names which may not have been statistically key in any one corpus may have been considered key when the frequency at which they occurred is coupled with other references to the same character from other games. Similarly, there is still unequal representation in the series as a whole: as the total raw frequency at which these male names occur is 3.1 times higher than the raw frequency at which female names occur. This number is actually higher than all previous games. Thus, it could be argued that on a broad level, there is an unequal representation, though CD Projekt Red appears to be giving more prominence to a select number of female characters in each game, this does not necessarily hold true throughout the series.

There were 3.5 times as many references to male social actors in the series as a whole—which is a lower ratio than in *The Witcher 1* and *The Witcher 2*, but not as less as *The Witcher 3*. However, the collective raw frequency of the terms denoting male social actors was 9.5 times more frequent than the terms for female social actors. This is higher than the frequency at which words denoting a male social actor occurred compared to female social actors in both *The Witcher 2* (5.8 times more frequently) and *The Witcher 3* (5.2 times more frequently). The level is more similar to the data presented in *The Witcher 1* (9.8 times more frequently). Thus, although there is a diachronic change within a small number of keywords from each game individually, overall, the data still demonstrates unequal representation at a quantifiable level.

Within the words denoting gendered social actors, there appears to be a dichotomy not just in the corpus as a whole, but across the keywords for each game individually. *Witchers* and *sorceresses* are positioned dichotomously: men hunt monsters up close while women have to cast spells from a distance (terms like *wizard* or *warrioress* could have been used to denote roles for men who fight from a distance and women who fight up close, but these were very infrequent). To some degree, this could support the notions of Bergstrom et al. (2012) as well as Yee et al. (2011), who argued that different roles within videogames are gendered, with melee roles typically being associated more with masculinity and healing/ranged roles being associated with femininity.

Furthermore, in all three games and the corpus as a whole, *king* is a keyword, but royalty honorifics for women are not—with the exception of *princess* in *The Witcher 1*. However, even with this exception, *princess*(es) are not afforded the same power as *kings*—that is to say, kings are the patriarchs, while princesses wait to become matriarchs. Indeed, there are words for male social actors such as *master* which appear as key within the corpus as a whole, suggesting that there is more representation of male characters in positions of power. Indeed, returning to the individual games, *king*, *king's*, *lords*, *master*, and *sire* all occur as keywords in at least one game. With the exception of *princess* in *The Witcher 1*, none of the gendered keywords across the corpora refer to women in inherent positions of power. Therefore, the games show a trend both quantitatively and in terms of lexical semantics for not depicting women in positions of power.

Analysing *Trophy*

I have already argued that the quantification of keywords gives a broad picture of how gender is represented, but the frequencies at which keywords occur alone do not quite reveal how they are used. For the last section of analysis in this chapter, I now move from the frequencies of keywords and the lexical semantics of these keywords towards qualitative analyses of individual keywords (similar to the work of Milani, 2013; Heritage & Koller, 2020).

In order to investigate words that reveal something about the representation of gender, all keywords (for each game and the corpus as a whole) were analysed with a mixture of examining the statistically significant collocates of those keywords (and frequencies of those collocates), collocational networks, and close reading of extended concordance lines. Although I do not report on all the findings of these methods (primarily due to limitations of space), these triangulated methods allowed for a deeper understanding of the data. In the following subsection, I highlight how these methods can be implemented in the analysis of one keyword.

The analysis below is a case study of the term *trophy*, as it is a non-gendered keyword which is imbued with tacit gender bias. This gender bias was only discovered after examining collocations and collocational networks for non-gendered keywords. Therefore, this case study demonstrates how a non-gendered keyword was analysed because often scholars choose to examine words which will show something about gender from the beginning. Usually, by picking a word which is known to relate directly to gender and/or sexuality, an analyst will easily be able to answer the question 'yes, but is it gender?' (Swann, 2002, p. 43). As I touched upon in Chapter 1, Swann argues that, as interesting as some uses of language may be, these uses do not always indicate that there is some sort of gender bias or gender-work at play. So, while women might be represented as 'x', it might also be the case that they are represented in such a way because of 'y' other identity or 'z' phenomenon. This is one of the reasons why so many analyses focus on explicitly gendered terms, such as *man/woman* (see Pearce, 2008), because by doing this, the analyst is able to clearly say 'yes, well this analysis does relate to gender'. However, with this, words which might show something interesting in terms of the representation of gender might be overlooked in favour of other words which clearly answer the question 'yes but is it gender?' from the onset.

The point raised above is not to invalidate the previous corpus studies which have examined explicitly gendered terms, such as *man/woman* (see Krendel, 2020; Pearce, 2008) or *girl/boy* (see Krendel, 2020; Taylor, 2013). However, I wish to draw attention to the fact that it is much less frequent to examine either gender-neutral or non-gendered words for how they relate to other gendered phrases. One exception to this is the work of Hunt (2015). In Hunt's work on the representation of gender in children's literature, she takes gender-neutral body parts (such as *hands* and *feet*) and examines what gendered characters do what with their bodies. Hunt's work demonstrates that the differences in how characters move their bodies are influenced by the gender of the characters in those pieces of literature. For example, in the *Harry Potter* series, the female characters are often discussed in terms of being helped to their feet more than male characters, and regularly carry less important objects than their male counterparts.

The analysis presented in this section demonstrates the fruitful nature of looking beyond just lexical semantics for body parts and shows the use of corpus analytical methods on a category of word which might be otherwise overlooked (because *trophy* is a noun which does not normally denote a living being). The analysis below also shows the fruitful nature of collocational networks, which are regularly under-utilised in discourse analyses of gender (though, see Baker, 2014; Heritage & Baker, 2021; Taylor, 2016).

First, the collocates of *trophy* were examined. There were multiple collocates which met the established traditional thresholds for significance discussed in Chapter 3. Therefore, the top 40 collocates were analysed. The statistical measures implemented for collocation were: 5 $\geq$ frequency of occurrence within a 5L-5R window and at least MI $\geq$ 3; T-score $\geq$ 2. I decided to triangulate the statistics implemented: by also comparing the MI scores against the T-scores. If a collocate was statistically significant by MI score, I also checked it against the T-score for that collocate. If it was not significant by T-score, I still analysed the collocate but paid less attention to it than collocates that were statistically significant by both. These collocates are outlined in Table 6.11 below. Of these 40 collocates, 7 were explicitly gendered (these are highlighted in bold). Of these 7, 5 were the names of female monsters and 2 were male pronouns. These gendered collocates are highlighted in bold in the table.

Table 6.11 Top 40 collocates of the word *trophy*

Number	Word	Frequency	Frequency (L)	Frequency (R)	MI score	T-score
1	trophy	80	40	40	12.819	8.763
2	the	63	27	36	3.738	7.228
3	a	39	35	4	4.250	5.929
4	from	26	1	25	6.263	5.035
5	to	22	3	19	3.215	4.204
6	take	21	19	2	7.274	4.554
7	it	10	3	7	3.741	3.362
8	**hag**	**9**	**6**	**3**	**10.426**	**2.998**
9	collect	9	2	7	9.572	2.824
10	nekker	8	5	3	9.891	2.826
11	for	8	3	5	3.366	2.564
12	wyvern	7	3	4	10.957	2.644
13	cockatrice	7	4	3	10.372	2.644
14	arachas	7	4	3	10.120	2.826
15	your	6	3	3	3.556	2.249
16	warrior	6	3	3	8.684	2.443
17	**nightwraith**	**6**	**3**	**3**	**11.635**	**2.449**
18	kill	6	6	0	5.991	2.412
19	grave	6	3	3	8.957	(N/S)
20	forktail	6	3	3	10.588	2.644
21	ekimmara	6	2	4	11.220	2.448
22	chort	6	3	3	11.149	2.448
23	but	6	2	4	3.827	2.283
24	this	5	4	1	3.463	2.040
25	**succubus**	**5**	**3**	**2**	**9.301**	**2.233**
26	**siren**	**5**	**2**	**3**	**11.694**	**2.235**
27	on	5	4	1	3.494	2.045
28	ice	5	2	3	9.234	2.232
29	**his**	**5**	**3**	**2**	**3.477**	**2.043**
30	**he**	**5**	**2**	**3**	**3.281**	**(N/S)**
31	griffin	5	3	2	8.592	2.444
32	giant	5	3	2	9.109	2.232
33	fiend	5	2	3	10.149	2.234
34	**erynia**	**5**	**2**	**3**	**13.279**	**2.236**
35	earth	5	1	4	9.012	2.232
36	drowner	5	3	2	10.471	2.235
37	doppler	5	2	3	10.234	2.234
38	cave	5	2	3	8.384	2.230
39	as	5	4	1	3.781	2.090

(continued)

Table 6.11 (continued)

Number	Word	Frequency	Frequency (L)	Frequency (R)	MI score	T-score
40	troll	4	2	2	7.489	(N/S)

Something to be careful of with this collocational analysis is the fact that *trophy* collocates with *trophy*. This is because of how the data is structured—multiple trophies are discussed next to each other (as they are collectable items).

One of the most striking things about Table 6.11 is the number of monsters which are statistically significant collocates of *trophy* (as mentioned, 5 were gendered but there were 17 monsters as collocates). Indeed, a concordance line analysis revealed that these monsters, or at least body parts of these monsters, were collectable trophies. For example:

> The witcher learned that the **female troll** had been killed by one Dmitri, who then sold **her head** as a **trophy** to Sendler (The Witcher 2)
> Take a **trophy** from the **shrieker.** Investigate the site of the monster's attack using your Witcher Senses. (The Witcher 3)

Of the 17 words which denoted a monster whose body parts are trophies for the character, 5 are exclusive terms for female monsters, and none are exclusive terms male monsters. This is to say that monsters such as *troll* could refer to male and female trolls, but in folklore and mythos *sirens* are exclusively gendered as women.[4] Furthermore, the only gendered pronouns which occur in this list are both male pronouns. Initially, this could suggest some male dominance and entitled ownership over female (monster) bodies. Indeed, concordance lines for these pronouns and the word *trophy* suggest as much:

> **He** went off to see the alderman, brandishing **his** newly won **trophy**. The Harpy Queen. (The Witcher 2)

[4] There are a number of monsters that could have been included which are gendered as male social actors, such as *incubi* or a *satyr.*

When **he** showed the beekeeper the **trophy he** had **taken** from the hound, he received a handsome reward. (The Witcher 3)

However, it is important to remember that the main playable character is male, and references to his previous actions may have also encouraged this use of pronouns. Indeed, both examples above reference Geralt taking the trophy.

With regard to the statistics, it is also interesting to see how by MI-score the female monsters surpass Durrant and Doherty's (2010) suggestion of an MI $\geq$ 6 but not the suggestion of a T-score threshold of $\geq$ 7.5. Thus, it is possible to argue that, with regard to collocational strength, these terms are worth examining as they appear to meet the criteria for being 'psychologically meaningful'. Nevertheless, all the monsters are considered statistically significant by the traditional thresholds. One area for debate is the inclusion of the word *he* as a statistically significant collocate. By the traditional threshold of MI $\geq$ 3, *he* was significant, but by T-score it was not. This collocate has been included even though it only passed one statistical significance threshold. However, given the frequency of collocates which denoted female monsters (in addition to the high MI-scores they exhibited), the following section focuses on these as opposed to the male pronouns.

A collocational network analysis confirmed that female monsters were discussed with regard to their status as collectable trophies. A collocational network is a visual representation of multiple collocates, using lines to indicate which words frequently occur near or next to one another (Brezina et al., 2015; see also Heritage & Baker, 2021). I highlight this in Fig. 6.1, which shows a collocational network of the words *trophy* and *succubus*. Although only appearing within the top 150 keywords of *The Witcher 3*, in the full corpus, *trophy* is still key despite being below the arbitrary 150 cut-off the corpus as a whole. Across all three games, *trophy* occurs 88 times and has a log-likelihood value of 137.845 ($P \leq 0.00001$) while *succubus* occurs 65 times and has a log-likelihood value of 114.403 ($P \leq 0.00001$). Thus, *succubus* is also statistically key, even though it is not present in any of the keyword lists provided in this chapter as it is below the 150 cut-off point.

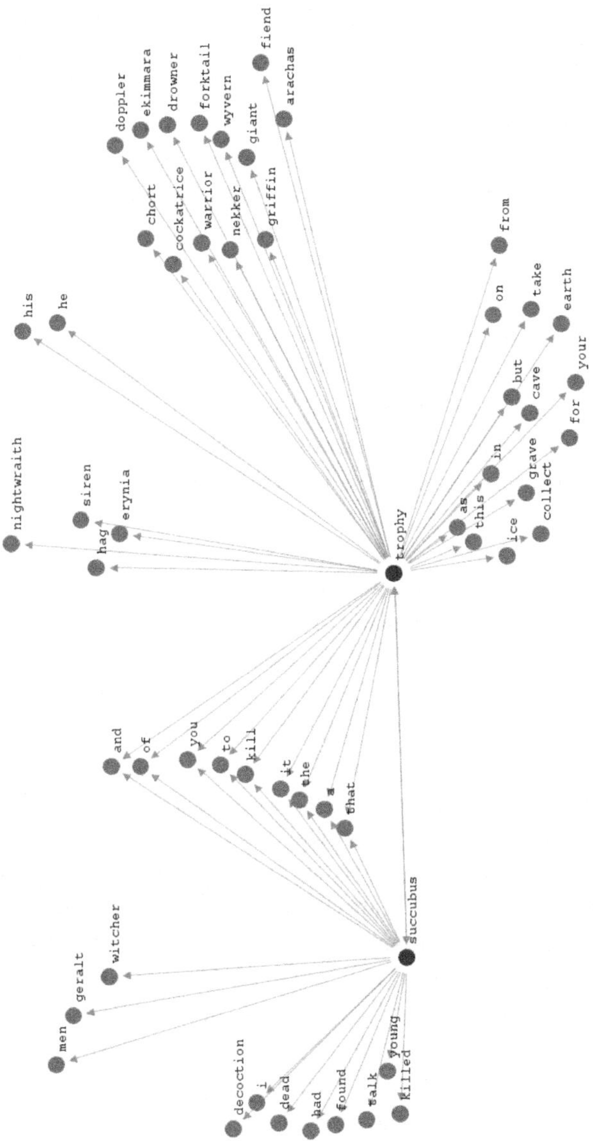

Fig. 6.1 The collocational networks of *trophy* and *succubus*

In Fig. 6.1, I have manually organised the collocates into male/female words, gender-neutral, and non-gendered groups. This has been done for ease of viewing. This is an important point for scholars not familiar with collocational networks. Usually, when a collocational network is provided, it will place words randomly in relation to other collocates, and the closer they are to the node word would indicate the collocational strength. This has deliberately not been included here, because the semantic groups which the collocates belong to clearly demonstrate how gender biases can be linked to certain terms, and this point is more relevant than the collocational strength.

To some degree, this collocational network analysis confirms the need for caution and to consider the main character (*Geralt*), as his name and profession (*witcher*) are 2 of the 3 gendered collocates for the word *succubus*. The other gendered collocate, *men*, occurs due to the succubus' role in lore, to lure (typically heterosexual) men into sexual temptation and possibly death. This is also evidenced in the concordance lines for this collocation:

> Ele'yas hired the witcher to kill a succubus, a monster that seduced and killed young **men**. The **succubus**, however, claimed that the jealous elf was actually the murderer. (The Witcher 2)

In scholarly research which examines the roles of monsters in folklore and fantasy literature, some argue that the character of a succubus has been represented in problematic ways. As Cunningham (2016) states, female defiance of stereotypical sex roles is a trope associated with 'monsters' in the horror genre, such as the brides of Dracula, who attempt to seduce Jonathan Harker into both sexual temptation and death (see Stoker, 1897). Furthermore, women who do this are positioned on the negative side of a dichotomy, where they are the 'villain' and the main character is the 'hero'. Some scholars would thus argue that succubi are problematic from the onset as they are set to deviate from stereotypical gender roles and will become villains.

Yet, it appears as though characters like the *succubus* are even more problematic and multi-layered than simply defying stereotypical roles. The inclusion of such a monster may enforce a heteronormative idea that a woman's body and sexual prowess has power over men and that this power can lure men to their demise (see Rudman & Glick, 2012, p. 254). Within the context of *The Witcher* games, the character is also problematic because a male equivalent of the succubus, an incubus, does not occur.[5] This lack of a character ignores the sexual desires and fantasies of women and men who are sexually attracted to men. Interestingly, even though there are queer female characters, none are lured by the succubus, thus adding to a problematic and archaic ideology that women's bodies are to be used for the sexual gratification of heterosexual men (Rudman & Glick, 2012, pp. 253–256). Indeed, this use of perceived heterosexuality could play a role in 'maintaining the gender hierarchy that subordinates women to men' (Cameron & Kulick, 2003, p. 45). Not only is the character of a succubus an inherently sexualised character, but her body is a trophy for the player to claim.

In order to further explore how succubi are represented within the game, the extended concordance lines for the term *succubus* were explored. The concordance lines demonstrate that men were often employed to deceive, ward off, or kill a succubus (20 out of 65 occurrences). For example:

> I'm to **get rid** of the **succubus** (The Witcher 1)
> That's precisely who I need to **lure** a **succubus** (The Witcher 2)
> Ele'yas hired The Witcher to **kill** a **succubus** (The Witcher 2)

Typically, the verbs used about succubi relate to the succubus being the recipient of some form of mental action (such as being lured) or a material action (such as being killed). They are not spoken to, or patients of similar processes, but they are acted upon or deceived (see also differences in verbs for transitivity in relation to gendered social actors in Chapter 5).

Furthermore, a close reading of concordance lines revealed succubui are presumed guilty of murder, and their punishment for this presumed crime is that they are to be deceived before being killed. Even if a succubus was innocent, some concordance lines suggest that their fate

[5] There were no results for this term in the corpus.

is more likely to be death than salvation (10 out of 65 occurrences). For example:

> This clue suggested that the succubus - **guilty or not** - was **too dangerous to be left alive** (The Witcher 2)

Concordance lines like this give weight to a negative representation of female monsters. Despite being autonomous within the videogames, the actions associated with female monsters like succubi, regardless of whether or not they are guilty of them, position women who break the conventional norms of society as evil and as though they deserve to be killed. It is wholly possible to represent monsters in positive or neutral ways—and indeed, other monsters within *The Witcher* series are represented in positive ways. For example, *godlings* are another monster within the series and are described as 'hard-working and clever creatures [who] gladly perform small services for those in their care' (The Witcher 3). Thus, negative representations of female monsters like the *succubus* is a choice made by the scriptwriters.

This finding raises questions about whether or not all trophies are presented in such a way, and about how other trophies can be gendered. Therefore, an additional concordance line analysis of the term *trophy* was conducted, which revealed that trophies are usually represented as positive things:

> **Great trophy** but hide it from women (The Witcher 1)
> **lovely trophy** though I'd prefer to see the head of some racist (The Witcher 1)

In both examples, the noun is pre-modified with positive adjectives to convey judgement on the trophy (i.e. 'great' and 'lovely'). The first example is particularly gendered and suggests that trophies are bloody and that women are too squeamish about viewing these. In turn, this reflects a stereotype of what women (dis)like.

Elsewhere in the concordance line analysis, it appeared as though it is usually the main character who is instructed to go and *take* a specific trophy (31 out of 88 occurrences):

Take a trophy from the **noonwraith** (The Witcher 3)
Take a trophy from the **water hag** (The Witcher 3)

In both these examples, the imperative forms are used and are likely to have come from people requesting the help of the main character. Though, it is also interesting to see the verb *take*, suggesting that there is some degree of entitled ownership, and as though the main male character will be stealing something that does not belong to him. Therefore, it is possible to suggest that the word *trophy* is typically positive, with players being pushed towards killing certain monsters in order to gain parts of their bodies as trophies. These body parts often come from monsters which are either exclusively female or monsters which could be either male or female. In other words, there are no trophies which come from male-only monsters (such as from an incubus).

With regard to how gender is used in relation to trophies, typically, it is assumed that a man would be the one to collect a *trophy*:

The cockatrice slain, **Geralt** took a **trophy** from its corpse (The Witcher 3)
any **man** who comes to me without a **trophy** shall receive no gold (The Witcher 3)
there's a **trophy** like that in my **uncle's** dining hall (The Witcher 1)

Indeed, this notion could echo archaic and problematic ideologies that men are the hunters/gatherers, while women stay at home. In the only times that language about female characters occurs with the word *trophy*, it is in a negative way (such as they are too squeamish about bearing the sight of a trophy or they themselves are the trophy), so this indicates that there is gender bias within the trophy reward system of the game.

Importantly, this work does also echo some of the work of Hunt (2015), in that the body parts are what become the trophies (even if it is less explicitly discussed). Therefore, body parts in relation to gendered social actors appear to be ways of examining how those characters are represented. While Hunt has used corpus methods to search for explicit terms relating to the body, this analysis has uncovered it through analysing a word which was not explicitly related to the body.

Conclusions

In this chapter, I demonstrated how an analyst might choose to employ corpus-driven methods to investigate how gender is represented in both individual games and across a videogame series. I primarily used keywords and the frequencies of these keywords, which indicated that at a quantitative level there are still unequal representations of gender—with words denoting male characters being more frequent than words denoting female characters. In comparison with the previous literature which has used visual content analysis, the findings presented in this chapter demonstrate that male characters are referred to more frequently than female characters. While previous visual content analyses showed that male characters might be up to four times more likely to occur than female characters, the findings of this chapter showed that they could be referred to up to 9.8 times more frequently than female characters. I also demonstrated how the analytical procedures were implemented with the analysis of the non-gendered keyword *trophy*. I argued that by analysing this term and collocates/collocational networks of this term, it was possible to uncover a gender bias that some gender/sexuality scholars may have otherwise overlooked.

Although *trophy* is ostensibly a non-gendered word, I demonstrated that *trophy* had gendered associations, and these associations are problematic. This led to a further analysis of one of the female monsters which collocated with *trophy*—*succubus*. A collocational network analysis revealed that this monster was discussed in relation to men and being possessed by men. Often, non-gendered words like *trophy* are overlooked by gender scholars because they do not inherently suggest anything to do with gender (see Swann, 2002). However, this chapter has shown the need to also consider non-gendered words for their gendered associations, as collocates and collocational networks could reveal that non-gendered words are used for gendered concepts (similar to Hunt's, 2015 work on how seemingly non-gendered body parts showed that there was some gender bias in the *Harry Potter* series). However, beyond this, I have also demonstrated some of the ways keyword lists can be separated by how they represent gender.

Ultimately, this chapter has demonstrated multiple ways that people might want to approach the representation of gender within a videogame series such as *The Witcher*. I have demonstrated that the application of corpus methods allows an analyst to go beyond what can be gained through a visual content analysis alone.

I have also demonstrated that there are diachronic changes in how gender has been represented in the past 8 years, which in turn has a number of implications for what texts should be analysed. Should it be the case, therefore, that we have to be even more careful with what videogames we analyse? 8 years may not seem like a long time, but as shown in this chapter, even at a quantifiable level, there were several changes in how gender is represented. In the next chapter, I explore diachronic change in a videogame series in more detail. I take two versions of the same online game. Since 2004, the videogame has continued to develop, with new expansions being added every 2–3 years. The first version was initially released in 2004 but re-released in 2019. Language, representations, and play mechanics were kept the same as when it was initially released. I contrast how gender is represented in this re-released version of the game to the 2018 'live' version of the videogame. Therefore, I examine the difference a 15-year gap within the same videogame can create.

Ludography

CD Projekt Red. (2007). *The Witcher*. Warsaw, Poland: CD Projekt Red.
CD Projekt Red. (2011). *The Witcher 2: Assassination of Kings*. Warsaw, Poland: CD Projekt Red.
CD Projekt Red. (2015). *The Witcher 3: Wild Hunt*. Warsaw, Poland: CD Projekt Red.

Bibliography

Baker, P. (2006). *Using corpora in discourse analysis*. Bloomsbury.
Baker, P. (2014). *Using corpora to analyse gender*. Bloomsbury.

Beasley, B., & Collins Standley, T. (2002). Shirts vs. skins: Clothing as an indicator of gender role stereotyping in video games. *Mass Communication & Society, 5*(3), 279–293.

Bergstrom, K., Jenson, J., & de Castell, S. (2012). What's 'choice' got to do with it? Avatar selection differences between novice and expert players or World of Warcraft and Rift. In *Proceedings of the International Conference on the Foundations of Digital Games* (pp. 97–104).

Brezina, V., McEnery, T., & Wattam, S. (2015). Collocations in context: A new perspective on collocation networks. *International Journal of Corpus Linguistics, 20*(2), 139–173.

Brown, F. (2020). *The Witcher series hits 50 million sales*. PC Gamer. https://www.pcgamer.com/uk/the-witcher-series-hits-50-million-sales/. Accessed February 2021.

Burgess, M., Stermer, S., & Burgess, S. R. (2007). Sex, lies, and video games: The portrayal of male and female characters on video game covers. *Sex Roles, 57*(5–6), 419–433.

Buss, S. (2005). Valuing autonomy and respecting persons: Manipulation, seduction, and the basis of moral constraints. *Ethics, 11*(5), 195–135.

Cameron, D., & Kulick, D. (2003). *Language and sexuality*. Cambridge University Press.

Coffey-Glover, L. (2019). *Men in women's worlds: Constructions of masculinity in women's magazines*. Palgrave Macmillan.

Csimbi (2012). *Csimbi's tools* [computer software]. Csimbi's tools. https://sites.google.com/site/csimbi/home. Accessed February 2021.

Clark, T. (2019). *Netflix's 'The Witcher' dethroned 'The Mandalorian' as the biggest TV series in the world*. Business Insider. https://www.businessinsider.com/witcher-passed-mandalorian-as-biggest-tv-show-in-the-world-2019-12?r=US&IR=T. Accessed February 2021.

Cunningham, L. (2016). Queerness and the undead female monster. In C. Miller & A. Bowdoin Van Riper (Eds.), *The laughing dead: The horror-comedy film from bride of Frankenstein to Zombieland* (pp. 154–168). Rowman and Littlefield.

Durrant, P., & Doherty, A. (2010). Are high frequency collocations psychologically real? Investigating the thesis of collocational priming. *Corpus Linguistics and Linguistic Theory, 6*(2), 125–155.

Gestos, M., Smith-Merry, J., & Campbell, A. (2018). Representation of women in videogames: A systematic review of literature in consideration of adult female wellbeing. *Cyberpsychology, Behavior, and Social Networking, 21*(9), 535–541.

Gibbed. (2015). *Gibbed red tools*. Nexus Mods. https://www.nexusmods.com/witcher2/mods/768/. Accessed February 2021.

Grubb, J. (2020). *Netflix's 'The Witcher' helps fuel 554% growth in The Witcher 3 sales*. Venturebeat. https://venturebeat.com/2020/02/13/witcher-netflix-game-sales. Accessed February 2021.

Heritage, F. (2021). *Maidens and monsters: A corpus Assisted critical discourse analysis of the representation of gender in The Witcher videogame series* (Doctoral dissertation, Lancaster University).

Heritage, F., & Baker, P. (2021). Crime or culture?: Representations of chemsex in the British press and magazines aimed at GBTQ + men. *Critical Discourse Studies*. Advanced online publication: https://doi.org/10.1080/17405904.2021.1910052.

Heritage, F., & Koller, V. (2020). Incels, in-groups, and ideologies: The representation of gendered social actors in a sexuality-based online community. *Journal of Language and Sexuality, 9*(2), 152–178.

Holroyd, J. (2009). Relational autonomy and paternalistic interventions. *Res Publica, 15*(1), 321–336.

Hunt S. (2015). Representations of gender and agency in the harry potter series. In: P. Baker & T. McEnery (Eds.), *Corpora and discourse studies: Integrating discourse and corpora* (pp. 266–284). Palgrave Macmillan.

Ivory, J. (2006). Still a man's game: Gender representation in online reviews of video games. *Mass Communication & Society, 9*(1), 103–114.

Jones, O. (2020). Boris Johnson's message to the working class: good luck out there. *The Guardian*. https://www.theguardian.com/commentisfree/2020/may/12/boris-johnson-working-class-good-luck. Accessed February 2021.

Krendel, A. (2020). The men and women, guys and girls of the "manosphere": A corpus-assisted discourse approach. *Discourse & Society, 31*(6), 607–630.

Milani, T. (2013). Are 'queers' really 'queer'? Language, identity and same-sex desire in a South African online community. *Discourse & Society, 24*(5), 615–633.

Miller, M., & Summers, A. (2007). Gender differences in video game characters' roles, appearances, and attire as portrayed in video game magazines. *Sex Roles, 57*(9–10), 733–742.

Paaßen, B., Morgenroth, T., & Stratemeyer, M. (2017). What is a true gamer? The male gamer stereotype and the marginalization of women in video game culture. *Sex Roles, 76*(7), 421–435.

Partington, A., Duguid, A., & Taylor, C. (2013). *Patterns and meanings in discourse: Theory and practice in corpus-assisted discourse studies (CADS)*. John Benjamins.

Pearce, M. (2008). Investigating the collocational behaviour of MAN and WOMAN in the BNC using Sketch Engine. *Corpora, 3*(1), 1–29.

Rudman, L. A., & Glick, P. (2012). *The social psychology of gender: How power and intimacy shape gender relations*. Emerald Group Publishing.

Sapkowski, A. (1992). *Sword of destiny* (Miecz przeznaczenia). English edition: 2015. Gollancz.

Sapkowski, A. (1993). *The last wish (Ostatnie życzenie)*. English edition: 2007. Gollancz.

Sapkowski, A. (1994). *Blood of elves (Krew elfów)*. English edition: 2009. London: Gollancz.

Sapkowski, A. (1995). *Time of Contempt (Czas pogardy)*. English edition: 2013. Gollancz.

Sapkowski, A. (1996). *Baptism of fire (Chrzest ognia)*. English edition: 2014. Gollancz.

Sapkowski, A. (1997). *The tower of swallows (Wieża Jaskółki)*. English edition: 2016. Gollancz.

Sapkowski, A. (1999). *Lady of the lake (Pani Jeziora)*. English edition: 2017. Gollancz.

Scharrer, E. (2004). Virtual violence: Gender and aggression in video game advertisements. *Mass Communication & Society, 7*(4), 393–412.

Scott, M. (2016). *WordSmith tools version 7*. Lexical Analysis Software.

Sinclair, J. (2004). *Trust the text: Language, corpus and discourse*. Routledge.

Stoker, B. (1897). *Dracula*. Archibald Constable and Company.

Swann, J. (2002). Yes, but is it gender?. In L. Litosseliti & J. Sunderland (Eds.), *Gender identity and discourse analysis* (pp. 43–67). John Benjamins.

Taylor, C. (2013). Searching for similarity using corpus-assisted discourse studies. *Corpora, 8*(1), 81–113.

Taylor, C. (2016). *Mock politeness in English and Italian: A corpus-assisted metalanguage analysis*. John Benjamins.

Toh, W (2015). *A multimodal discourse analysis of video games: A ludonarrative model* (Doctoral dissertation, National University of Singapore).

van Leeuwen, T. (2008). *Discourse and practice: New tools for critical discourse analysis*. Oxford University Press.

Yee, N., Ducheneaut, N., Yao, M., & Nelson, L. (2011). Do men heal more when in drag?: conflicting identity cues between user and avatar. In *Proceedings of the SIGCHI conference on Human factors in computing systems* (pp. 773–776). Association for Computing Machinery.

Zaitsev, D. (2015). *Lua Utilis for the Witcher 3*. Github: https://github.com/hhrhhr/Lua-utils-for-Witcher-3. Accessed February 2021.

7

Gendered Character Speech in *World of Warcraft*

Beware the Daughter of the Sea

It is 2018 and I get a notification on my phone: there is a new video that the friends I am with (who are also avid gamers) and I must watch immediately. We scurry about to turn out the lights, load up the video, and a ghostly woman's voice starts to echo through the room: '"Beware, beware the Daughter of the Sea". "Beware", I heard him cry. His words carried upon the ocean breeze as he sank beneath the tide'. We sit in silence, our mouths almost on the floor amazed at the beauty of the video, which continues in the form of a sea shanty sung by deep male voices about someone called 'the Daughter of the Sea'. It comes to an end and we hear the ghostly woman's voice return to whisper 'Beware, beware the Daughter of the Sea. Beware, beware, of me'. We sat in silence, in shock and awe, at the beauty of this new promotional video for the next expansion of *World of Warcraft* (see Gregory, 2018).

In this chapter, I turn to explore how gender is represented through what gendered characters say. The video I indicated above demonstrates two different ways gender can be constructed through language: the first is a representation of 'the daughter' of the sea—whom we can suggest

F. Heritage, *Language, Gender and Videogames*,
https://doi.org/10.1007/978-3-030-74398-7_7

is someone to be wary of. We could probably say there is some sort of gendered representation going on here (though, we would need more data to do a full-scale analysis). However, there is also a second representation here: at points, the ghostly woman is speaking about herself (in this case, the ghostly woman is a main character called Lady Jaina Proudmore). We can thus look at how individual characters who are gendered use language and what they talk about.

The previous two chapters examined how characters were represented in videogames by looking at the language around gendered terms and how frequently gendered characters appeared. These methods of examining representation are useful because they also remove some of the essentialist bias associated with earlier research into language and gender (e.g. Lakoff, 1973, 1975). However, there is an undeniably large body of research which does examine how men and women speak, and the implications of these ways of speaking (see, e.g., Baker, 2014; Baxter, 2014; Kitzinger, 2009).

Men and Women Speak

Within the study of language and gender, there is a deep history of looking at how men and women speak. These examinations also have a history of being intertwined with variationist sociolinguistics (see, e.g., Tannen, 1990, 1994). Variationist sociolinguistics is concerned with the idea that there are reasons for variations in language, and one of these reasons might be due to the differences in the gender identities of the speaker(s) (see, Van Herk, 2012). However, this idea has been criticised because this notion makes it easy to not only homogenise entire groups, but also allows analysts to be relatively essentialist in their approach to language and gender (essentialism is discussed in subsequent paragraphs, but see Giora, 2002 for a discussion of these critiques; see also Chapter 2). There is thus a constant tension when examining the language used by people of certain identities—because there might be quantifiable differences which are caused because of gender identity, the way people of those identities have been socialised, and what they believe the social expectations are for themselves. However, we cannot claim that all these people will be representative of all others with those identities, and so while we can see patterns across data sets, we regularly have to be careful when looking at language usage rather than representations. In order to understand this problem further, we first need to understand the idea of essentialism.

Although I mentioned and touched upon essentialist ideas earlier, it is worth fleshing out this concept before we can fully appreciate the critiques of it. To appreciate this idea, we need to return to the work of Plato and Aristotle—specifically their work on forms and essences. Building on Plato's work relating to how we experience reality, Aristotle argued that there are some attributes that are necessary to the identity or function of a given entity. An essential property of a triangle, for instance, is that the sum of its internal angles amounts to 180 degrees (this example is discussed in more detail in White, 1972). Applied to gender identity, this could be demonstrated by phraseological constructions such as 'you have "x" feature; you must therefore be "y" gender'. However, there is a growing body of research which suggests that 'x' feature and 'y' identities are never stable categories (see Bing & Bergvall, 1996), mismatches regularly occur, and there are several ways that these ideas can be defied. A non-linguistic example of an essentialist ideology as manifested through language use might be if someone says/believes that if 'you have a penis; you must therefore be male'. There are several transgender/non-binary people with penises, and so the linking of these two is redundant. Outside of this, there are also people who were born intersex who might have penises that do not match their identities. If a man were to lose his penis in an accident, he would probably still consider himself and man and be considered a man by others. These examples demonstrate that the link between categories, as they relate to gender, is unstable (see also Butler, 1990).

We can demonstrate this and problematise essentialist ideas a step further and apply this notion to the way people speak—does this mean that men with high-pitched voices are actually women? Does this mean because women were 'born that way', that they cannot swear? The answer to both of those questions is a resounding 'no'. Our physiological makeup does not impact the way we use language at a lexical or grammatical level. It might possibly affect how we can sound—but a number of drag queens can demonstrate how problematic viewing pitch as an indicator of identity is, as many are also able to modulate their voice in order to conform or reject ideals associated with gender and pitch, and some can regularly do this in a split second (see, e.g., Barrett, 2017).

So, now we have covered why focusing on how people use language can be problematic, it is now worth turning to examine why it can be beneficial. We can use how people speak to examine how people approach certain topics and get at underlying ideologies that they may have towards these topics. Levon (2015) demonstrates how tone and pitch can get to underlying ideologies towards identity in his work on sexuality and sociolinguistics in Israel. In his work, he draws attention to Igal, a 40-year-old orthodox Jewish man who, despite being married to a woman and having children, has sex with men. Levon argues that this participant's use of a phenomenon called creaky voice was a way of negotiating the conflict between his sexual and religious identities. Therefore, we can see that the language features used by this individual occur when his identity is negotiated. This is much more in-depth and provides a more nuanced account for examining identity construction through language rather than saying 'this person uses creaky voice so must have sex with men'.

Elsewhere, others have examined speech styles of female leaders (see, e.g., Baxter, 2012; Holmes & Schnurr, 2006). This kind of research examines the use of 'masculine' and 'feminine' styles of communication, with a view of looking at how stereotypes associated with the way men/women speak are conformed to/rejected in certain situations. For example, there are some occasions where female leaders feel they need to use humour and irony via speech styles associated with masculinity, while other occasions may call for a more feminine style. Important in this kind of work is that the analysts do not examine 'women's language' (Lakoff, 1975, p. 43), but rather examine interactional styles of these women. Something that previous analysis has done very well is to acknowledge that even the women who use these speech styles can change their style depending on the context and that even within the same context different people might use different speech styles (see, e.g., Baxter, 2012).

In a similar vein, Baker (2014) used corpus methods to examine how female academics negotiated conflict in classroom settings, and how they would phrase their disagreements during conflicts in order to appear less offensive. Ultimately, he argues that the ways the women in his corpus negotiated disagreement was varied, and although there were some overarching similarities, Baker also draws attention to the fact that it was not possible to draw conclusive arguments about a set style of disagreement. This again speaks to the importance of considering individual differences and the need to consider different contexts.

However, where this chapter and the previous research differs is that previous researchers have examined living participants—participants who are naturally producing language, or are producing language in as close to a naturalistic environment as one might reasonably expect under the pretence of being recorded for an academic study. When we examine how gendered characters in videogames speak, the dynamics change. Scriptwriters have the chance to edit language before the player encounters it. Once an initial sentence is written, they are able to go back and change speech styles they think are not 'masculine' or 'feminine' enough, and ultimately are able to show how they believe characters 'should' speak. Although I have previously critiqued the study for its ambiguous methodology, Goorimoorthee et al.'s (2019) work on accent distribution in the *Dragon Age: Origins* videogame (Bioware, 2009) demonstrates this point well with regard to racialised characters. They argued that different races would use different accents and that the representation of accents constituted subconscious 'othering' of certain races within the videogame. In other words, the language presented to players is something which is carefully constructed by the directors and scriptwriters. The language can be edited if these people in a position of power believe that it is not appropriate to their visions (this point is similar to the issues in magazine articles, discussed in Jeffries, 2007). Therefore, what is said by gendered characters is a way of representing how the scriptwriters (in a position of power) believe how people of that gender should/would speak in those contexts, and this can be repeated throughout the game.

Rather than examining phonological features (something which is very hard to do with a corpus), this chapter examines speech styles of male and female characters. In particular, in this chapter, I use data from the Massively Multiplayer Online Role-Playing Game (MMORPG) *World of Warcraft* (*WoW*)(Blizzard, 2004–onwards).

World of Warcraft: Background

Warcraft: Orcs & Humans (Blizzard, 1994) is a real-time strategy (RTS) game. In the game, the player takes the role of either the Human inhabitants of Azeroth or the invading Orcs. Players are given a number of objectives, such as building items, collecting materials, or destroying objects, ultimately with the aim of defeating the opposing army. The game was so popular that it spawned two additional sequels, each with an additional expansion: *Warcraft II: Tides of Darkness* (Blizzard, 1995), which came with the expansion game *Warcraft II: Beyond the Dark Portal* (1996), and *Warcraft III: Reign of Chaos* (2002), which came with the expansion *Warcraft III: The Frozen Throne* (Blizzard, 2003). There were several stories involved within these RTS games and, considering the story has been written into several books, graphic novels, and videogames, it is not possible to cover all of the lore of this videogame series within such a short space.

These games were hugely successful at the time they were released, which ultimately led Blizzard to create an MMORPG based around them. Thus, in 2004, *WoW* was born. *Wow* was a 3D representation of the *Warcraft* universe. To describe all the gameplay mechanics would not be possible within this space, but to give some context, I will attempt to summarise the basic choices players had to make. Players had to create their own characters, which could be either male or female. They were able to pick one of nine classes (druid, hunter, mage, paladin, priest, rogue, shaman, warlock, warrior) and one of eight races (discussed subsequently). Certain classes could only be played if the player's character was a certain race, such as how only human characters could be paladins, or how if a player wanted to play as a druid they could only play as a night elf or tauren. When players came to pick what race they wanted their character to be, they also had to consider the 'faction' to which that race was aligned. The player could join either the Alliance (by selecting a human, dwarf, gnome, or night elf), or the Horde (by selecting an orc, troll, tauren, or undead). The Alliance and the Horde were enemies and would regularly fight against each other. This meant that if players chose a character who was in the Horde, they would not have access to storylines only available to members of the Alliance and vice versa.

Similarly, there were certain quests and storylines that only people of a particular class could gain access to, so the choices a player made at the very beginning of the game were clearly very important.

At the time of release, *WoW* received high praise—earning a total of 93/100 on Metacritic (Metacritic, 2004). With fan websites tracking the metrics of subscribers, it was assumed that 8 million subscriptions were active by the end of the first version of the game (referred to as *Vanilla WoW*) (see Gamasutra, 2011). Since *Vanilla WoW*, there have been an additional eight expansions (at the time of writing) and at one point, *WoW* had amassed more than 12 million subscribers.

WoW, and communities who play *WoW*, have since been the subject of extensive academic investigation. These investigations span a number of fields, ranging from medicine (see, e.g., Balicer, 2007; Lofgren & Fefferman, 2007) to theorycraft—i.e. looking at how people apply theoretical mathematical models to in-game results (see, Paul, 2011), and, importantly for this book, to language and gender studies (see Braithwaite, 2014; Ensslin, 2012). In particular, within the linguistic research into *WoW*, Braithwaite's (2014) research investigated attitudes towards feminism via how players of *WoW* discussed a character whose language was changed from the beta to 'live' version of the game, in order to be more gender-inclusive. Ensslin (2012) similarly examined how players use metaphors about gender on an online forum dedicated to *WoW*. However, these studies have typically focused on the language around *WoW* (see Chapter 2).

Therefore, this chapter attempts to examine how language has been used within *WoW*, with particular regard to how gendered characters enact certain speech styles. However, before this can be fully discussed, first, I will outline and justify the data used in the corpora.

WoW Quests

In *WoW*, players are given 'quests' from non-playing characters (NPCs). These NPCs are typically represented through gendered bodies—i.e. there are typically male and female avatars. While there are some characters and races which may exist outside of this perceived gender binary, it is fair to say that the vast majority of humanoid characters fall into this distinction. Additionally, characters are typically not discussed in terms of being transgender or non-binary. In fact, it was not until the *Shadowlands* expansion (2020) that Blizzard introduced the first transgender character to the series (WoWhead, 2020a).

These NPCs (and a few items in the game) would occasionally have a yellow '!' above them. This would mean that the player could click on that character (or less frequently item) to receive a 'quest' (i.e. a task for the player to complete). There is a vast range of quests, including (but not limited to) taking medicine to another character in a different location, killing a boss, or collecting 'x' amount of flowers. Broadly speaking, these quests are tasks that the player completes in order to receive experience points (which allows them to level up), gold (used as in-game currency), items/objects that may make playing the game easier in some way, or a combination of the three.

In both of the versions of *WoW* which are used in this chapter (discussed in a later section), there were about 850–1,000 quests per faction (WoWhead, 2020b, 2020c). These quests were scattered throughout the playable world, and so a number of players may have only completed a handful of these. While there were some quests which could be taken by any faction (or were re-written for the opposing faction), there were also some quests that one faction could complete but the other could not. Therefore, the questing experience of all players can be different, and while there may be some quests which the majority of one faction completed, these are not necessarily universal experiences.

When a player collects a quest from an NPC, they would be presented with an initial 'description' dialogue box. This would give the player an indication of what task(s) needed to be completed, and clues as to where to complete them. Players would then complete these tasks and return the quest to either the same or a different NPC, depending on the quest or task. Thus, there are also some important considerations to do with gender here: who is responsible for shaping the player's narrative? Who is setting tasks for the player? And who are they interacting with?

While undertaking the task that the quest giver hands to the player, they can talk to the NPC whom they would hand the quest to in the end—this will allow for a 'progress' dialogue, where the NPC will ask about the player's progress. Players are usually unable to respond to this. Finally, once the players have completed the quest, when they talk to whomever they hand the quest into (i.e. whom they speak to in order to complete the quest), they will also be presented with some additional dialogue.

These quests thus contribute to the immersion of the in-game world. They allow for information that the player would not normally get from just killing monsters in the forest. But more than that, they are ways to characterise gendered characters and ways to characterise members of certain races and factions.

What *WoW* Games to Analyse

One problem with *WoW*, from a researcher's perspective, is that it has such a rich history of expansions and these expansions reflect different views in society. When I started writing this monograph, the most recent expansion was *Battle for Azeroth* (2018–2020) (henceforth, I refer to this expansion as *BFA WoW*). However, while revising the manuscript, a new expansion, *Shadowlands* (2020) was released. This highlights a conundrum for linguistic researchers working with data that is regularly updated: do we take what is current when we are doing the work, or do we wait for the most up-to-date expansions?

I decided to take the former expansion for reasons of practicality. However, there was a second reason for choosing *BFA WoW*. Halfway through the *BFA WoW* expansion, Blizzard released *World of Warcraft Classic* (2019), a re-released version of the original game from 2004 to 2007 (henceforth, I refer to this re-release as *Classic WoW*). Blizzard had several opportunities here: they could have kept all the language from the original game the same as what was available to players (this was the option they went for), they could also have updated certain problematic quests, or they could have updated the game in its entirety. Given that Blizzard decided to keep everything the exact same as what players experienced 15 years prior, this, therefore, provides a perfect data set for diachronic comparison. Thus, I take *BFA WoW* not only because it was the most recent at the time data collection started, but also because it is likely to have been directly compared to *Classic WoW* given the time at which it was released. While it could be possible to take a sample of quests from each expansion and use these to see more incremental changes, by taking the greatest contrasting points in time it is possible to see the more 'extreme' differences.

Constructing the Corpus

In order to build the *WoW* corpus, I used the website *WoWHead*. As mentioned in Chapter 4, *WoWHead* asks players to install an add-on to their computer. When playing the game, this add-on scrapes the data a player interacts with, such as the language in quests. Therefore, the data is crowdsourced from thousands of players worldwide. This data is then stored on the website for others to access—usually to help them complete quests or find specific items.

For this analysis, I took two versions of *WoWhead*—one version which was dedicated to documenting the quests from *Classic WoW* and one version dedicated to *BFA WoW*. Within these, I was able to select whether or not the quests were available to Horde or Alliance players. For each faction, I then took 200 random quests. This meant that I took 400 quests from *Classic WoW* and 400 quests from *BFA WoW*.

Rather than take say 100 quests from female quest givers and 100 male quest givers (and then repeat this for each faction), I took these 400 at random, as this is a more accurate reflection of the kind of quests that players interact with. While it could be useful to take equal sample sizes of male and female quest givers, this does not reflect the state of gendered quest givers (i.e. doing so would ignore biases in terms of the frequencies at which players interact with avatars who have gendered bodies).

Once these distinctions were made, I sorted the quests available to each faction (this was a function available on *WoWhead*). Once I had selected the subset of quests I wanted *WoWhead* to display, the website displayed about 1000 quests for each faction, separated across 10 webpages on the website. Once this was done, for every webpage of 100 quests, I copied and pasted the titles of the quests into an excel file and assigned each quest title a sequential number (1–100). I then used a random number generator 20 times to randomly select which quests from each page would be included. I did this until I had 200 quests for each faction within each version of the game. Once I had narrowed down my subset of quests, I followed the links through to individual webpages for the quests. On *WoWhead*, the website is structured so as each quest has its own webpage, which details what language is shown to the player, who gives the quest, and who the quest is handed into.

I then copied and pasted the data on the website into separate text files. I then also used some basic XML tagging in order to better separate the different elements. I separated these elements into (1) the quest title, (2) the description (i.e. the text given to the player upon accepting the quest), (3) the progress text (i.e. the text given to the player after they have accepted the quest but before they complete the quest, including if they talk to the character before the requirements of the quest are met), and (4) the completion text (i.e. what is said to the character once they have met the requirements and just before they gain their rewards). These different parts of the quest were also tagged for the gender of who presents such text using the tag 'gender = "m/f/i"'. Here, 'm' relating to male characters saying the dialouge, 'f' relating to female characters, and 'i' relating to items. An example of a quest text and how it was structured in the corpus is below:

<quest title > Surena Caledon </quest title>
<description gender = "m">
I had a student named Surena Caledon. She stood where you stand now, eager to learn of warlock magic, and possessing no small bit of talent. More than that she was young and pleasing to the eye. Had I seen it then, the traitorous trollop!
The thieving wench ran off with one of the Defias, Erlan Drudgemoor. While her loss is of little importance, I gifted her a bloodstone choker that I must have.
Her life means nothing to me now. You will find her at the Brackwell Pumpkin Patch. Retrieve what is mine.
</description>
<progress gender = "m">

Even the older and wiser can be unmanned by the wiles of youth and beauty, [name]. A piece of advice you would do well to remember throughout your life.
</progress>
<completion gender = "m">
Surena was talented, but not enough so to gain mastery of [class] magic on her own. It's a shame to see talent wasted, but sometimes it is necessary.
I hope my investment in you will bear different results.
</completion>

In this example, note how '[name]' and '[class]' are placed in square brackets. This is because the code of the game allows these terms to be filled into match the player's character (even though this quest will obviously fill in [class] with 'warlock').

As can be seen in the above example, there is clearly gender bias within this quest alone—a male character is discussing how attractive he found a female character and then refers to her as 'the traitorous trollop'. Arguably more important than the interesting use of alliteration in this example is that this kind of representation of both men and women within the game could be considered problematic. A male character appears to be obsessed with a woman, pays particular attention to her physical appearance, uses derogatory terms towards her, and calls for her execution. If this kind of representation is normalised, this could further contribute towards negative societal views of women and could normalise ideas about what is acceptable to call women who wrong men. It is also problematic because it paints a woman as using her sexuality as a means to commit a crime (theft). However, as noted in Chapter 2, there is a need to analyse beyond just this quest alone (even though a lot of qualitative analysis could be conducted on it) and examine whether or not these trends run across quests.

In order to determine whether or not the person being spoken to was male, female, or an item (which I also used as a tag for other non-gendered humanoid beings), I looked up the character on *WoWhead*. When scraping the data from each quest's webpage, there was almost always a hyperlink to show who gives the quest and to whom the quest

Table 7.1 Quest givers, quest receivers, and sizes for the *WoW* sub-corpora

Faction	Male quest giver	Female quest giver	Item quest giver	Male quest receiver	Female quest receiver	Item quest receiver	Word count
	Classic WoW						
Alliance	155	36	9	160	35	5	26,831
Horde	160	32	8	166	31	3	26,447
	BFA WoW						
Alliance	116	69	15	115	79	6	18,065
Horde	129	64	7	126	71	3	18,440
TOTAL	560	201	39	567	216	17	89,783

is handed. Usually, the character was obviously gendered, but if I could not tell, I searched other quest texts that referred to that character and examined the pronouns used for that character. In one case, I also went and found the NPC using my character. Something else to be wary of is that in the later games, Blizzard added in 'world quests', which were quests which would automatically appear on the player's screen. Players could also occasionally hand quests in without seeing an NPC. These 'world quests' were excluded from the *BFA WoW* corpus.

Once I had done this across all 800 quests, I was able to extract all the details relating to who gives quests and to whom quests are handed in. These details, along with the size of each corpus, are outlined in Table 7.1.

Frequencies of Who Is Interacted With

The initial frequencies suggest that male characters are more likely to give and receive quests. In the samples taken from both factions in *Classic WoW*, 77.5–80% of the quest givers were male, while 80–83% of the people quests were handed into were male characters. Comparatively, only 16–18% of the quest givers in *Classic WoW* were female characters, while 15.5–17.5% received the quest. Clearly, in *Classic WoW*, players were much more likely to interact with male characters in comparison to female characters. The difference in how frequently male characters are interacted with in comparison to female characters suggests an unequal representation at a quantitative level. If players are only ever engaging with male characters, they may conceptualise the 'default' *WoW* NPC as a male avatar—which in turn normalises the backgrounding of female characters.

There has also been an obvious diachronic change across the two versions of *WoW*—with many more women giving quests in *BFA WoW* in comparison to *Classic WoW*. In the sample taken from *BFA WoW*, 58-64.5% of quests were given by male characters, and 57.5–63% were accepted by male characters. By contrast, 32–34.5% of the characters who gave quests were women (an increase of approximately 100%). Similarly, in terms of female characters who receive quests, this has increased to 35.5–39.5% of the sample (an increase of 129%).

Another area to consider is the gendered characters across factions. In this sampling, I only elected to include quests which were specific for Horde or Alliance—rather than quests which could be taken by both Horde **and** Alliance. This was to see whether differences were created by different factions—something particularly important considering in *Classic WoW* the leaders of the Alliance and Horde were both men, while in *BFA WoW* one leader was a woman and one was a man. Therefore, one of the reasons why I separated the corpus by faction was in case this change to one faction being led by a female character had a causational effect on the frequency of women who gave quests—and it did not appear to (in both *Classic WoW* and *BFA WoW* there are actually fewer female Horde characters who give and receive quests than female Alliance characters).

However, there might be some causational effect between one of two interconnected variables. First: there may be more women giving quests because more women may have been included in *WoW*. This would not be surprising, considering there have been 15 years of feminist critiques of videogames. Second: in comparison to *Classic WoW*, in *BFA WoW* there are more female leaders of each race (who are also likely to provide the player with quests). In *Classic WoW*, there was one leader for each race comprising the Alliance and Horde (8 in total)—of these leaders there was one female leader in each faction. In *BFA WoW* there were a greater number of playable races (and each race still had its own leader(s), meaning there were more of them). In *BFA WoW* there were 11 playable races for each faction with an additional race which is neutral and can join either faction. Of these 11 playable races for each faction, 4 in each faction were led by female characters. Therefore, not only has there been an increase in the number of female quest givers/receivers interacted with, but also in the number of characters who are female leaders.

While the increase in how many women give and receive quests (as well as the increase in the number of female leaders) is good progress, there is still unequal representation at a quantifiable level. Indeed, even in *BFA WoW*, where women are much more represented in comparison to male quest givers, they are still about ½ as likely to give quests or receive quests. To some degree, this also calls back to the work discussed in Chapter 6. In Chapter 6, I demonstrated that there was a diachronic change in how frequently female characters were referred to—and I argued that while it is good that it is getting better, there is still a long way to go until a point of equality is achieved.

Who Says What?

While analysing these frequencies is useful—because it allows for a 'big data' overview that a researcher might not get if they took a small non-representative sample, it does not necessarily tell us about the language used by these characters. Is it the case that women of the Alliance only ever talk about things like flowers and magic? While male characters only talk about killing and brute strength? Is there a faction difference? And has anything changed?

There are several ways to go about answering these questions—but in the subsequent analysis, I take two different approaches. First, I take eight keyword lists for all the possible sub-corpora. These sub-corpora (variants) are listed below:

1. *Classic WoW*—male Alliance characters
2. *Classic WoW*—male Horde characters
3. *Classic WoW*—female Alliance characters
4. *Classic WoW*—female Horde characters
5. *BFA WoW*—male Alliance characters

6. *BFA WoW*—male Horde characters
7. *BFA WoW*—female Alliance characters
8. *BFA WoW*—female Horde characters.

This allows for an indication of what words are more likely to occur within each sub-corpus. While each corpus is only approximately 4,000–12,000 words, meaning that in theory each corpus could be manually read through, keeping track of this over c.90,000 words would probably be too difficult, and so the quantification offered by keyword lists might prove useful. In order to generate these keywords, unlike the research conducted in Chapter 6, I use the VG2014 corpus discussed in Chapter 5 as the reference corpus. One reason for this is because it is considerably bigger than the *WoW* sub-corpora, and in a similar genre. The second method I implement is tagging of semantic domains (discussed in a later section in more detail). Tagging for the semantic domains still uses corpus software but allows for a different picture of what semantic domains are being drawn on in characterisation.

What Do Women Talk About?

To start the analysis, I generated keyword lists for the language used by female characters. I used the same keyword statistics discussed in Chapters 3 and 6, apart from the minimum frequency of occurrence (this was set to 3, given the size of the corpora). For the sake of space, I have not reported on the different statistical levels here, though all words in the lists provided were statistically key. The top 20 keywords for each sub-corpora, as organised by statistical significance (BIC score), are listed below in Table 7.2.

One of the most noticeable changes between *Classic WoW* and *BFA WoW* is the increase in lexemes which approximate dialectal words using phonological spelling—such as *Tae* (approximating Scottish) or *De* (approximating Caribbean Jamaican English). The use of words which approximate the phonological aspects of Caribbean Jamaican English is particularly prevalent in the Horde speakers in *BFA WoW*. To some degree, this highlights the need to look at intersecting identities: not only

Table 7.2 Top 20 keyword lists for all Alliance and Horde female characters in *Classic WoW* and *BFA WoW*

Classic WoW				*BFA WoW*			
Alliance		Horde		Alliance		Horde	
Word	**Hits**	**Word**	**Hits**	**Word**	**Hits**	**Word**	**Hits**
Cenarion	7	Gelkis	8	We	104	De	114
Remedies	7	Xavian	7	Horde	16	Dat	39
Totem	6	Stonetalon	7	Coven	8	Dis	36
Salve	6	XT	6	Us	42	Loa	22
Corruption	8	Will	41	Our	47	Trolls	19
Speak	13	Ratchet	5	Will	53	Dey	13
Jer'kai	5	Hillsbrad	5	Tae	6	We	88
Marsh	5	Felwood	5	Tortollans	6	Blood	27
Will	39	Cenarion	5	Has	38	Zuldazar	9
Infliction	4	Venture	5	Ashvane	5	Horde	11
Gizmonitor	4	Ordanus	4	Jaina	5	Dese	8
Extracts	4	Morrowgrain	4	Pike	5	Jakra'zet	8
Vyletoungue	4	Zapper	4	Stormwind	4	Dem	8
Clasp	4	Serpentbloom	4	Tidesage	4	Will	54
Knowledge	9	Satyrs	4	Drust	4	Have	72
Spider	4	Shop	5	Scepter	4	Ben'jin	7
Gems	5	Awake	4	Azshara	4	Naga	9
Bring	13	Emberstrife	4	Ankoan	4	Ateena	6
Titans	3	Magram	4	Blighted	5	Talanji	5
Wool	3	Horns	5	Naga	**5**	Maka'fon	5

are the speakers women, but they are also more likely to be members of the Troll race—which typically use accents associated with Caribbean Jamaican English. This also opens up new lines of inquiry for sociolinguistic research—particularly with how dialectal features are conveyed in the language of videogames, how these map on to personalities, and whether there are any subtle (gendered) biases within these (also expanding on the work of Goorimoorthee et al., 2019).

Further, Alliance women in *Classic WoW* are more likely to use lexemes which relate to health care—such as *remedies*, and *salve*, while these do not appear in the keyword list for the Horde women in *Classic WoW* or the keyword list for women of either in *BFA WoW*. Thus, there could be a difference between what Alliance women in *Classic WoW* and what both Horde women in *Classic WoW* and Alliance women in *BFA WoW* were expected to talk about (this point about health care and healing lexis is discussed in more detail in a subsequent section of this chapter).

Women in *BFA WoW* are also more likely to talk about races—such as *Tortollans*, *Drust*, *Ankoan*, and *Naga* in comparison to women in *Classic WoW*. Neither Horde nor Alliance women in *Classic WoW* had words denoting a race within their top 20 keywords. This could possibly reflect the ever-growing nature of *WoW*, with several more (playable) races added, it is logical that members of those races will be spoken about. However, when contrasting these to what male characters talk about (discussed in a subsequent section), it appears as though women are more likely to talk about these races. This shows not only a difference between what women in *Classic WoW* spoke about but also a difference between what male and female characters in *BFA WoW* discuss (keywords for the language used by male characters are discussed in the next section).

A difference between female characters in *Classic WoW* and *BFA WoW* is that the keyword list generated from the language used by the female characters in *BFA WoW* was more likely to contain the names of characters who are central to the storyline. In *BFA WoW* these include names such as—*Ashvane*, *Jaina*, and *Talanji*. While the names of some characters appear in the keywords for both the Alliance and Horde women in *Classic WoW* (2 names in each keyword list—*Jer'kai* and *Vyletoungue* for the Alliance; *Xavian* and *Ordanus* for the Horde), these characters are not central. That is to say, the actions of the characters in the keyword lists for the language used by female characters in *BFA WoW* have a lasting impact on the narrative, such as how *Jaina* and *Talanji* become leaders of the Alliance and Horde (respectively). *Ashevane* and *Jaina* are both bosses, who require several players to beat. These kinds of characters are clearly different to low-level NPCs that provide a single quest (such as *Xavian*) or need to be killed as part of a low-level quest (such as *Ordanus*).

In terms of characters referenced, one element which is noticeable across both factions from a diachronic perspective is the fact that women in *BFA WoW* are more likely to reference a female leader—*Jaina* for the Alliance and *Talanji* for the Horde. Interestingly, both are magic users, and so it could be that the female leaders who get the most recognition are those who can use magic. I have previously argued (Heritage, 2020,

2021) that women in games are typically associated with magical powers, and male characters are associated with physical strength. Therefore, this kind of representation might be crossing over into leadership positions and referenced as such by gendered characters. An additional consideration is that each female leader is mainly referenced by women of the same faction—that is to say, women of the Alliance do not reference the magical strength of the female Horde leader (*Talanji*) and vice versa.

Across the Horde and Alliance, we see a number of similarities in both *Classic WoW* and *BFA WoW*. This is important given that a number of the exact words are not identical, but the concepts they denote are. This idea is discussed in more detail in a later section.

What Do Men Talk About?

While it can be useful to study 'x' social group's use of language in its own right, sometimes we need to be careful because 'y' feature might be caused by elements such as genre. Therefore, it can often be worthwhile comparing different social groups—in this case, it can be useful to compare how women speak to how men speak in *WoW*. In order to do this, the same process for the previous section was followed, and keyword lists for male characters are presented below in Table 7.3.

In comparison to female characters in *Classic WoW*, male characters appear to be more likely to talk about place names. In the keyword list for male Alliance characters in *Classic WoW*, 8/20 keywords are place names, while in the keyword list for male Horde characters in *Classic WoW*, 6/20 refer to place names. In *Classic WoW*, the keyword list for the women of the Alliance contained no place names, and the keyword list for women of the Horde contained four names.

This difference in reference to place names continues through to the keyword lists for men of both the Horde and Alliance in *BFA WoW*. In the keyword lists for Alliance women in *BFA WoW*, there were two references to place names. For Horde women in *BFA WoW*, there was only one word denoting a place name. By contrast, 6/20 of the keywords for male characters of the Alliance in *BFA WoW* refer to place names. However, only one word denotes a location in the keywords for male

Table 7.3 Top 20 keyword lists for all Alliance and Horde male characters in *Classic WoW* and *BFA WoW*

Classic WoW				*BFA WoW*			
Alliance		**Horde**		**Alliance**		**Horde**	
Word	**Hits**	**Word**	**Hits**	**Word**	**Hits**	**Word**	**Hits**
Stormwind	38	Will	222	Horde	22	De	200
Will	167	Horde	29	Jaina	14	Dis	63
Ogres	19	Bring	64	Our	80	Dat	53
Ironforge	17	Barrens	21	Kul	11	Loa	35
Bring	51	Scarlet	21	Ashvane	9	Dey	23
Hiccup	14	Scourge	22	Ritual	17	We	182
Uldaman	13	Must	87	Fate's	8	Trolls	24
Duskwood	13	Ashenvale	14	Zandalari	8	Dere	20
Kalimdor	12	Blackrock	13	Ram	9	Dem	20
Gnomergan	12	Lich	13	Boralus	7	Da	21
Troggs	12	Crusade	12	Irontide	7	Will	114
Darnassus	12	Lard	11	Tiras	7	Dese	18
Defias	11	Da	12	Brewfest	6	Blood	40
Must	74	Scholomance	10	Dagor	6	Zandalari	13
League	11	Orgrimar	10	Tol	6	Zuldazar	12
Cenarion	9	Warchief	10	Freehold	6	Zul	12
Thunderbrew	9	Pendant	12	Cannons	7	Horde	15
Explorers	9	Spirit	28	These	42	Titan	14
Morrowgrain	9	Venom	11	Pretties	5	Meat	16
Blackrock	8	Needles	9	Proudmoore	5	Hir'eek	10

characters of the Horde in *BFA WoW*. This is the same word found in the keyword list for women of the Horde in *BFA WoW*—*Zuldazar*. Therefore, it is possible to argue that, in terms of keywords denoting locations, there are greater differences in the keywords used between male and female characters of the Alliance in *BFA WoW* than members of the Horde.

One difference, in comparison to female characters of the Alliance in *Classic WoW* and male characters of both the Horde and Alliance in *BFA WoW*, is that male characters do not appear to reference items relating to healing. While I noted that female characters of the Alliance were likely to talk about *remedies* and *salve*(*s*), words denoting similar concepts did not appear in the keyword lists for male characters in *BFA WoW*. Therefore, there is a difference in what male characters were saying in both 2004–2006 and 2018–2020 compared to what female characters were saying in 2004–2006. Indeed, this use of language resonates with previous visual content analysis, which suggested that male characters were more likely to be blacksmiths and female characters were more likely to be herbalists (see Bergstrom et al., 2011).

For male characters of both the Horde and Alliance in *Classic WoW*, there are a number of keywords relating to foes—such as *ogres*, *troggs* (a kind of monster), and *Defias* (an enemy sect). The focus on enemies also continues through the keywords for the male characters of the Alliance from *Classic WoW* to *BFA WoW*, with some keywords relating to potential enemies—such as *Horde*, *Irontide*, and *Zandalari*. It should be noted, however, that some of these terms also occurred as keywords for female speakers of the Alliance in *BFA WoW*—such as *Drust*. Importantly, male characters of the Horde do not reference such enemies (with the possible exception of *Zul*, though *Zul* starts the storyline as a friendly character). Therefore, we might possibly draw the conclusion male characters in *Classic WoW* were more likely than female characters to talk about enemies. This has since changed, and female characters of the Alliance in *BFA WoW* (and male characters in *BFA WoW*) are now likely to also talk about enemies. Therefore, there are some changes, and one might argue that this is a step towards equality in *BFA WoW*.

For male Horde characters, there has been a similar shift to terms which approximate the phonological features of Jamaican English (similar to female characters of the Horde). The likely reason for this is the change in the storyline—from one which focuses on the Horde based in Kalimdor and the Eastern Kingdoms of Azeroth (the main world) to one which focuses on the Horde's campaign in Zandalar (the Troll empire). Interestingly, male characters of the Horde in BFA appear to use more dietic references using phonological approximation—both male and female characters share 6 dietic references in their keywords, but male characters also have two more—*dere* (there are) and *da* (the). Male characters of the Horde do not have their female leader's name in their keywords, but they do have the names of two male Loa[1] (*Hir'eek*

[1] Loa are not to be confused with the spirits associated with Haitian and Louisianan voodoo. In *WoW*, they are beats who are comparable to demi-gods.

and *Rezan*) and a male character who betrayed their faction (*Zul*). Therefore, even in *BFA WoW*, there are differences in what—and who—male and female characters of the Horde talk about.

Summary from Keywords

Given that there are 8 different sub-corpora, keeping track of these findings can be difficult. As such, it is worth highlighting some of the core takeaways from the analysis of what male and female characters talk about in both *Classic WoW* and *BFA WoW*. These findings can be summarised as follows:

1. Female Alliance characters in *Classic WoW* were more likely to talk about healing and nature
2. Female characters in *BFA WoW* (both Horde and Alliance) were more likely to talk about races than female characters in *Classic WoW*
3. Female characters in *BFA WoW* talk about more important named characters than female characters in *Classic WoW*
4. Female characters in *BFA WoW* talk about the female magic user who is a leader for their faction (i.e. Horde characters talk about *Talanji* and Alliance characters talk about *Jaina* but not vice versa).
5. In *BFA WoW,* male characters of the Alliance were more likely to talk about place names
6. Male characters are more likely to use terms to refer to enemies
7. There are words which are written to be read in accents. These phonological approximations occur across all data sets but are most prominent in male Horde characters.
8. Male characters of the Horde in *BFA WoW* reference Loa, but not their leader.

From Frequencies to Semantic Domains

I mentioned earlier that the above approach looks at keywords which denote similar concepts—and I manually categorised them into semantic categories (e.g. locations). However, I was only able to do this for keywords, which are typically frequent within a given corpus. This means that words which might be infrequent but denote similar concepts might not be captured. These similar concepts could paint a very different picture of what characters say—and the concepts they denote may not have shown up in the top 20 keywords. One way to combat this is to do an analysis of semantic domains instead. In order to generate the semantic domains which gendered characters draw upon, I conflated the language used by Horde and Alliance gendered characters in each version of the game. In other words, I made four files: one for male character's speech in *Classic WoW*, one for female character's speech in *Classic WoW*, one for male character's speech in *BFA WoW*, and one for female character's speech in *BFA WoW*.

Once these files were grouped together, they were individually uploaded into Wmatrix—an online piece of corpus software hosted at Lancaster University (see Rayson, 2008). Wmatrix contains two different automatic taggers for corpora: one is a POS (part of speech) tagger called CLAWS (see Fligelstone et al., 1997; Garside, 1987, 1996). CLAWS is able to detect the different grammatical senses which words are used in and has an approximately 96–97% rate of accuracy. This can be useful for certain forms of analysis—such as transitivity analysis. However, the second piece of software, which is used for the following analysis, is the USAS tagger. USAS is a multi-tier structured tagging system with 21 major discourse fields—which is further subdivided into subdivisions to allow for finer-grained quantification of semantic domains (see Piao et al., 2004, 2015; Wilson & Rayson, 1993).

This brought up a list of the most frequent semantic domains—of which, I took the top 20 for each sub-corpus. When doing this kind of analysis, the semantic tagger only shows the semantic tag name (e.g. M2 or Z3), which meant each had to be located in the tag-set. Once this was done, overly generic categories which would not help much in terms of semantic analysis (typically those within the Z category, such as Z5 (grammar bin) or Z99 (unmatched)) were removed. This then led to the top 20 categories for each sub-corpus, discussed below in Table 7.4.

Immediately, one noticeable difference in terms of the semantic field gendered characters draw on is that there is little semantic shift within

Table 7.4 Top 20 semantic domains for male and female character's speech in *Classic WoW* and *BFA WoW*

Female Characters		Male Characters	
Classic WoW	***BFA WoW***	***Classic WoW***	***BFA WoW***
Location and direction	Location and direction	Being	Being
Time: Future	Getting, giving, and possession	Location and direction	Location and direction
General actions	General actions	Getting, giving, and possession	Getting, giving, and possession
Moving, coming, and going	Time: Future	Time: Future	Time: Future
Obligation and necessity	Moving, coming, and going	Time: Past	Time: Past
Religion and the supernatural	Obligation and necessity	Moving, coming, and going	Negative
Putting, taking, and transporting	Negative	Obligation and necessity	Moving, coming, and going
Negative	Religion and the supernatural	Objects generally	Obligation and necessity
Helping/hindering	Anatomy and physiology	Religion and the supernatural	Putting, taking, and transporting
Evaluation: Good/bad	Religion and the supernatural	Putting, taking, and transporting	Religion and the supernatural
Anatomy and physiology	Life and living things	Anatomy and physiology	Power, organizing
Personal names	Physical attributes	Evaluation: Good/bad	Objects generally
Geographical terms	Putting, taking, and transporting	Power, organizing	Personal names
Power, organizing	Power relationships	Personal names	Helping/hindering
Knowledge	Thought and belief	Geographical terms	Living creatures generally

(continued)

Table 7.4 (continued)

Female Characters		Male Characters	
Living creatures generally	Investigate, examine, etc.	Knowledge	Anatomy and physiology
Quantities	Helping/hindering	Living creatures generally	Evaluation: Good/bad
Groups and affiliation	Evaluation: Good/bad	Calm/Violent/Angry	Warfare, defence and the army; Weapons
Places	Groups and affiliation	Education in general	Calm/Violent/Angry
Plants	Personal names	Warfare, defence and the army; Weapons	Crime, law and order: Law & order

each gendered group—that is to say, there are only a few semantic domains which are unique to each gendered group within each version of the game. Female characters draw on similar semantic domains in both *Classic WoW* and *BFA WoW*, as do male characters.

Female Characters' Semantic Domains

Female characters in both *Classic WoW* and *BFA WoW* shared 12 semantic domains. These were: Groups and affiliation; Personal names; Religion and the supernatural; Location and direction; Putting, taking, and transporting; Negative; Helping/hindering; Evaluation: Good/bad; General actions; Obligation and necessity; Anatomy and physiology; and Time: Future. In each version of the game, there were 8 semantic categories which were unique to the language used by women. In *Classic WoW*, these were: Places; Knowledge; Geographical terms; Living creatures generally; Moving coming, going; Plants; Quantities; and Power, organizing. In *BFA WoW* these were: Physical attributes; Life and living things; Thought and belief; Investigate, examine, etc.; Moving, coming, and going; Power relationships; and Getting, giving, and possession.

Broadly speaking, for women in *Classic WoW* and *BFA WoW*, the kind of semantic domains which are drawn upon are relatively similar. However, in *Classic WoW*, one area of interest was how women were more likely to talk about plants and living creatures. An examination of the concordance lines around these semantic domains revealed that female characters in *Classic WoW* would typically talk about things such as herbs with healing properties, as well as animals which needed saving. For example:

> this rare **herb** found only in Thousand Needles **will help light the dormant sacred fire of life**
> All around Darkshore are **sickly deer;** use the salve on them and cure **their malaise**

In *BFA WoW*, one semantic domain female characters were likely to draw upon was 'Life and living things'—which bears some similarity to the semantic domain of 'Plants and living creatures'. However, the beings referred to were not necessarily sickly passive animals which the adventure is sent to help heal, but it included monsters who need to be slain or living creatures who have items, etc. The difference between the semantics drawn upon within these kinds of categories, therefore, is that women in *Classic WoW* were more likely to talk about wanting to heal and help nature, while women in *BFA WoW* were more likely to talk about things that live, which might need killing or talking to. To some degree, this finding, particularly as it relates to the representation of women in *Classic WoW*, could echo the notions put forward by scholars such as Yee et al. (2011), who argued that players of *WoW* would perceive healing as a feminine trait.

Male Characters' Semantic Domains

By contrast to female characters, male characters shared 17 semantic domains, and each version had 3 unique semantic domains. The shared semantic domains were: Putting, taking, and transporting; Religion and the supernatural; Personal names; Objects generally; Location and direction; Time: Past; Living creatures generally; Calm/Violent/Angry; Evaluation: Good/bad; Moving, coming and going; Warfare, defence and the army; Weapons; Being; Obligation and necessity; Anatomy and physiology; Time: Future; Getting, giving, and possession; and Power, organizing. The semantic domains unique to men in *Classic WoW* were: Knowledge; Geographical terms; and Education in general. While the semantic domains unique to men in *BFA WoW* were: Negative; Helping/hindering; and Crime, law and order.

Something striking with the male characters is just how little difference there is in terms of the semantic domains which are drawn upon between *Classic WoW* and *BFA WoW*. One reason for this might be due to differences in what is/was acceptable characterisation for women in comparison to what is/was acceptable characterisation for men. I would argue that the attitudes towards how men have been characterised in videogames over the past 15 years have not changed much, while the representation of women (in particular) has been a heated topic of debate—and has meant that the representation of women has changed a lot in other videogames (see, e.g., the change in how Laura Croft was represented, discussed in MacCallum-Stewart, 2014). When masculine speech styles are seen as the 'norm' this can take longer to change—but when feminine speech styles are seen as 'problematic', it is easier to correct what is seen as 'problematic' rather than the 'norm'.

One area of change in the semantic domains that men draw upon is how men in *BFA WoW* draw on the semantic domain of 'Law and order', but men from *Classic WoW* do not. Within this category, the language in the concordance lines reveals that the words typically related to violence and the prison system, such as:

> De punishment for de **crime** of mutiny is **death**
> the honor of **getting rid of our prisoners** with your most potent venom!

In other words, while law and order could cover more neutral constructions such as 'this person has been arrested for the crime of loitering', it typically is used to discuss the more extreme crimes, such as 'mutiny'. There are also examples of violence towards other characters, especially if they are criminals (e.g. 'getting rid of [...] prisoners'). This kind of violence is a far cry from the more peaceful nature of some of the semantic domains which are drawn on by female characters in *Classic WoW*, which demonstrates the stark contrast between the gendered expectations of female characters in *Classic WoW* and male characters in *BFA WoW*.

There is a difference in the kind of language male characters draw upon to discuss 'Warfare, defence and the army, and weapons' between *Classic WoW* and *BFA WoW*. In *Classic WoW*, the words in this semantic category typically relate to men wanting to help war efforts from afar, for example:

> I knew him, well, **before he left for the war**, but that was the **last time I saw him**
> If you **seek a weapon**, warrior, then you should seek Thun'grim. **To find him, first travel to the Crossroads** to the west

However, the concordance lines for this semantic domain reveal that discussion of war in *BFA WoW* becomes more focused on men who participated in war or who died in war:

> The Zandalari fleet is decimated, and **King Rastakhan is dead. Our war with the Horde is almost over**
> The **enemy has turned our forward cannons around on us**. Scuttle that equipment to stop the bombardments!

There thus appears to be a difference in the level of involvements players, and by extension the male characters they interact with, have in wars.

A Difference Within a Similarity

One area I want to draw attention to is within the similarities in semantic categories. As noted in previous chapters of analysis, and by scholars such as Taylor (2013), it is often easy to look at differences in how gender is represented—but similarities can often reveal other interesting dimensions to representations of gender. One such area of similarity is that male and female characters in both *Classic WoW* and *BFA WoW* draw on the semantic domain of anatomy and physiology. However, when we look closer, we see a difference in the kind of words drawn upon in this semantic domain. Female characters in *Classic WoW* typically talk about anatomy and physiology through discussion of *blood* (11 instances), *hands* (11 instances), and *head*(s) (6 instances). Women in *BFA WoW* typically talk about *blood* (26 instances), *head*(s) (12 instances), and *snout*(s) (7 instances). By contrast, male characters in *Classic WoW* were more likely to talk about anatomy and physiology through the use of words such as *eye*(s) (36 instances), *skeleton*(s) (26 instances), and *skull*(s) (18 instances). Male characters in *BFA WoW* were more likely to talk about *blood* (49 instances), *ear(s)* (15 instances), and *skull(s)* (5 instances).

There, thus, appears to some differences and similarities in the kind of anatomy that male and female characters talk about. Interestingly, men and women in *BFA WoW* both discuss *blood* (as do women in *Classic WoW*). However, there are several different words that characters in these groups use. I would argue that discussion of skeletons and skulls carry implicature of death. In *Classic WoW*, women do not talk about body parts which would indicate death (unlike words such as *skeleton* and *skull*). One reason for this could be that such body parts are more extreme than *snouts*, and so there could be an implication that women might be too squeamish to talk about this topic. Thus, while there are similar semantic fields drawn upon, some of the lexemes within these fields could reveal an underlying bias of what writers think male and female characters are likely to talk about (or what they feel these gendered characters should talk about).

These are just some of the differences within a similarity between male and female characters. Therefore, while in the lists of tagged semantic domains, there are a number of similar semantic domains which both male and female character draw on, the kind of language within these semantic categories is different. This could reflect broader ideas of what is accepted for male/female characters to talk about, and although there may be a move to making the semantic domains more equal, language within these may still be bound up with some cultural norms.

Discussion

The above analysis demonstrates that there are both similarities and differences in what male and female characters talk about in *World of Warcraft*, and how this has changed over time. One of the main points to take away from this chapter is that I have demonstrated that there are differences in the language used by male and female characters—both in *Classic WoW* and *BFA WoW*. These differences range from the frequencies at which players interact with gendered characters to the words gendered characters use and the kind of semantic domains they draw upon. However, there are also a number of similarities—as well as differences within areas which we might immediately think are similarities (see Taylor, 2013).

Importantly, it should be noted that the data does not appear to be as simple as 'men always say "a" and women always say "b"'. While I have tried to capture this by demonstrating similarities (and by showing how some similarities can actually contain subtle differences), one issue with the above analysis is that such a quantification of the language used by multiple gendered individuals almost risks people conflating these usages with the idea of men and women's language. Therefore, I want to use this section to discuss some of the problematic aspects of corpus-based sociolinguistic approaches to gender as it pertains to language use: that it can be hard to pin similarities/differences down to gender alone. Such large-scale quantification of usage by gender will invariably gloss over the performative nature of gender (i.e. how it is constructed in each context), and so large-scale corpus studies can, at times, be in conflict with the discursive and constructivist nature of identity.

However, can we really claim that the language analysed in this chapter is only looking at the language used by gendered individuals? Something to remember is that these characters do not exist in real life. They will not have had the experiences of growing up and internalising ideologies of gender, and so can they really be said to be 'performing' it? We need to take a step back and remember that these characters are carefully constructed by employees at Blizzard Entertainment. Part of the way these characters are constructed included their gender, and what is an appropriate way for that character to speak. Such an analysis of the speech patterns as separated by gendered characters, therefore, blurs the line between usage and representation.

One connected issue which overhangs this research is the question of 'yes, but is it gender?' (Swann, 2002). This is difficult to answer in a sociolinguistic analysis which focuses on usage, because looking just at words used or the semantic domains drawn upon does not necessarily reveal that something has become 'gendered'. However, given the amount of male and female character's language which has been analysed, we could probably make the argument that the amount of data shows trends across a large enough proportion of gendered characters to make some tentative claims. The claims made above must also be considered in the context of the different games: I am not saying that all female characters are more likely to use 'x' across all videogames, but that it is more likely within this specific corpus.

There are also, of course, a number of other dimensions to this corpus that could be explored. I have not included these in this chapter, simply due to limitations of space. We could, for example, examine the differences between female characters who only use certain varieties of English, such as Jamaican English and those who use 'standard' English (note, I use 'standard' here to refer to the kind of language which is used as a barometer by prescriptivists—even though it is a written version that reflects RP and is not inherently better nor the 'norm'). There are also other intersecting identities which could be considered different dimensions, such as the age of characters, locations of characters, and perceived ethnicities.

Conclusions

In this chapter, I have attempted to show some of the ways we could combine corpus sociolinguistics (with a focus on usage) as applied to videogames. While corpus approaches to sociolinguistics are not new (see, e.g., Baker, 2010; Baker & Heritage, 2021), it is less often applied to data which is scripted and said by characters (though, see, e.g., Baker, 2008). While trying to avoid an essentialist approach to language use, I have focused on how characters are constructed, and the kind of language that they use across gendered characters. This chapter demonstrates several ways future researchers might want to explore such issues—ranging from the implementation of wordlists to semantic domain analysis.

I have, hopefully, shown how this kind of research can produce vast amounts of rich data—and how interpreting this data can be complex and not always clear cut. However, I also hope that I have emphasised enough that this is not necessarily a bad thing, and that there are a number of similarities across what gendered characters say, in addition to some differences. These similarities and differences can be elicited through a number of corpus methods. While keywords and/or semantic domains as tagged using a semantic tagger like USAS give a quantitative indication of similarities or differences, they should simultaneously be explored via concordance line analysis.

Therefore, this chapter demonstrates different ways which one might want to take lines of future research. While there has already been some fantastic analysis of how gender is represented in the paratext of *WoW* games (see, e.g., Braithewaite, 2014; Ensslin, 2012), little has been done in the way of analysing gender within *WoW* (similar to arguments made in earlier chapters). This chapter shows that it is possible, and different methods could be applied to similar data.

While this chapter contributes to the aforementioned gap in the research literature, it certainly is not without some limitations. One area where future scholars might want to continue this work is to examine how language is used by players to construct gendered characters. For example, how do people who roleplay on *WoW* construct their gendered identity? Additionally, how do communities of practice discuss gendered characters? There were also a number of issues around how broad some of the USAS tags are—for example the tag 'negative' does not really give a full overview of the kind of semantic domains which characters have drawn upon, and there are some issues around how some words were placed in an uncategorisable bin—most likely because they were game-specific language, such as the names of locations. Future research might therefore want to look at developing a modified tagging system for fantasy videogames, like *WoW*. There are several avenues for research, and this chapter has contributed in part to bridging the gaps in the literature.

Ludography

Bioware. (2009). *Dragon age: Origins*. Redwood City, California: Electronic Arts.

Blizzard Entertainment. (1994). *Warcraft: Orcs & Humans*. Irvine, California: Blizzard Entertainment.

Blizzard Entertainment. (1995). *Warcraft II: Tides of darkness*. Irvine, California: Blizzard Entertainment.

Blizzard Entertainment. (1996). *Warcraft II: Beyond the dark portal*. Irvine, California: Blizzard Entertainment.

Blizzard Entertainment. (2002). *Warcraft III: Reign of Chaos*. Irvine, California: Blizzard Entertainment.

Blizzard Entertainment (2003). *Warcraft III: The frozen throne*. Irvine, California: Blizzard Entertainment.

Blizzard Entertainment. (2004–2006). *World of warcraft*. Irvine, California: Blizzard Entertainment.

Blizzard Entertainment. (2018–2020). *World of warcraft: Battle for Azeroth*. Irvine, California: Blizzard Entertainment.

Blizzard Entertainment. (2020–current). *World of warcraft: Shadowlands*. Irvine, California: Blizzard Entertainment.

Bibliography

Balicer, R. D. (2007). Modeling infectious diseases dissemination through online role-playing games. *Epidemiology, 18*(2), 260–261.

Baker, P. (2008). *Sexed texts: Language, gender and sexuality*. Equinox.

Baker, P. (2010) *Sociolinguistics and corpus linguistics*. Edinburgh University Press.

Baker, P. (2014). *Using corpora to analyse gender*. Bloomsbury.

Baker, P., & Heritage, F. (2021). Corpus approaches to sociolinguistics. In A. O'Keefe & M. McCarthy (Eds.), *The Routledge handbook of corpus linguistics* (2nd edn.). Routledge.

Barrett, R. (2017). *From drag Queens to Leathermen: Language, gender, and Gay male subcultures*. Oxford University Press.

Baxter, J. (2012). Women of the corporation: A sociolinguistic perspective of senior women's leadership language in the UK. *Journal of Sociolinguistics, 16*(1), 81–107.

Baxter, J. (2014). *Double-voicing at work: Power, gender and linguistic expertise*. Palgrave Macmillan.

Bergstrom, K., McArthur, V., Jenson, J., & Peyton, T. (2011). All in a day's work: A study of World of Warcraft NPCs comparing gender to professions. In *Proceedings of the 2011 ACM SIGGRAPH Symposium on Video Games* (pp. 31–35).

Bing, J., & Bergvall, V. (1996). The question of questions: Beyond binary thinking. In: V. Bergvall, J. Bing, & A. Freed (Eds.), *Rethinking language and gender research: Theory and practice* (pp. 1–30). Addison Wesley Longman.

Braithwaite, A. (2014). 'Seriously, get out': Feminists on the forums and the War (craft) on women. *New Media & Society, 16*(5), 703–718.

Butler, J. (1990). *Gender trouble*. Routledge.

Ensslin, A. (2012). *The language of gaming*. Palgrave.

Fligelstone, S., Pacey, M., & Rayson, P. (1997). How to generalize the task of annotation. In R. Garside, G. Leech, & A. McEnery (Eds.), *Corpus annotation: Linguistic information from computer text corpora* (pp. 122–136). Longman.

Gamasutra. (2011). *Seven years of world of warcraft*. Gamasutra. https://www.gamasutra.com/view/news/128323/Seven_Years_Of_World_Of_Warcraft.php. Accessed February 2021.

Garside, R. (1987). The CLAWS word-tagging system. In R. Garside, G. Leech & G. Sampson (Eds.), *The computational analysis of english: A corpus-based approach* (pp. 30–41). Longman.

Garside, R. (1996). The robust tagging of unrestricted text: The BNC experience. In J. Thomas & M. Short (Eds.), *Using corpora for language research: Studies in the Honour of Geoffrey Leech* (pp. 167–180). Longman.

Giora, R. (2002). Theorizing gender feminist awareness and language change. In B. Baron & H. Kotthoff (Eds.), *Gender in Interaction: Perspectives on femininity and masculinity in ethnography and discourse* (pp. 329–343). John Benjamins.

Gregory, D. (2018). *Warbringers: Jaina. World of Warcraft promotional cinematic*. Blizzard Entertainment's YouTube channel. https://youtu.be/Fo7XPvwRgG8. Accessed February 2021.

Goorimoorthee, T., Csipo, A., Carleton, S., & Ensslin, A. (2019). Language ideologies in videogame discourse: Forms of sociophonetic othering in accented character speech. In A. Ennslin & I. Balteiro (Eds.), *Approaches to videogame discourse: Lexis, interaction, textuality* (pp. 269–287). Bloomsbury.

Heritage, F. (2020). Applying corpus linguistics to videogame data: Exploring the representation of gender in videogames at a lexical level. *Game Studies 20*(3).

Heritage, F. (2021). *Maidens and monsters: A corpus assisted critical discourse analysis of the representation of gender in The Witcher videogame series* (Doctoral dissertation, Lancaster University).

Holmes, J., & Schnurr, S. (2006). 'Doing femininity' at work: More than just relational practice 1. *Journal of Sociolinguistics, 10*(1), 31–51.

Jeffries, L. (2007). *Textual construction of the female body: A critical discourse approach*. Palgrave Macmillan.

Kitzinger, C. (2009). Doing gender: A conversation analytic perspective. *Gender & Society, 2 3*(1), 94–98.

Lakoff, R. (1973). Language and woman's place. *Language in Society, 2*(1), 45–80.

Lakoff, R. (1975). *Language and woman's place*. Harper and Row.

Levon, E. (2015). Conflicted Selves: Language, religion and same-sex desire in Israel. In E. Levon & R. Beline Mendes (Eds.), *Language, sexuality, and power: Studies in intersectional sociolinguistics* (pp. 215–240). Oxford University Press.

Lofgren, E. T., & Fefferman, N. H. (2007). The untapped potential of virtual game worlds to shed light on real world epidemics. *The Lancet Infectious Diseases, 7*(9), 625–629.

MacCallum-Stewart, E. (2014). "Take That, Bitches!" Refiguring Lara Croft in feminist game narratives. *Game Studies, 14*(2).

Metacritic. (2004). *World of Warcraft*. Metacritic. https://www.metacritic.com/game/pc/world-of-warcraft. Accessed February 2021.

Paul, C. (2011). Optimizing play: How theorycraft changes gameplay and design. *Game Studies 11*(2).

Piao, S. Rayson, P. Archer, D., & McEnery, T. (2004). Evaluating lexical resources for a semantic tagger. In *proceedings of 4th International Conference on Language Resources and Evaluation (LREC 2004)* (pp. 499–502).

Piao, S., Bianchi, F., Dayrell, C., D'Egidio, A., & Rayson, P. (2015). Development of the multilingual semantic annotation system. *In proceedings of the*

2015 Conference of the North American Chapter of the Association for Computational Linguistics—Human Language Technologies (NAACL HLT 2015) (pp. 1268–1274).

Rayson, P. (2008). From key words to key semantic domains. *International Journal of Corpus Linguistics, 13*(4), 519–549.

Swann, J. (2002). Yes, but is it gender? In L. Litosseliti & J. Sunderland (Eds.), *Gender identity and discourse analysis* (pp. 43–67). John Benjamins.

Tannen, D. (1990). *You just don't understand: Women and men in conversation.* Morrow.

Tannen, D. (1994). Communication between the sexes. In C. Davidson & L. Wagner-Martin (Eds.), *The Oxford Companion to Women's writing in the United States* (pp. 471–472). Oxford University Press.

Taylor, C. (2013). Searching for similarity using corpus-assisted discourse studies. *Corpora, 8*(1), 81–113.

Van Herk, G. (2012). *What is sociolinguistics?* (2nd edn.). Wiley.

White, N. P. (1972). Origins of Aristotle's essentialism. *The Review of Metaphysics, 26*(1), 57–85.

Wilson, A., & Rayson, P. (1993). Automatic content analysis of spoken discourse. In C. Souter & E. Atwell (Eds.), *Corpus based computational linguistics* (pp. 215–226). Rodopi.

WoWhead. (2020a). *Pelagos, WoW's First transgender character, on his identity in Shadowlands.* WoWhead. https://www.wowhead.com/news=316944/pelagos-wows-first-transgender-character-on-his-identity-in-shadowlands. Accessed February 2021.

WoWhead. (2020b). *World of warcraft classic quests.* WoWhead. https://classic.wowhead.com/quests/. Accessed February 2021.

WoWhead. (2020c). *World of warcraft battle for Azeroth quests.* https://www.wowhead.com/quests/battle-for-azeroth/. Accessed February 2021.

Yee, N., Ducheneaut, N., Yao, M., & Nelson, L. (2011). Do men heal more when in drag?: conflicting identity cues between user and avatar. In *Proceedings of the SIGCHI conference on Human factors in computing systems* (pp. 773–776). Association for Computing Machinery.

8

Conclusions

Game Over

The work presented in this book has been situated at the intersection of three fields: language and gender studies (specifically from a critical discursive perspective), ludolinguistics, and corpus linguistics. I have used corpus methods to investigate how gender is represented and how discourses of and about gender have been (re)produced in the form of linguistic representations within multiple popular videogames.

This final chapter discusses and summarises the key findings from each of the analysis chapters of the book and tries to tie together some of the more overarching findings found within the analysis chapters. However, I wish to stress that while the analysis has uncovered some interesting findings with regard to the representation of gender, some caution is also needed. Therefore, I would like to start this chapter by noting some of the broad conclusions before I discuss some limitations of the research, as well as how future research might aim to use corpora, or incorporate corpus methods, to overcome these limitations.

F. Heritage, *Language, Gender and Videogames*,
https://doi.org/10.1007/978-3-030-74398-7_8

What Can We Conclude from the Research?

This monograph has demonstrated that corpus methods can be utilised in the exploration of how gender is represented in fantasy videogames. Although corpus linguistics, language and gender studies, and videogame studies all have a rich history of high-quality research, the work presented here is, to the best of my knowledge, the first monograph to combine all three disciplines. The findings, when compared to previous research, demonstrate that not only are women underrepresented at a visual level, but they are underrepresented in terms of how often they are referred to. Across all three chapters of analysis, something which was striking was the difference in frequencies at which nouns and pronouns referring to male/female social actors occurred. Male social actors were sometimes up to 9.8 times more likely to appear in some series—but usually this was between 4 and 6 times more likely. While previous research had indicated that men were likely to be up to 4 times more frequent at a visual level (see, e.g., Gestos et al., 2018; Ivory, 2006; Paaßen et al., 2017), the research demonstrated that frequencies at which words denoting gendered characters are also unequal at a linguistic level.

Typically, male characters occupied positions of power and regularly enacted violence. However, female characters were often limited in their positions of power, and while they occasionally enacted violence, were much more likely to be spoken about in terms of their relation to others or their mental abilities. Ultimately, these representations can sustain problematic views of gender: that it is acceptable for men to be violent and that they should rely on their abilities to fight, rather than their abilities to think and study. Similarly, repeated representations of women as uninterested in fighting, or as healers/users of magical abilities, can contribute to what we think is (un)acceptable behaviour for women. Both these representations feed into ideals of hegemonic masculinity (see Connell, 2005), in that conforming to normative gendered behaviours seeks to further sustain the hegemony.

The findings have also suggested that men are more likely to be agents of verbs (Chapter 5) and were more likely to initiate quests (Chapter 7) in comparison to women. Both findings suggest a problematic representation of gender: that women are considerably less likely to be agentive and the agents of change. Previous work has discussed women as passive participants because they are victims or 'damsels in distress' (see, Sarkeesian, 2014). The analysis presented in this book builds on this previous research and takes the ideas behind it a step forward. By doing close (systemic functional) linguistic analysis of the clauses containing a reference to a gendered social actor, we are able to move from very subjective interpretations based on overarching narrative structures (such as those provided by Sarkeesian, 2014) to more fine-grained (and I would argue more objective) identification of how women are passivised. However, something to remember is that women are not always passivised, but they are much more so in comparison to male characters. This kind of research could, in theory, be done without the use of corpus methods. It would be possible, for example, to take one small section of a videogame and look at the clauses within that section. However, this might miss several occurrences of different verbs—and there is no guarantee that a verb within that section would occur with a reference to a (gendered) social actor. Therefore, by implementing corpus methods, it is possible to refine our data (via part-of-speech tagging the data and looking at how verbs collocate with social actors) and to look across a broader selection of texts. This refined data set then provides a much 'cleaner' starting point for close analysis as possible. Hopefully, the analysis has shown that this is one of the fruitful applications of corpus methods to this kind of data.

From a methodological standpoint, this book has demonstrated the validity of using corpus methods on videogame data and that a variety of corpus methods can be implemented in the study of videogames. While previous studies had examined the language around videogames, I argued that there was a dearth in the ludolinguistic research—that research which looked at the language within videogames often used problematic methods to collect the data. However, there was an even greater dearth in the literature because there are multiple different methods within corpus linguistics which could have been applied to this kind of data. The field of corpus linguistics is not a single methodology, rather it is a collection of methodologies. Therefore, while I have demonstrated that some methods reveal interesting information about how gender is represented in videogames, more research is needed to apply different corpus methodologies to videogame data.

Elsewhere, I also hope that this monograph has provided researchers with some ways to gather data from videogames. Something I demonstrated in Chapter 4 was that there are multiple ways to collect videogame data. However, videogame data can be difficult and/or time-consuming to get. I have demonstrated that while string/text dump files, as extracted by computer software, can provide the most data which is the most representative, it is often 'messy'. I have also demonstrated that there are other ways to collect the data, although sometimes a lot of additional work is required to check the data and/or code it. Broadly speaking, I would recommend one of three methods to collect the data. I implemented these three methods across the chapters of analysis and have reproduced them below:

1. Play through the videogame(s) and transcribe the data (this method and method (2) were implemented in Chapter 5);
2. Use computer software to extract the language from the videogame(s) (this method was implemented in Chapters 5 and 6);
3. Use fan websites which have either data mined the language—i.e. implemented the same procedure as (1) or which have gathered the data in a way which does not edit spelling, grammar, etc. (this was the method implemented in Chapter 7).

While it is also possible to get data from fan transcripts, such a method runs the risk of others changing the language, which in turn can make corpus analyses problematic. Thus, while I have argued that this method can be used, it is not one I would recommend unless the three methods above are not possible. It might be the case that future studies develop new ways of collecting data, or ways of making such data more widely available, which is something that I would wholly welcome.

Some Limitations

This book is not without limitations, and there are several aspects of corpus approaches to gender in videogames to be wary of. In this section, I turn to some of these limitations and discuss possible lines for future research to address them.

One of the first limitations I want to draw attention to is how time-consuming building corpora of videogames can be and how there is a compromise between accuracy of tagging and amount of data that can be tagged. Anecdotally, extracting the text dump files for parts of the corpora in Chapter 5 and the whole corpora for Chapter 6 was a relatively seamless process, and gathering the data before it was cleaned could take as little as a few hours. The data for Chapter 7—which was considerably smaller—took in excess of 75 hours to collect and add the XML annotations to. Thus, despite being a fraction of the size of *The Witcher* corpora used in Chapter 6, the data took at least 5 times longer to code and annotate. I am aware that students might want to use this book as a starting point for their own studies but might have time constraints on assignments. Therefore, for students who might be looking at conducting a similar analysis, this kind of manual collection and annotation might yield too little data in too much time. Thus, time constraints around collection and annotation are something to bear in mind as a potential limitation for future research.

An additional limitation of some data is that many of the text dump files are not tagged for speakers or are tagged in a way which does not provide meaningful metadata to the analyst. This can be difficult if a researcher wants to do an analysis like the variationist sociolinguistic approach demonstrated in Chapter 7. Additionally, what should be done with the language which is automatically generated for NPCs—such as 'lovely weather today'? Often, this automatically generated language can occur with any gendered character, and so different playthroughs might present slightly different data. This can be problematic when tagging who says what within text dump files. This is one of the reasons why it is possibly best to use text dump files for analysing how gendered social actors are represented, rather than how they speak within a videogame.

A different way to overcome the problem with the language generated by NPCs is to ignore what is randomly generated and examine what is specifically scripted for certain NPCs. In Chapter 7, I specifically only looked at NPCs who did not have randomly generated dialogue, but who were quest givers/receivers. This also meant that they were characters with whom players were likely to interact. This allowed for analysis at a quantitative level in terms of what roles gendered characters play, but also analysis of differences in terms of the kind of language that gendered characters were likely to use (this is also discussed in a later subsection). However, sometimes specific language from such NPCs is not as obvious as quest giver/receiver, so selecting such data can be difficult in other videogames.

Singular Modes of Communication

Throughout this book, I have focused specifically on how language is used to construct representations of gender. This was primarily done because other research which examined the representation of gender in videogames focused on representation as communicated through visual modes (see, e.g., Matthews et al., 2016). While there had been some previous research into multimodal approaches to gender in videogames, these were typically limited to the modes of visual communication and auditory communication (see, e.g., Machin & van Leeuwen, 2016). The reason for choosing to look at language was to make the case that, as a communicative mode, language should not be overlooked—and thus, to contribute to filling this dearth of literature.

However, relying on analyses of a single mode—be that visual, linguistic, or auditory, can be problematic. Therefore, something I really wish to impose is that, while corpora can often reveal interesting and pertinent findings about the language used to represent gender, data such as this is inherently multimodal. Corpus methods can thus offer a lens into representation from one angle, but for a full picture of how gender is represented in a videogame, or series of videogames, additional work is required in different modes of communication. One way to do this could be to combine multimodal critical discourse analysis and corpus linguistics, or to triangulate visual corpora with lexical corpora. Although there are visual corpora, these are often much smaller by comparison (see, e.g., Abuczki & Ghazaleh, 2013; Schembri et al., 2013) and when they are used, they typically relate to sign language (see Fenlon et al., 2015; Schembri et al., 2013). Outside of sign language corpora, multimodal corpora which contain visual elements are still in their infancy (see, e.g., Christiansen et al., 2020; Knight & Adolphs, 2020). Once this field has matured more, it would be good to combine the methods of multimodal corpora with lexical corpora.

Elsewhere, while other studies have examined how sound can be gendered, and how identity is enacted through sound, it would be good to be able to do so with corpus methods. While phonological corpora have been compiled and utilised in a variety of different research fields (see, e.g., Durand, 2017; Gut, 2009; Vella & Grech, 2021), the current research appears to focus around accent/dialectal research in addition to second language acquisition. What appears to be less common, however, is phonological corpus research which examines gender and how gendered characters in different media are represented in terms of their voices. It could be the case, for example, that all female characters in a game are represented as using high rising terminal (raising the tone of their voice at the end of a sentence). Application of corpus techniques on a tagged corpus (like the one used in Chapter 7) could reveal useful phonological patterns around gendered representations. One way into this data might be to use sound files which often accompany a videogame when downloaded to a computer. These files could be transcribed and uploaded to corpus software, and manual mark-up could be included to best see different phonological patterns with a corpus approach. This could bear some similarities to the work conducted by Goorimoorthee et al. (2019) but might add a different dimension to the analysis.

Videogames, Paratext, and Triangulation

Throughout the first chapters of this monograph, I argued that we need to look beyond paratext and actually apply corpus methods to the language used within videogames. I specifically argued that the differences in genre and register might create different representations and that we cannot understand how gender is represented in one text by only analysing a second.

However, I do not seek to completely invalidate the research conducted on videogame paratext—and indeed, I think it is an entirely useful field. This monograph demonstrates some of the ways that representations can be examined within videogames, how we can get data to conduct at such investigations, and how some videogames represent gender. It would be good for future research to triangulate the methods demonstrated in this monograph with data from paratext of certain videogames. Doing so could examine where representations cross genres and registers around videogames. For example, it would be interesting to compare how representations of gender in videogames such as *The Witcher* (Chapter 6) compare to reviews of the game, the language used in the television series, and the book series. Similar to the previous section on single communicative modes, sometimes it can be useful to compare communicative modes as represented in different genres and registers. It would also be interesting to conduct multimodal analyses as assisted by corpora in both videogames and the paratext of videogames.

Developments in Technology

In a previous subsection, I alluded to the fact that, while I would like to have conducted a multimodal analysis on this data, visual corpora are comparatively small, and the field in general is still relatively new. I now want to draw attention to an issue around technology as it relates to corpus linguistics and the analysis of videogames, as this is currently a barrier to further research.

As it stands, the technology does not currently exist to manually tag quests for the gender of the character who is speaking. Additionally, advances in technology are required to tag where the data comes within the videogame, and to transcribe (as well as tag) all permutations of a videogame. As technology develops, it might be possible to automatically play through every permutation and record this in a separate document for a corpus. In a similar vein, there is currently no single piece of technology which can extract all the text files from every videogame, and this can be difficult when trying to build much bigger reference corpora. As I demonstrated in Chapters 6 and 7, using software to extract text files from *The Witcher* proved to be much faster and yielded a much larger data set. One avenue of progress which might be good would be for people, who are experts at coding and natural language processing (NLP), to create user-friendly software that can extract language files with ease.

Elsewhere, there are still several issues with corpus software itself, and corpus software is ever developing. For example, as can be seen in this monograph, I have had to triangulate corpus software to gain a full picture of how gender is represented within a corpus (such as using both CLAWS and WordSmith7). Certain elements of some pieces of software are more adept at some things than others, and this can often mean that people who are new to corpus linguistics might not always know what piece of software to use for what, nor know the benefits of using one piece over another. However, I understand that there are current constraints within each piece of software, and the addition of more tools within a piece of software will inevitably slow down the speed at which it can run. One of the exciting aspects of corpus linguistics is that the field will only continue to grow as new technologies become available. It makes sense, therefore, that any corpus study will also be able to develop as technology progresses.

Challenging Binaries

Throughout Chapter 2, I argued that gender is not a binary concept: that it is something which is fluid and negotiated through discourse. However, as can be seen from the three chapters of analysis, it is regularly presented as such: that statistically speaking, only men and women are present in these mainstream games. Characters who are non-binary are underrepresented or not represented at all. While it might be the case that there is good non-binary gender representation in some other games, especially games developed by queer indie game developers—such as the character TOMCAT in the game *2064: Read Only Memories* (MidBoss, 2015), this does not always appear in AAA games. Indeed, as I noted in Chapter 7, it was not until late 2020 when *WoW* introduced its first transgender character (and even then, *WoW* had been updating the game multiple times a year for 16 years).

What would be good for future analyses could be to compare the representation of non-binary characters (or lack thereof) in AAA games to the representation of these kinds of characters in games developed by queer game designers. Even more broadly, it would be interesting to compare how gender, sexuality, and intersecting identities are represented in both kinds of videogames. Identities are invariably tied to what we write and produce, and so it would also be important to look at the identities of the writers of videogames and the kinds of representations they create. Some representations may undergo a process of filtration from editors, and so policies implemented in individual companies would also need to be considered.

While I have also tried to examine different types of gender performances, such as different types of masculinity, this does not necessarily mean that these are the only types of gender performance presented in the videogames. Therefore, additional research might want to consider the other types of gender which are performed within videogames. It could be the case that certain types of characters are more likely to enact one stylised gender performance in comparison with others. One criticism of corpus linguistic methods is that it can often be at ends with the situationally constructed nature of gender performativity. While such repeated patterns can be brought to the fore, there might be other patterns which can be observed through different analytical techniques, such as conversation analysis. Therefore, while corpus linguistic methods appear to offer some ways of examining certain gender performances, they may be less appropriate for others.

There are also additional issues in corpus linguistics which make examining the representation of non-binary characters challenging. One such issue is the use of 'they'. While 'they' and its possessive form 'their' can be used to refer to a single person (such as in 'I believe someone has left <u>their</u> coat here' or 'Kat told me <u>they</u> really like birds that look like dinosaurs'), it can also be used as a third-person plural pronoun (such as in 'The British public want what is in their best interest' or 'I'm chaperoning a local youth group today. They are going to a theme park'). By contrast, male/female pronouns are almost always singular (with the exception of 'he', which can be used as a gender-neutral marker, although the popularity of this is falling out of use). One of the challenges for corpus linguistics in the future might be to create software which can read the co-text to make judgements on whether or not a third-person pronoun is singular or plural. While some work has been done on transgender (including non-binary) identities using CADS methods (see, e.g., Zottola, 2021), more work is still needed to address the dearth of literature in this area.

More Games, More Data

Before finishing this monograph, something I would like to draw attention to is the number of videogames which I have analysed. In total, this book has used data from 13 different videogames for corpus analyses (I used two versions of *WoW* and a sample of *The Witcher 3* was used in VG2014). Importantly, I did not claim that the analysis was applicable to all videogames, and any claims made in this book are specifically about the data presented within the corpora. Importantly, the analysis presented in this book provides a 'snapshot' into how gender is represented within videogames of the same genre—but it is just that, a representative sample. However, this does raise the point that more research is required across a wide range of videogame texts. At the minute, thousands of videogames are released every year—by both professional companies and indie developers. Much larger corpora could be built and tagged in order to investigate representations across a broader data set. However, to do so would take a lot more time and resources.

Something which could be done in future might be to use larger samples from videogames (like the data presented in Chapter 6) and compare the representation of gender across videogame series. It would be interesting, for example, to compare a series of videogames which did very well in terms of their sales figures to ones which did less well. It could be that the language plays a role in whether or not a game is viewed as successful—and the success of a videogame might also be linked to the representation of gender. For example, is it the case that people are boycotting a videogame because they know that it contributes to maintaining problematic views of gender and/or sexuality? Until such research is conducted, we will not be able to say with certainty.

A different area I alluded to earlier was that the representation of gender and sexuality might be different when contrasting games from queer indie developers in comparison with mainstream studios. This is another avenue of inquiry that future researchers might want to investigate, as there might several differences created by the intended target audience and the register of the games. There are also differences in what is expected of developers within each, as well as differences in timescales. Queer indie developers are not the only kind of videogame developers outside of those who produce AAA games but may be more inclined to tackle issues of gender and/or sexuality in different ways due to their own identities.

Similarly, it is very difficult to know who wrote what on some of these videogames. For all we know, the writing team on some of the videogames might possibly be entirely male, entirely female, a mix, have non-binary people working on the project, and so on. Depending on what is available, future scholars may wish to look at the language in games for which they know the authorial team. This could then possibly allow for a deeper understanding of what gendered writers believe is acceptable to include in the representation of gendered characters.

Directions for Future Research

While the previous sections have drawn attention to some very specific lines of research as a means to address some of the limitations presented in this book, it is worth turning to more general directions for future research. That is to say, there are a number of elements of this monograph which are useful and could be elaborated on with different types of data, or that different corpus methods/discursive frameworks could be implemented on the same data.

One direction I would like to see future research go is towards genre-based analyses of different videogames. It might be useful to examine the language in 'point and click' videogames in comparison to, for example, MMORPGs. Doing so might provide an idea of where representations are most problematic or indicate the genre/register-based norms. Future scholars might want to implement corpus-based genre/register analysis, such as Multi-Dimensional Factor Analysis (see, Biber, 1992). This kind of research allows analysts to examine the kind of grammatical patterns associated with particular registers of text—and this could be applied to data which is gendered. For example, someone might want to compare games designed by queer game designers to mainstream games and examine the register features of each.

While I have primarily analysed the text which companies have approved, future research might want to use corpus methods to examine gaming communities via in-game chat features (building on the work of people such as Baker, 2008). This could be particularly helpful to understand not only how gender is represented by people with the power to decide what to include in the game, but how communities enact gender in a non-moderated way. This could also be useful in terms of corpus-based research into online communities of practice.

Finally, gender is just one of the many intersecting identities that people represent and perform every day. While I have elected to examine the representation of gender in this monograph, there are several other identities that future research will still need to examine with corpus methods. Although some work has been conducted on the phonological representation of racialised identities (see Goorimoorthee et al., 2019), to the best of my knowledge, no work has been conducted on corpus approaches to the representation of ethnicity in videogames. This might be harder to conduct, given that explicit markers might not always be present in language around ethnicity (i.e. pronouns denote the gender of an individual, but, in English, they are not usually embedded with identities relating to ethnicity). Moreover, work will be needed to look at some intersections of identity—such as how age and gender intersect within videogames (though, see Heritage, 2021 for a discussion of age and gender in *The Witcher* series). Even beyond the representation of gender—other identities intersect and so these will also need to be investigated.

Directions for Implementation in Industry

One thing which I would really like for this book to do is to make it outside of dusty university library shelves. This book is directly critical of some of the practices of writing implemented by videogame scriptwriters, and so I would like for it to also influence the way they represent gender and characterise gendered individuals.

Before discussing the implications of the findings for videogame developers, it is worth noting the research brings forth philosophical questions about what videogame creators should be doing in terms of the representation of gender within their games and my own views on how videogame companies could represent gender. I believe that, whenever appropriate, videogame developers should strive to make male and female characters equally diverse and with a wide range of different types of positive and negative gender representations. In other words, while problematic representations do exist (and it is not possible to always have all characters represented in a positive way), there should be a reasonable balance regarding how male and female characters are represented. I believe that there is space for more traditional and problematic representations because such representations reflect aspects of the real world, and so excluding them could make the videogames appear overly artificial or even moralising. Nevertheless, over-reliance on stereotypical representations creates a perpetual cycle, in which problematic gender roles become fossilised as part of the genre and sociocultural knowledge. Therefore, I would argue that it is necessary for videogame developers to create multi-dimensional representations of gender, which represent gendered characters in equal ways, as a method of progressing views towards gender.

There are several ways in which videogame companies could prevent the fossilisation of stereotypical representations, including creating and discussing non-binary gendered characters, creating dialogue which challenges players who make overtly sexist choices, and not positioning female social actors in the patient position in transitive clauses as frequently as they occurred in the data presented in Chapter 5. The implementation of new policies, as based on evidence provided in this monograph, could serve as a starting point for bettering the representation of gender in this genre. However, videogame companies might also choose to take some of the methods demonstrated in this book and apply them to their own data.

Even if developers were to only examine lexical frequencies (similar to the work conducted in Chapter 5), this could indicate some of the sub-conscious biases of the writing team. This is one method which is both practical and quick to conduct: if a team sees that they have 4 times as many references to male characters than female characters, then they might want to consider addressing this gender imbalance. Other writing teams might also want to examine the use of gendered nouns or pronouns as a way to examine whether or not their writing demonstrates bias, via examining the collocates and transitive verbs that these gendered terms occur with (such as the work conducted in Chapter 5). Similarly, this is a method which could reveal how agentive they have made their characters and could create more complex and realistic representations of gender (such as the work in Chapter 6). Writers might also want to look at what their gendered characters are saying and if there is a bias in the kind of semantic domains gendered characters are drawing on (see Chapter 7). Importantly, although these methods are quick to conduct (and can give initial indicative information), they can be further elaborated on for more nuanced investigations by videogame writers.

Finally, I would like to see a number of videogame companies reach out and consult (corpus) linguists when appropriate. There are a number of additional methods (not discussed in this book due to limitations of space) which can be used to investigate representations. In addition, there are several (corpus) linguists who look at more than just the representation of gender, and the expertise of such a diverse field could provide useful guidance for additional characterisation, representations, and content. Other (corpus) linguists also have familiarity with several disciplines, such as business communication, or with similar text types, and these could prove useful to videogame developers.

Concluding Remarks

All forms of media, videogames included, have the potential to be insidious. A single videogame alone will not necessarily completely change a person's mind about identity, but repeated patterns and exposure to problematic representations might have an incremental effect (Baker, 2006, p. 13) and ultimately impact a person's ideology. While videogames are a fun and exciting form of media, we must remain critical of the power structures inherent within them and discuss how these power structures can normalise ideologies based around identity. This is not to say that people cannot simply enjoy videogames, but rather that critical media awareness is an important step in recognising when representations are unequal and the impact of such unequal representations.

There were several reasons why I wrote this monograph. However, one of the primary reasons was to address a dearth of literature in the study of language within videogames. I saw that a number of studies which claimed to look at the representation of gender 'in' videogames actually looked at the representation of gender 'around' videogames. In other words, rather than take the language used within videogames, many studies looked at videogame paratext as a proxy for looking at the language within the videogame itself (see, e.g., Carrillo Masso, 2011; Ensslin, 2012). When studies did look at the representation of gender 'in' videogames, these were typically visual content analyses, although representations can cross semiotic modes, and the semiotic mode of language was often overlooked. I have demonstrated some of the ways that corpus linguistic methods can be applied to authentic data from within videogames. As a discipline which is focused around representativeness and statistically driven linguistic analysis, corpus linguistic methods offer a rigorous way to examine how language is used to represent identity within such a medium.

Ultimately, videogames are an ever-developing form of mass media, with the power to (re)produce and normalise representations of gender. Some of the representations which are being normalised in videogames could be damaging to an individual's perceptions of gender. The internalisation of these gender-based norms and ideologies has implications for player's own identities and how they navigate these outside of videogames, specifically how they (re)produce the sociocultural knowledge about gender, as normalised in these games, to other contexts. This form of media is being consumed by more and more people, and representations in such a wide-reaching medium cannot remain unchallenged. I hope that this book indicates the value of considering the ways that gender can be represented within them, in addition to some of the ways that such representations can be investigated.

Ludography

MidBoss. (2015). *2064: Read only memories*. San Francisco, California: California.

Bibliography

Abuczki, Á., & Ghazaleh, E. B. (2013). An overview of multimodal corpora, annotation tools and schemes. *Argumentum, 9*(1), 86–98.

Baker, P. (2006). *Using corpora in discourse analysis*. Bloomsbury.

Baker, P. (2008a). *Sexed texts: Language, gender and sexuality*. Equinox.

Biber, D. (1992). The multi-dimensional approach to linguistic analyses of genre variation: An overview of methodology and findings. *Computers and the Humanities, 26*(5–6), 331–345.

Carrillo Masso, I. (2011). The grips of fantasy: The construction of female characters in and beyond virtual game worlds. In A. Ensslin. & E. Muse (Eds.), *Creating second lives: Community, identity and spatiality as constructions of the virtual* (pp. 113–142). Routledge.

Christiansen, A., Dance, W. & Wild, A. (2020). Constructing corpora from images and text. In S. Rüdiger & D. Dayter (Eds.), *Corpus approaches to social media* (pp. 149–174). John Benjamins.

Connell, R. (2005). *Masculinities* (2nd edn.). Polity Press.

Durand, J. (2017). Corpus phonology. In M. Aronoff (Ed.), *The Oxford research encyclopaedia of linguistics* (pp. 1–20). Oxford University Press.

Ensslin, A. (2012). *The language of gaming*. Palgrave.

Fenlon, J., Schembri, A., Johnston, T. & Cormier, K. (2015). Documentary and corpus approaches to sign language research. In E. Orfanidou, B. Woll.,

& G. Morgan (Eds.), *The Blackwell guide to research methods in Sign language studies* (pp. 156–172). Wiley.

Gestos, M., Smith-Merry, J., & Campbell, A. (2018). Representation of women in videogames: A systematic review of literature in consideration of adult female wellbeing. *Cyberpsychology, Behavior, and Social Networking, 21*(9), 535–541.

Goorimoorthee, T., Csipo, A., Carleton, S., & Ensslin, A. (2019). Language ideologies in videogame discourse: Forms of sociophonetic othering in accented character speech. In A. Ennslin & I. Balteiro (Eds.), *Approaches to videogame discourse: Lexis, interaction, textuality* (pp. 269–287). Bloomsbury.

Gut, U. (2009). *Non-native speech: A corpus-based analysis of phonological and phonetic properties of L2 English and German.* Peter Lang.

Heritage, F. (2021). *Maidens and monsters: A corpus assisted critical discourse analysis of the representation of gender in The Witcher videogame series* (Doctoral dissertation, Lancaster University).

Ivory, J. (2006). Still a man's game: Gender representation in online reviews of video games. *Mass Communication & Society, 9*(1), 103–114.

Knight, D., & Adolphs, S. (2020). Multimodal corpora. In M. Paquot & S. T. Gries (Eds.), *A practical handbook of corpus linguistics* (pp. 351–369). Springer International Publishing.

Machin, D., & van Leeuwen, T. (2016). Sound, music and gender in mobile games. *Gender and Language, 10*(3), 412–432.

Matthews, N. L., Lynch, T., & Martins, N. (2016). Real ideal: Investigating how ideal and hyper-ideal video game bodies affect men and women. *Computers in Human Behavior, 59*(1), 155–164.

Neumer, C. (2001) *Hironobu Sakaguchi Interview*. Stumped Magazine. https://www.stumpedmagazine.com/interviews/hironobu-sakaguchi/. Accessed February 2021.

Paaßen, B., Morgenroth, T., & Stratemeyer, M. (2017). What is a true gamer? The male gamer stereotype and the marginalization of women in video game culture. *Sex Roles, 76*(7), 421–435.

Sarkeesian, A. (2014). *Tropes vs. women. Feminist frequency: Conversations with pop culture*. YouTube. https://www.youtube.com/watch?v=X6p5AZp7r_Q. Accessed February 2021.

Schembri, A., Fenlon, F., Rentelis, R., Reynolds, S., & Cormier, K. (2013). Building the British sign language corpus. *Language Documentation and Conservation, 7*(1), 136–154.

Vella, A., & Grech, S. (2021). What can a corpus tell us about phonetic and phonological variation? In A. O'keeffe & M. McCarthy (Eds.), *The Routledge handbook of corpus linguistics* (2nd edn.). Routledge.

Zottola, A. (2021). *Transgender identities in the press: A corpus-based discourse analysis*. Bloomsbury.

Index

F. Heritage, *Language, Gender and Videogames*,
https://doi.org/10.1007/978-3-030-74398-7

The manufacturer's authorised representative in the EU is Springer Nature Customer Service Centre GmbH, Europaplatz 3, 69115 Heidelberg, Germany. If you have any concerns regarding our products, please contact ProductSafety@springernature.com

Printed and bound by CPI Group (UK) Ltd, Croydon, CR0 4YY

30/09/2026

02225455-0008